Performance Philosophy

Series Editors
Laura Cull Ó Maoilearca
University of Surrey
Guildford, UK

Alice Lagaay
Hamburg University of Applied Sciences
Hamburg, Germany

Will Daddario
Independent Scholar
Asheville, NC, USA

Performance Philosophy is an interdisciplinary and international field of thought, creative practice and scholarship. The Performance Philosophy book series comprises monographs and essay collections addressing the relationship between performance and philosophy within a broad range of philosophical traditions and performance practices, including drama, theatre, performance arts, dance, art and music. It also includes studies of the performative aspects of life and, indeed, philosophy itself. As such, the series addresses the philosophy of performance as well as performance-as-philosophy and philosophy-as-performance.

Series Advisory Board:
Emmanuel Alloa, Assistant Professor in Philosophy, University of St. Gallen, Switzerland
Lydia Goehr, Professor of Philosophy, Columbia University, USA
James R. Hamilton, Professor of Philosophy, Kansas State University, USA
Bojana Kunst, Professor of Choreography and Performance, Institute for Applied Theatre Studies, Justus-Liebig University Giessen, Germany
Nikolaus Müller-Schöll, Professor of Theatre Studies, Goethe University, Frankfurt am Main, Germany
Martin Puchner, Professor of Drama and of English and Comparative Literature, Harvard University, USA
Alan Read, Professor of Theatre, King's College London, UK
Freddie Rokem, Professor (Emeritus) of Theatre Arts, Tel Aviv University, Israel
http://www.performancephilosophy.org/books/

More information about this series at
http://www.palgrave.com/gp/series/14558

Spencer Golub

A Philosophical Autofiction

Dolor's Youth

Spencer Golub
Department of Theatre Arts
  and Performance Studies
Brown University
Providence, RI, USA

Performance Philosophy
ISBN 978-3-030-05611-7   ISBN 978-3-030-05612-4   (eBook)
https://doi.org/10.1007/978-3-030-05612-4

Library of Congress Control Number: 2018963738

This Palgrave Macmillan imprint is published by the registered company Springer Nature
Switzerland AG
The registered company address is: Gewerbestrasse 11, 6330 Cham, Switzerland

CONTENTS

Contents

CHAPTER 1

Preface

This book represents a thought experiment on the theme of uncertainty.
It takes as its premise G. E. Moore's notion of mutually incompatible
statements in relation to life being held together by a shifting first-person
subject that hypothesizes narrative as a single subject through-line.
It recalls Wittgenstein's idea of "family resemblance" as a genre rather
than biological or genealogical classification. "Family resemblance" both
centers and de-centers the idea of "family" as a stable unit of common
singularity. In the guise of memory and family history, I offer my imagining mind's "elective affinities" (to borrow from Goethe who borrowed
from science) in which resemblances are observed but observations are
in large part invented. I undo history and memory for the purpose of
discovering the self via reconstruction, which engenders another language game of family resemblance in which a single self metastasizes
from a family cell (or cells). The self becomes its own family of resemblances and non-resemblances as well. I do things with philosophy (and
employ literature *as* philosophy) but embed philosophy in experience,
in errors of naming and recall, as in family relations and family history
and other indices of the so-called real. *Dolor's Youth* treats selected incidents as found objects and objects as life events drawn from my own
and other characters' lives. It is a work of hypothetical embodiment, a
"life" not of record but of slippage. "Life" lived as philosophical error.
It tries not to tell you but to show you this and to perform the task of
self-discovery without the benefit of an integrated self. To go where

© The Author(s) 2019
S. Golub, *A Philosophical Autofiction*, Performance Philosophy,
https://doi.org/10.1007/978-3-030-05612-4_1

obsessive-compulsive self-overturning takes me and see how the individual self moves away from "I" and into the interspace this "I" inhabits.

Wittgenstein called G. E. Moore's statement, "I went to the pictures last Tuesday but I don't believe that I did," a "paradox" but many others labeled it "absurd."[1] The problem rests in subject more than in il/logic, or to state it differently, in the apparency of the former rather than of the latter. Moore's statements are so widely disputed because they are scanned as one might any other sentence, by looking for subject–object agreement and for where the thought begins and where it ends. The problem, insofar as it is a problem at all, is that a thought oscillates through the sentence that puts the subject at risk by doubling its appearance and rendering it unrecognizable both to the reader and to itself. A doubled and redoubled "I" is the present book's semantically actual agent, its subject in search of a subject position, a position from which it can be framed as an integrated subject, opposed by the counter-agency of the subject itself. The subject of this book is at a loss to know who he is other than someone else and so employs fictions to create or re-create (his) character. These others tessellate, sometimes even under the sign of the same Hebrew name borne by three non-Jewish characters drawn from real life so as/as if to attest to the ambiguousness of the narrator's own ambiguous Jewish identity (not so much as Wittgenstein but of the same order). Changing family names and family members accrue generational loss that inexactly matches cause and effect. The multiple, alternative selves who (are) set forth in this book and clamor for its authorship, have ghost-written the statement, "*p and I do not believe that p.*"[2] It is a statement that is forthright in its embarrassed negotiation of lower-case and upper-case subjecthood ("p" and "I").

The question broached by another Moore statement, "It's raining outside and I don't believe it" is a contestation of outside and inside, and more commonly among philosophers, between knowing and believing.

---

[1] Wittgenstein's last words appeared in Norman Malcolm, *Wittgenstein: A Memoir* (New York: Oxford University Press, 1962) and again in the biography of record, Ray Monk's, *Ludwig Wittgenstein: The Duty of Genius* (New York: Penguin Books, 1991); G.E. Moore, "A Reply to My Critics," in Paul Arthur Schilpp, ed., *The Philosophy of G.E. Moore* (Evanston: Northwestern University Press, 1942), 543.

[2] G.E. Moore, *Selected Writings*, ed. T. Baldwin (London: Routledge, 1993), 211, paraphrased in Mitchell Green and John N. Williams, "Introduction," in Mitchell Green and John N. Williams, eds., *Moore's Paradox: New Essays on Belief, Rationality, and the First Person* (New York: Oxford University Press, 2007), 3.

But it is furthermore a contestation between an "and" and the "but" which is sometimes put in its place or else is overlaid upon the "and" in the reader's mind to spin it round to something that appears on the surface to be only slightly less illogical. I feel something not entirely dissimilar in thinking about the title of the celebrated cine-paradox that is simultaneously called *Last Year at Marienbad* and *Last Year in Marienbad* (*L'année dernière à Marienbad*). Many people use the titles interchangeably, and if you Google the latter you will get a complete pull-down menu under the title *Last Year in Marienbad* but/and when you click on any of the menu options you are taken to the site of *Last Year at Marienbad*.[3] The title has been auto-corrected minus any evidence that the original title entry was incorrect. In fact, the number of entries that appear under the "incorrect" title leads the reader to believe that his misremembering of the film title is correct. Given the film's non-agreement of protagonistic memory (predicated on the assumption that memory *is* the protagonist), the contestation of *at* and *in* here appears to be all the more subject-driven. You not/remembering transpires at/in the story of the narrative trying to recall itself, without necessarily taking or having taken place. There may be only *semantic* memory, which may only be memory in/of itself, its figuration, the sounds it makes when we speak it, the shapes it makes when we write it down as sentences, words, and letters. And as/in the stories of our life. I believe what I say in much the same way that the speaker in/of Moore's paradox believes what he says or rather what "I" says, whoever "he" is, whatever "I" have made of "him," or of whatever "I" am also made.

We know what we know according to evidence but we are in a position to manipulate this evidence to suggest that there is proof of life where no life exists and to doubt this existence in the past as well as in the present. There is, in fact, no evidence, only *further* evidence, something based on presupposition. But on what is presupposition based? As to the self, we have not even the certainty that we do at a glance that something else, something other (a chair or a table) exists in the material world. Even in cases like this, we can lose sight of material reality between glances without anything other than the object itself to sustain us. It is all tied to perception, of course but as Roy Sorenson notes, parsing and paraphrasing Schopenhauer, "like the eye, the 'I' is the 'center

---

[3] "*à*: could mean *of, at, to, in, for, on*." https://www.quora.com/What-does-à-mean-in-French.

of all existence' and yet is not present to consciousness or experience."[4] We cannot *see* it. Reality itself might disappear in the blink of an "I." In a discussion of Moore's Paradox, I misread the first part of "mercury exists in a solid state only at a temperature less than 38.86 degrees below zero Fahrenheit" as "*memory* exists only in a solid state."[5] Despite its uncertain provenance, this new statement is true insofar as I believe it. The solidity of memory being here extruded from an overriding state of mercuriality is all the "evidence" "I" need to go on as to who I am and am not, who I was and was not. I am not stating facts. I am making an argument, offering a counterproposal that on its own terms cannot be refuted. What would your (or my) evidence for doing so be?

Dolor's Youth appears in the wake of my book *The Baroque Night* (2018), which concludes with the statement, "a man's got to believe in something"—a tough guy remark spoken in the voice of a neo-noir character run through my own voice modulator (or perhaps the reverse). I had a desperate need to be *somebody*, and since the character in question had just expired in my retelling, I stole his identity and ended the book before I got caught. I am risking apprehension by continuing my life as an identity thief even more directly in *Dolor's Youth*, wherein I become characters I *might actually* have been, some but not all of whom were raised in the Jewish faith. I use "faith" here as something larger than and not always commensurate with myself, a character trait, as something with which to be identified as if "I" am a genre (I imagine) unto myself. Was I in this as with my "self" persuaded by other people's arguments as I often am by a book, only to "change my mind" after reading another book that convinces me of its case or of my having misread the first book? In *On Certainty*, Wittgenstein, himself relates this to the question of family, the bête noire of *Dolor's Youth*.[6] Wittgenstein, whose family was as accomplished as it was fatally broken, wrote: "I believe that I had great-grandparents, that the people who gave themselves out as my parents really were my parents, etc. This belief may never have been expressed: even the thought that it was so, never thought" (*OC* §159). Wittgenstein intends for this to support his idea that there are things

---

[4] Roy Sorenson, "The All-Seeing Eye: A Blind Spot in the History of Ideas," in Green and Williams, eds., *Moore's Paradox: New Essays on Belief, Rationality, and the First Person*, 45.

[5] Morris Lazerowitz, "Moore's Paradox," in Schilpp, ed., *The Philosophy of G.E. Moore*, 371.

[6] Ludwig Wittgenstein, *On Certainty*, ed. G.E.M. Anscombe and G.H. von Wright and trans. Denis Paul and G.E.M. Anscombe (New York: Harper & Row, 1972).

we instinctively "know" without proof, even without prior mental representation, before thought but not aforethought.[7] This is a part of the a priori world that predates our subjective worlding, which informs the first statement of the *Tractatus*, "The world is everything that is the case."[8]

In terms of the individual, doing precedes thinking and yet doing is not precisely experience because that again would necessarily fold in the accountability of proofs. By arguing that some things are not so much anti- as extra- or a -evidentiary, Wittgenstein pursues a creative mandate for philosophy that can be lost in the abundancy of his philosophy's somewhat tortured idea (after and sometimes anti-G. E. Moore) of "common sense." Wittgenstein believes that philosophers have been deleterious to philosophy by overthinking it and through it, the world. And so, I have taken Wittgenstein not so much at his word (because I not only support but indulge in and rely upon misreading) but as a thought-prompt, as I have done before in my book, *Incapacity: Wittgenstein, Anxiety, and Performance Behavior* (2014). I have now taken up the challenge of what it has been like to live without proof (as do we all) and with an overly developed sense of my own self as being unprovable by the evidence of real life. This continues an argument I have made in *The Baroque Night*, which flips the positions of reality and unreality on the authenticity spectrum. But I am now going further by illustrating that the self is *not* one of those elemental things that simply *is* without us knowing it for a fact or even as an intuition. The self is something that exists only in the fictional world that we call unreal. To speak of *true* fiction makes sense to me personally. To speak of *real* fiction is simply a matter of genre classification. What would make fiction be *not real fiction*? "I" am a genre classification, which, then, is to say that not all of what I have to say here is true *and* all of it is meant to be real.

"'True fiction' is a contradiction in terms," writes Bruce Duffy at the start of his (nevertheless) persuasive literary adaptation of Wittgenstein's life, *The World As I Found It*. The title was Wittgenstein's although it was not meant to be autobiographical, but instead to speak to the slippage of the "I." Looking back on his work four years following its initial publication, Duffy sees in Wittgenstein's self-effacing passage, "a poet's

---

[7]The case for this manner of reading Wittgenstein's last and unfinished book is made clearly and persuasively in Danièle Moyal-Sharrock, *Understanding Wittgenstein's On Certainty* (New York: Palgrave Macmillan, 2004).

[8]Ludwig Wittgenstein, *Tractatus Logico-Philosophicus* (1922), 1.

song of origins and disappearances, of words and then word-covering silence."[9] Duffy is here paraphrasing the concluding statement of the *Tractatus* ("What we cannot speak about we must pass over in silence.") to characterize its opening passage, returning to "origin" and the "I" as structural devices working together to create a fictional reality. On this theme, Duffy cites Rimbaud (another of his literary biographical subjects), who wrote at age sixteen, "It is wrong to say: I think. One ought to say: People think me. I is someone else."[10]

I am by nature a non-problem solver who employs heuristic methods in my writing to dis/articulate the nature and extent of my self-doubt. This much I know about the self—it is a heuristic project that defies heuristic shortcuts. ("'I know'," writes Danièle Moyal-Sharrock speaking for Wittgenstein, "conveys a grammatical, not an epistemic certainty."[11]) The "methods" I employ may block as in obscure or dematerialize inroads to understanding and meaning-making, at the same time recasting blocking as in staging interventions, that necessarily invent a de facto self for its agency and figurations. My perverse heuristic is a model of insufficiency rendered normative for me by a Gyntian desire in the face of external prompts *to be insufficient*, to go roundabout. The ongoing struggle for clarity unsurprisingly results in a decoherence that ensures irresolution, which keeps what is after all the philosopher's game inside of me alive and kicking, kicking its host body, its host mind—as in, "I have a body." And "I have a mind." But not, necessarily, "I have a self that has/had a life."

This is not a work of philosophical skepticism that sets out to prove a negative as in the Cartesian skeptical idea that life is an illusion put in our minds by some external demon and so not our own. Danièle Moyal-Sharrock, who has written clearly and persuasively on late (the so-called Third) Wittgenstein and about *On Certainty*, in particular, characterizes basic skeptical thought experiments on doubt and belief as "behaviors"—doubt-behavior and belief-behavior. She says that such thought experiments "must be regarded as fiction, *not possibility*...a thought that runs wild...on the uncharted track of imagination is not a 'possibility'; it is a thought."[12] This is, at least for me, where philosophy and

[9] Bruce Duffy, "Preface," in *The World As I Found It* (New York: New York Review Books, 1987), i and 558.

[10] Ibid., 556.

[11] Moyal-Sharrock, *Understanding Wittgenstein's On Certainty*, 26.

[12] Ibid., 176 and 178.

performance philosophy track differently. My two previous books of performance philosophy deal with what could be called pain-behaviors and reality-behaviors, presenting fiction, and hybridity not as unreasonable alternatives to reality but as real possibilities that the imagination entertains beyond the point at which the "pure(ly)" philosophical thought-experiment stops. That does not make what my version of performance philosophy (I cannot/do not speak for the field in general) delusional nor even quasi-systematic. I offer instead a web of thought-correspondences that does not lose contact with reality but rather expands what is thought, how that thought is lived, and how that thought *in its fullness* reveals the lyricism of our humanness that more logical analysis, I feel, does not capture. I try to do real-time thought experiments in which writing creates meaning (as if) for the first time and what philosophers call "nonsense" takes its rightful place in philosophy's performance.

A CHAPTER BREAKDOWN AND SELF-CRITIQUE FOR PHILOSOPHICAL READERS

Field-State

This short chapter serves as the book's introduction. Beginning with the trope of Anne Frank's secret annex and with that of the reader, it discovers that the space of self-enclosure can be read like a book with pages missing and new pages inserted that treat past time as pastime. This begins the narrative of finding replacement parts for a past that ghosts influence where causal links have long-since disappeared. A homeland is fictionally cited/sited/sighted from which nothing and no one can firmly derive any real sense of origin. Thus, begins a major theme in the book regarding the inauthenticity and possible irrelevance of origins. This puts history on notice, as it does logical thought and its various delivery systems.

Non-Disclosure

"I did not grow up," this chapter's first words, contest personal biography and cite *DOLOR'S YOUTH* as a self-contesting title. (This can also be read as an apophatic statement in which the assertion of what something or someone is not may enable useful forms of speculative discourse.)

I immediately call the self into question as a sort of placeholder for bigger historical narratives that are in effect all origin stories and so, I think, suspect. I posit the Kantian manifold as a model of/for synthesized selfing that is by nature dialectically self-interrogating. How does becoming a self lose itself in the becoming "as" as opposed to the being "the"? There is a trauma ghosting this "story" that begins to push its way to the surface at the mention of Martin Amis's novel *Time's Arrow* that tells its tale backwards to the inexactness of trauma as a historically "real" point of origin (which leaves me in a difficult place of apparent alignment with a cultural nemesis). A Jewish mindset replaces Jewish historical experience and the idea of post-someone-else's-traumatic experience presents as a hypothetical condition. Who or what then constitutes the first-person subject's community—the "we" of the "I"—and can they ever become synonymous, and does this idea of "becoming" render this an impossible proposition? Do fictional/fiction's genealogies provide models for rapprochement with the impossibility of our own ambitions or do they further alienate these ambitions from any claim of truth-seeking and truth-telling? Is Moore's paradox a means of making sense of what the "I" narrates in its concealed and unconcealed states of personhood? Can the "I" make truth claims for what is not ostensibly real? Suddenly, something very real intervenes—cancer, odd in that it is recurring after nineteen years, enough time in which a child could grow to its maturity with foreknowledge of the trauma it contains, and said cancer takes on both your identity and an identity of its own (or vice versa). The most real paradoxically presents itself as being the most metaphoric identity you possess (or that possesses you). Is this cancer the instantiation of some more distant trauma that precedes not just your childhood but your birth? Is this cancer a clue to the "we" to which you as an "I" belong? If so and even if not, it both dominates your mind and becomes your mindset. Life itself and its prehistory become carcinogenic, as the self begins to multiply and get renamed and "I" enter into films. Keywords that will circulate throughout this text are introduced: "atom/ic" (bomb), "cell" (cancer), "family cell" (cancer, betrayal), "friend" (betrayal of memory, cancer again). Melancholia is personified. The original family name is revealed and chaos is introduced into the family rendering its history hypothetical.

Cowbird

Amnesiac, dysmorphic, and otherwise duplicitous character conditions broach an embodied philosophy of "inessentialism" by embracing the self as being something that is written. "My cancer" narrates some of its origin story, paradoxical in that its origin as in its cause cannot be ascertained and because cancer by its very nature does not practice integration so much as re-creation and decreation, "de-selfing." This then somewhat false narrative delivered from real events further usurps and subverts the subject's role in its own narrative. In E. M. Cioran's formulation, self-consciousness cancerously gnaws at health by infusing it with thought about itself. Cancer casts us as its narrative's neurotic character, and "I" enter into (primarily) Jewish-American fiction. Hallucinated lives and counter-lives append to the struggle between the physical body and its metaphoric embodiments. "Anne Frank" returns as her own fictional character, cancer serving now as an experimental cure for self-limitation and "Anne Frank" as a testimony not to survivor guilt but to survivor fear. The cowbird arrives to give a name to a species of subject that curates some other species' eggs (history, origins), to usurp the biographies even of those who are yet unborn. Writing, like cancer's x-ray and chemical treatments, performs a possibly toxic curative agency. Cowbirdman enters the ranks of neurotic, self-canceling superheroes who will recur in the book's narrative as alternative selves.

Generational Loss

In my usage, generational loss constitutes an erosion of certainty in the act of asking the question how a thing that you know, that you think you have always known is made and how the autobiographical "hinge" (as Wittgenstein called it) can be broken. Can inner experience demand of empirical knowledge that it account for itself as being what it says it is—real? Is the idea of "family" commensurate with its actual content? Is the apparent discontinuity of individual character an indication of the gap between belief and thought? Obsessive-compulsive disorder presents here as a Wittgensteinian family resemblance of psychophysical stuttering and (like-minded cancerous) metastasizing form. The unhinging of belief in grounded definition(s) renders origin not so much false as merely isomorphic, with contested relationship. Anxiety is, in the sense of forms or creates, a pseudo-hinge. Hypnagogia and "paraphase" (Joseph McCarthy's term) come between the self and the scenes it dreams (up) for itself not only in but beside time. Leibniz's principle of "sufficient reason" argues the possibility of being "otherwise" alongside Moore's paradoxical construction of how the appearance of being otherwise is explicable by means of a shifting subject. OCD reflects and expresses the stuttering mind. Might OCD be a genre concept on the Wittgensteinian theme of family resemblance (and of *OC—On Certainty*)?

Form of Life

This chapter takes as its premise Wittgenstein's "form of life," a philosophical imprimatur of cultural emplacement in language and identity formation. "I" as a form of life and as a form not so much of self-expression but as a stand-in for "self" as only a form of expression. A lack of what is called in relation to Wittgenstein "objective certainty" enables further shifting of the subject position and a series of maskings and unmaskings, self-impersonations and self-corrections. I try on my Jewishness as an Ashke (non)normative ilk-boy in genre fictions and so manifest the anomaly of not/being who or what I am. The idea that "the comedic equivalent of assimilation is masking, impersonation—the humor com[ing] from our apprehension of the mask and the simultaneous knowledge of the true identity behind it" (David E. Kaufman), is realized in the person of comedian Lenny Bruce with whom I share a hometown as a figurative place of origin. "Friendship, this relation without dependence, without episode, yet into which all of the simplicity of life enters" (Maurice Blanchot) is tested in the partnership and afterlife of Dean Martin and Jerry Lewis and found to be a historical romance rendered unsustainable by the "I" whose "friend" has forgotten him. What persists is only the mummified remains of friendship as a form of celebrity—the "I" celebrating validation from and through not just any other but "a friend." The "we"-ness of friendship joins the ranks of the other fictional varieties of "we"-ness—family, cancer, Jewishness, history, and origin.

Dog Anabasis

This chapter explores phantasmatic memory (the bite that leaves a mental, not a physical mark) and the contested origins of phobia (dog origin stories) in personal and culturally diasporic history. I acknowledge that I may be sustaining an obsession that more properly belongs to my predecessors, who have chosen not to be as obsessed as I am, not as obsessed with "I am." Can fear withstand rational consideration? Isn't this the point on which prejudice pivots? As the title of this chapter suggests, it is an uphill journey. Walking, meant to reinforce compulsive ritualized patterning to offset phobic imaginings, navigates between idea creation and thought dissipation. I experience the phantom dog bite as a reality "I" have devised to forestall further contact with what lies beneath the phantasmatically tattooed skin once it has been broken. I/"I" am like the dog insomuch as the horror is inbred.

I'm Not Like Everybody Else

In this final chapter, memory felled by the fever dream of a multitudinous reality, comes to rest. Narrative's split consciousness says it is the "everybody" that you are not like in all the names you give your thoughts and the one name you give yourself. Leon Wieseltier's observation that, "One of the primary methods for the transmission of tradition is the premature termination of childhood" takes me back to the traditional family gathering at which fictional characters are seated who test the integrity of "us" and so of "I" in memory. Did ritualized identity trouble the very origins it proclaimed? Did these troublings reveal themselves in the form of OCD rituals and cancer's recurrence? "Earliest childhood," Lawrence Kushner writes, "is living in the unity; adulthood is surviving the brokenness." Brokenness is, in the context of this book, not a final undoing but a continually being undone, the redoing of being undone in different names, different voices, and different selves that are always the same self, masked and anonymous, as if to say "'I' am nobody;" "'I' am no one."

CHAPTER 2

Field-State

Having to remain silent from 8 a.m. to 6 p.m. daily in the secret annex where she hides from the Nazis with her family and some fellow Jews, Anne (*The Diary of Anne Frank*, dir. George Stevens, 1959) became a voracious reader, traversing *A Tale of Two Cities* ("the saddest book I ever read") in a single nightless day. Anne would have been a reader anyway (she did bring the Dickens with her, after all) but she became something like the perfect reader due to her constrained circumstances. These are the most radically circumscribed conditions for the development of a reader and a writer. It is essentially what Otto Frank tells his daughter: "There are no walls, no locks, no bolts that anyone can put on your mind." (A front door left open almost seals the fate of those hiding in the secret annex.) A constrained life is a life lived in close-ups: the door, the lock, the face, the word, and the neurotic existentialism of self-regard, of having to devise the space and reasons for secrets, to nurture memories as traumas. Retreating into the smallest spaces I can create, whether a scene or a childhood map, burying my voice in my throat or stopping up my ears, walling out sound with inattention. Reading. Writing. Hiding.

Everybody has a secret annex, a locked room, sometimes not even a room but a closet or a space beneath the floor, somewhere hidden that protects you from "what's out there" and that conceals what is inside. I used to think I was searching in my own and other people's fictions for a secret room, not my own that would body forth with some truth about life and death, a first and last room. Now, I think I have found it,

S. Golub, *A Philosophical Autofiction*, Performance Philosophy, https://doi.org/10.1007/978-3-030-05612-4_2

or maybe it has found me, and it is not what I expected. I see myself as my own jailer, a prisoner to all I thought I had forgotten, criminally forgetting to "never forget." Like so many before me and so many after, I am now obsessively remembering and experiencing the full effect of having been hidden, constrained by a life spent thinking, speaking, hearing, reading, and writing in code. The ink has not yet dried on these new-old memories, this intergenerational origin story in which I play not just a part but a type. Jews are the people of the book and I, a first-generation Jewish American, am a person of the book of preexisting conditions.

I was taught about the Holocaust by my father, but I was a bad student. There was a soft syllabus—books that were of the sentimental historical and righteous anger variety, and nightly oral exams around the dinner table. But since I neglected to read the books my father gave to me or left for me to find, I hadn't any answers, or always the same answer: *I* (not *we*) can't live in the past. All the while, though, an ancestral history was gestating in me beneath layers of academic thinking, theoretical concern, and neurotic self-absorption. The catalog of guilt I had been amassing over the course of a lifetime finally arrived at the page entitled: "You Should Have Listened More to Your Father. (He Knew More Than You Gave Him Credit for.)" The first section heading under this title, "Why You Should Have Asked Him More Questions about His Past," speaks to my memory being impoverished by not having been more curious. I never considered how there was enough room for my father, his brother, and two sisters in my grandparents' small Bronx apartment. The only two bedrooms were always very dark, and I could at best imagine there were other rooms inside this darkness, like some deeper beyond, perhaps inside the dark wooden wardrobes, ominous in what might well have been a life-saving enormity—enough space in there to hide the other people they once were and their memories, not so much forgotten as put away. The hat boxes that were too high for a child to reach sat above them, nominally belonging to the people they now were on the outside—although I suspected that these boxes and the hats that might or might not still be inside them had lives all their own and if donned by my father's family in their present circumstances, the hats and their wearers would not recognize themselves or one another in the wardrobe's mirror.[1]

---

[1] Sholem Shachnah, the protagonist of Sholem Aleichem's "On Account of a Hat" (1913), experiences this when he accidentally switches hats with a Ukrainian official.

I became that mirror turned toward the street, the lookout of this particular un-settlement for double-parked cars that might represent attempts to block us in, to keep generations of my family from escaping. How would they come? Dropped off by military transport trucks on Davidson Avenue, dressed in full uniform and combat helmets? Would they try to slip among the double-parked cars on the street below so as not to be seen, where they nevertheless would be seen by me, the lookout? Would I be too horrified to speak, to alert my family to the imminent encroachment? Not that there was any means of escaping it or a preexisting and enduring immanence of same. Would they make a show of force, stream through the front doors of the apartment building (which at one point went missing) and proceed accordionly in single file up the leg-numbing heavy marble staircase that for me always seemed like punishment enough? Would they toss hand grenades or potato mashers up to the second-floor inlaid black-and-dingy-white tile floor, blowing us up or smoking us out? Did they care if they took us dead or alive? Would they ever lay eyes on the people whose lives they were destroying? Would they arrive in police cars whose two-note, high-low European sirens still strike fear in me whenever I hear them? Would two or three men in trench coats, maybe even hatless emerge from the cars, their pistols in pocket and at the ready? Would people staring furtively through barely parted lace curtains in neighboring buildings think that they could be next or thank God it is not them now? Do they have future generation agents like me to serve as *their* lookouts? (All of these images are, of course, montaged movie memories in which "I" have played this and other roles over and over again.) Perhaps they have come for the clothes hanging inside the wardrobe, as they did for my maiden aunt's dresses after her parents died and she moved into a one bedroom flat off the Brighton Beach stop in Russo-Jewish dementia. Once the dresses were gone, she did not so much die as join the missing. She did not ask if I remembered her, just said her name and I responded at once as if I did. Over the course of a phone conversation, I leapt in my mind through the faces of people she might be, only realizing after I hung up

---

Unable to accept himself in the identity he sees in the mirror, he illogically reasons that he's asleep. This gives new meaning to the sense that Sholem's resemblance to the man in the mirror is uncanny. Jeremy Dauber, *Jewish Comedy: A Serious History* (New York: W. W. Norton, 2017), 247–48.

that she was someone else I knew with her name many years before. She was writing a book about *her parents'* dementia.

There had been a "before" when they landed on Manhattan's Lower East Side where they first stayed after coming over from Belarus. But I assume or else think I was told they were living with other people which would have made for even less room. My mind's way around the absence of recorded memory is to imagine that the children grew up outside of their parents' Bronx apartment, on the street. Perhaps this was done to confound the people they thought were looking for them, who disguised as census takers sought to ferret out their nationality and ethnicity, along with the number of people living on the premises and their politics. Then again, the family had emigrated from a land of shifting borders, so they were accustomed to performing such sleight of hand, even shape-shifting into other names with alternative birthdates and histories that would stop a historian in his tracks but enables a serially neurotic narrative shape-shifting and repurposing of origins of my own.[2]

Having been born just after the war, I am of the first generation to be given the Holocaust as a birthright (to avenge the sober reality that I might never have been born at all had the Allies lost), the legacy of my parents' wartime "obsession with the Holocaust as a necessary sign of identity."[3] I was finishing college by the time Nathan Englander, who wrote these last words, was born, which only illustrates how intergenerational the narrative is. Maybe it's because the people he is describing in his short stories are old enough to be *his* parents—that is, old enough to be *me*. Englander has a story called "Everything I Know About My Family on My Mother's Side" in which he says that this "wouldn't even make a whole story."[4] Given the significance of maternal descent in constituting Jewish identity, I would find this strange were it not for my mother, a Jewish only child who grew up near (but in a better Bronx

---

[2] "'And what of the Jews?' asked Mendel. 'What trick is performed with the Jews?'... 'Sleight of hand,' she said... 'For a moment the magician stands, a field of Jews at his feet, then nothing.'" The discussion inverts the Nazi trope of extermination with Jewish magic on the way to the death camps. Nathan Englander, "The Tumblers," in *For the Relief of Unbearable Urges* (New York: Vintage, 2000), 41.

[3] Nathan Englander, "What We Talk About When We Talk About Anne Frank," in *What We Talk About When We Talk About Anne Frank* (New York: Vintage, 2013), 24.

[4] Englander, "Everything I Know About My Family on My Mother's Side," in *What We Talk About When We Talk About Anne Frank*, 132.

neighborhood than) my father but was fatherless from the age of roughly seventeen, being raised by a mother and her unmarried sister (a second maiden aunt) who collectively had no stories to tell. With all of this in mind, I need a new "before." I return to the darkness of the enormous wardrobe and sit myself down inside it. There, on the interior walls surrounding me on four sides, I project movie memories, peopled with Nazis and their German Shepherds, part of a subcategory of stories with images that scared and scarred me as a child growing up in my father's house. There are some of the Westerns I saw that helped comfort me, some puzzle films that raced my obsessive-compulsive mind in concentric circles only in reverse, romantic (including superhero) cine-opportunities to indulge my need to be someone else, even comedies testing the bond of friendship so alien to me. It is in all a recall much larger than my own, and it begins here.

It is perhaps ironic to situate the concept of origin in a Jewish cultural context in that so much of our history is diasporic, so much of our lineage concealed by those who believed it was dangerous to their health and alien to their religion to confess. I have a friend, a non-Jewish David, whose grandfather made a deathbed confession of his Jewishness. There is something provocative about linking origin and death in this way, something that makes Jewishness not so much an end as a means to reconsider a life. To me, it makes some kind of sense to employ intermedial origin as a diasporic condition and premise for reconsidering a life that has been Jewish in its doubting of premises upon which it could count and self-questioning to the point of casting individual identity as the most profound irony of all. How can you know who you are without the fiction of literature, of theater, of film, of memory? How do you keep these sources from combining, and finally, why would you? Diaspora as a condition of origin. Diaspora is who you are. You, your body, your body of work is always threatening to metastasize in acknowledgment of a basic condition. I have no alternative but *to be* alternative, to be not me but "I."

Waves of green grass high and wide, a sea of grass. Enough to make a man feel like he's wading into Nature's depths without a full understanding of what it is that envelops him. Being swept into and away from a static now whose natural cycles run inside it like a mill wheel. Everything seems to happen at a distance, in the tableau. The life outside the tableau never changes, just accretes its days and nights of waiting for the sea of grass to part, for the pictures to draw nearer, or the burning building to

be real and not merely a function of memory. How does one elude the
memory-scape? How does one first *see* it? We are all fire-starters, tele-
kinetically setting things alight, framing them like scenes from a hallucinated past. We create from the half-light of our consciousness events
that consume simple historical actions, add texture and luminescence,
double filters, ghostly appearances, material overlays, framed photos,
and mementos from other stories we have presumably already told. We
are seduced by tracking shots into thinking we are witnessing the movement of time. What we are actually seeing is the movement of work. We
are immersed in the strangeness of the vision of a life not lived earlier
but conceived as if it were. We create from this a family saga, a story
to be told in black-and-white and sepia-toned photos without any sense
of who would have taken them. Who else knew that I was doing this,
compiling a backlog of mis/remembered images? Who was responsible
for securing these images for posterity? Was the unknown photographer/
cinematographer a family member or friend? Was there even *one* friend?
Was there really ever any film in the camera? (I don't recall my grandparents possessing any photos, certainly none that they ever showed us.
And certainly, no camera. They *feared* the past and the future as they
would a final solution.) If no film, what was his game? Can one set out
consciously to compile a record of forgetting a non-appearance? Is it
one of those instances in which Nature grew over human events without leaving a trace of them ever having been there? Did the community
collude in the disappearance so as to hide in Nature from the horrors
of man? Did my grandparents' small Belarusian village help them bury
the photographic prints, the official records where they would not be
discovered, in the sea of grass, the waving field like something out of
Macbeth, appearing to be anomalous to any commonplace occurrence.
Perhaps it is better to hide than to be seen living, to keep to yourself, as
they say. Is self-protection a family credo, a behavior, a legacy in place of
a crest, for those whose lowly birth does not merit one? Did they sit atop
and stand behind wooden fences scanning the horizon for any sign of a
strange figure cutting through the grass like a scythe, beating a path to
their door, likewise concealed by a tangle of branches and shrubs? Were
they too busy lining up the long-shot to bother with framing those nearest to them? Did they gather at the Passover table, likewise waiting for
the Hebrew prophet Eliahu to appear? Were they looking at the grandchildren abstractly as being part of a wider fate tied to the self-consump-
tive action of sacrifice? Was the Passover table meant to host a séance?

Were the older generations in touch with spirits that we were not, of which we did not know? Were they protecting us from these spirits? Did the extent of our knowing or not knowing the words to the Hebrew prayers act as a defense or a dissolvent of these ancient forces? Were these forces drawing the Russian-born portion of my family back to the sea of grass? Had they left behind any relatives, of whom they lost sight in the tall weeds? Are some of them still sitting atop the wooden fence scanning the field *for them*, as if *they*, the emigrants, were the ones who disappeared? Those left behind are wrapped up in a makeshift combination of winter coats shorter than the nightdresses that reach their feet and drag in the snow. They are not dressed for going beyond their self-imposed border, their fence-line and remain uncertain as to whether life goes on out there in the tall grass, or whether it's just a medium, like time. Are the figures laboring to wrest themselves from time or rather to stay hidden in it? The distance we felt from my grandparents may have been something beyond which we could fathom or overcome. If the future was decided in the land they fled, where did that leave them? Were they, to themselves, already dead, and were we, their grandchildren, meant to be immortal? And, if so, does that make me abstract?

CHAPTER 3

Non-Disclosure

I did not grow up close to the land, like my landsman. I lived on, not off it but there was no "the" appended to "land" to denote a sort of bond of understanding. There were wooden frames of houses that were as yet incomplete but no rusted metal hulks or skeletal remains. Water occasionally pooled after a rain in my neighborhood but did not stand. Nature's magic and man's cruelty to man were as yet unknown to me. Alien sensory experiences were for the most part deferred. Not so, Ivan in *Ivan's Childhood* (dir. Andrei Tarkovsky, 1962), who crosses a destroyed Russian war-scape on foot and swims a river to reach military headquarters.[1] Ivan is in all senses a "reconnaissance agent," getting to know the lay of the land, with the eyes of a wise child only figuratively older than his years as this is a childhood alternatively dreamed and remembered by someone who is already dead. The blasted landscape of his youth has not escaped him except in story form. Houses left standing are only frames and doors are rendered ironic. Chimneys,

---

[1] Young Ivan is driven to serve in the military by his family's death at German hands. Russian Jewish boys as early as age twelve were conscripted into the military in a conscious state attempt to separate them from their living parents and break up the Jewish family. Alexander Herzen recalls the sad spectacle of Jewish boys "tramping in the mud for ten hours a day...being among strangers, nor father nor mother...they cough and cough until they cough themselves into their graves." Irving Howe, *World of Our Fathers: The Journey of the East European Jews to America and the Life They Found and Made* (New York: New York University Press, 2005), 6–7; Alexander Herzen, *My Past and Thoughts*, vol. 1, trans. Constance Garnett (London: Chatto and Windus, 1968), 219–20.

© The Author(s) 2019
S. Golub, *A Philosophical Autofiction*, Performance Philosophy,
https://doi.org/10.1007/978-3-030-05612-4_3

though free-standing, are baseless. Context is everything and nothing. Fields of time go on forever, with scarecrow trees frightened by self-immolating thought rising like dark pipe cleaners against the stark horizon. People don't walk, they trudge as I imagine they did in the always muddy shtetl into which my father was born on an uncertain date, where he marched behind the soldiers like Ivan, singing their songs in Russian, the captors' native tongue, their bayonets dreaming of whom they might hoist next.

Maybe this boy, my father, this child. I was as yet unknown to my family. Russia still lacked the distance from which it could be seen as an origin. Passages were not yet undertaken as storylines. Character names had not yet been created for us at Ellis Island that gave my unborn daughter her middle name without my realizing it at selection time. ("I" was already overlooking real-life experience and recreating names as if they were fictions.) Ivan resents (his) childhood for holding him back. Unafraid, he wants to be grown, like my father marching after soldiers, I guess. This "holding back" may sight a future no less a past, although in both cases may also be mistaken as to the order in which they occur. I did not have "Ivan's Childhood." But neither did Jerzy Kosinski (or "Ivan" for that matter), a Polish Jew who wrote his own autobiographical version of the wartime, war-torn childhood he might have had in *The Painted Bird* (1965) but did not. In the end and at its origins, the materiality of language is what is true...and also what is not true to the liar, lying being, after all, what we do not just to dissimulate but to *assimilate*, to be unoriginal, without origins.

From a Husserlian perspective, one could say about my growing up years that I allowed my ego's natural "attentive focus" to wander through levels of consciousness until it "fixed upon the givenness" of an "as if"-ness in which my mind could abide in an attitude of productive tolerance of my mortal fear of not being.[2] For me, this made writing a necessity, and in particular writing from inside the mind palace that has been under construction since childhood in which all my best thoughts adhere to image-recollections and fantastic memory reconstructions, to the evidential immateriality of "being (t)here" as a dubious mode of

---

[2] Edmund Husserl, *Ideas for a Pure Phenomenology and Phenomenological Philosophy. First Book: General Introduction to Pure Phenomenology* (*Ideas I*), trans. Daniel O. Dahlstrom (Indianapolis: Hackett Publishing Company, 2014), §101 and 204.

self-creation and self-citation.[3] The problem here and elsewhere is in the prefix, "self." Kierkegaard stated in 1849 that, "a self is the last thing the world cares about and the most dangerous thing of all for a person to show signs of having. The greatest hazard of all, losing the self, can occur very quietly in the world, as if it were nothing at all. No other loss can occur so quietly; any other loss—an arm, a leg, five dollars, a wife, etc.—is sure to be noticed." (Kierkegaard clearly did not have in mind here the loss or distortion of mental function that absents one from normative life behviors.) We are in thrall to all that we affirm and deny about the self, which is itself, Kierkegaard posits, inherently dialectic, a changing synthesis of what it finitely is and what it infinitely can or should be. "To become oneself is to become concrete. But to become concrete is neither to become finite nor to become infinite, for that which is to become concrete is indeed a synthesis." And in synthesis is born—ironically in the face of Kant's de-subjective selfing or de-selfing—the Kantian manifold. Remember Kant asserted that "the I is 'an entirely empty expression' which designates nothing more than 'the thought of an absolute, but logical unity of the subject' (CPR A, 356); it does not of itself exist as an ultimate substance or ground underlying knowledge and experience, but is simply a necessary logical function which accompanies it."[4] The self (which goes by the name of "I") is an entity that achieves maximum recognition through consciousness and other syntheses that can appear to be merely combinatory and not organic, as they note the evidence of appearance but not, as in the case of the arm or the leg, for example, disappearance. What can be seen to disappear is manifest but in terms of the self only symptomatic and so operates analogically under different, often hybridic names.[5]

There is a book by Hans Zischler called *Kafka Goes to the Movies* about which one reviewer wrote: "A more accurate title for this book might have been, 'What Kafka Would Have Seen Had He Gone to the Movies,' for as Kafka admitted 'I myself seldom go to the

---

[3] Husserl's idea that "*Making-clear-to-oneself*" is the result of two combined "*processes of rendering something intuitive and those of enhancing the clarity of what is inherently intuitive*" is useful in this regard. Husserl, *Ideas I*, §68 and 124.

[4] Imannuel Kant, *Critique of Pure Reason*, First Edition (1781), quoted in Howard Caygill, *A Kant Dictionary* (Malden, MA: Blackwell, 1995), 234.

[5] Ibid., 102; Søren Kierkegaard, *The Sickness Unto Death*, ed. Howard V. Hong and trans. Edna H. Hong (Princeton: Princeton University Press, 1983), 28 and 30.

cinematograph theater,' noting that his need for distraction 'drinks its fill from the [movie] posters.'"[6] The innocent construction "I myself" theatrically confirms what is not necessarily true, that the "I" and "myself" are one and the same, that if one of them goes to the movies, the other must go as well. But what if, as in Martin Amis's novel *Time's Arrow* (1992), "I" am cycling back without myself knowing where I am going or why? What if "I" or "myself" just decides to slip away? Perhaps I have something I must discover that is not ready to be reconstituted into myself. The self asks, "Why am I walking *backward* into the house?... What is the sequence of the journey I'm on? What are the rules? Why are the birds singing so strangely? Where am I heading?"[7] That Amis's novel will turn out to be about a former Nazi doctor who has so buried his past he does not initially know his own secret is not coincidental with some of the things I will discuss.

Generally speaking, we succumb to chronology (and to the chronological "I"), to the generational roll call of people and place names that bring comfort where the unknown, the unrecorded does not. Chronology, a function of causality roots us in famil(iarit)y and resolution. And yet, Robert Pinsky reminds us that "all people owe their being to origins multiple and unknown, a tangle of forgotten roots." What is more, his story of David, ancient king of the Jews "involves the mysteries of how a person belongs or does *not* belong [my *italics*] with another or with a family or tribe or people." You can, psychiatrists tell us, be born into the wrong family. I take my cue from shape-shifting King David and his "blurred chronology" (Was Goliath his *cousin*? Pinsky asks.), taking up various origin stories-identity narratives not limited to my own to interrogate these questions of does and does not, was and was not. I ask after Pinsky after David, "Who is the man—or, for that matter, if he is a figment then what is the figment?"[8]

Not only can we not trust chronology in a directional sense—i.e., we start at the beginning and conclude at the end—we cannot necessarily stop ourselves from beginning over and over again. The author of the preface to Marcel Bénebou's, *Why I Have Not Written Any of My Books*,

---

[6] Hans Zischler, *Kafka Goes to the Movies*, trans. Susan H. Gillespie (Chicago: University of Chicago Press, 2003); *Publishers Weekly*, 4 November 2002. https://www.publishersweekly.com/978-0-226-98671-5.

[7] Martin Amis, *Time's Arrow, or the Nature of the Offense* (New York: Vintage, 1992), 6.

[8] Robert Pinsky, *The Life of David* (New York: Schocken, 2005), 7, 12, 14, 15, and 65.

for example, attests that the book "is itself prefatory from beginning to end. Or more properly, from beginning to beginning, because wherever one finds oneself in this book, it always seems to be the beginning."[9] This is logical in its own way as the book's author, the presentable self, has stated "*I Have Not Written Any of My Books*" and so cannot keep tabs on what the book's structure is doing and undoing, except belatedly *as a reader.* The book begins with Bénebou, a Moroccan-born Jew, asking and synthesizing two enduring Jewish questions no doubt read aloud to him as a child. The first derived from one of the Four Questions posed at the *Pesach* (Passover) Seder, the second one of three interlocking questions aimed at establishing common humanity set forth by Shakespeare's Shylock: "How is this book [night] different from all other books [nights]?" and "Is it not made like them, of words and paper? When it is deciphered does it not make sense? When it is shredded, does it not make scrap?" ["Hath not a Jew eyes? Hath not a Jew hands, organs, dimensions, senses, affections, passions...? If you prick us, do we not bleed?"—*The Merchant of Venice*, III, i, 58–68.][10] Citation of sources here suggests that the writer comes only *after* the reader and implicitly that being read to comes even before that and that what was read to us is perhaps what ultimately remains. The stories we tell are the stories we hear, although whether I hear them *myself* when *I* hear them is open to question.

In *The Reader* (dir. Stephen Daldry, 2008 from the 1995 novel by Bernhard Schlink), a German teacher tells his students, one of whom, Michael, is inadvertently sleeping with a former concentration camp guard named Hannah Schmitz: "The notion of secrecy is central to Western literature. You may say the whole idea of character is defined by people holding specific information, which, for various reasons, sometimes perverse, sometimes noble, they are determined not to disclose." Karl Jaspers, *The Question of German Guilt* is on Michael's reading list for his law school class in 1958, so the question being posed is in part whether guilt is generational or intergenerational once the so-called one-time domestic secret of the Holocaust is now known by the German people who once denied or disbelieved it (did not claim it as *knowledge*

---

[9]Warren Motte, "Why I Have Not Prefaced Any of Marcel Bénebou's Books," in Marcel Bénebou, ed. and trans. David Kornacker, *Why I Have Not Written Any of My Books* (Lincoln: University of Nebraska Press, 1996), vii.

[10]Bénebou, *Why I Have Not Written Any of My Books*, 8.

because they had not directly seen or experienced it and having had it presented to them as a falsehood, on the order of an abstraction; pled the deniable "I," as in "'I' was only following orders."). Michael has served as Hannah Schmitz's reader. Hannah's sentencing hinges on her former young reader's evidence that she could not have written the report that sent camp prisoners to their death because she is illiterate (and so would have needed a writer as she later did a reader—a sort of commensurate "I"). Her shame at not being able to read surpasses her shame at having participated in sending people to their deaths to maintain order and keep chaos at bay. As such, she assumes the collective guilt of the six female guards who wrote the report in question. *I* was only following order(s), she might have said, but she feels she must atone to the letter not just of the law but to that of her moral illiteracy, as "I" is in itself an orderly construct. Who is this "*I*" and is she herself in on the secret? Were the actions of this *I* in character, and is character a generational conceit, a role one plays when circumstances demand? The other five former guards get several years in prison. Hannah gets life. Michael, the former reader, takes on the character of a guilt he has not in fact earned in the sense of deserved. (He did not know about Hannah's past when they were romantically involved.) Hannah and Michael's lives converge in other people's fictions which he reads into a tape recorder, providing her with an endless number of cassette tapes to fill the emptiness of her life in prison and to teach her to read for herself, to unconceal herself.

When Hannah is about to be released from prison after serving twenty years of her life sentence, Michael is contacted by her caseworker to see whether he will "take responsibility for" Hannah who has no family or friends and who, without Michael will have "no future at all." As the caseworker speaks on the phone to Michael, she scribbles some zig-zag energy lines, perhaps evoking the unconscious, emanating from a giant block, boldface (letter) "I." Is it a boldfaced "I"/lie, as in a first-person narrative about *someone else* taking responsibility? "Have you spent a lot of time thinking about the past?" Michael asks Hannah on a rare prison visit to arrange the circumstances of her life once she is released. It doesn't matter, she tells him. "The dead are still dead." Michael wonders aloud what she has learned and in so doing is asking for some secret door into her character. "I learned to read," she tells him, and the door, that same door behind which so many others hid to keep their lives secret, that door that sealed the fate of her concentration camp charges, closes shut. Hannah hangs herself in prison, using the stacks of books she accumulated as a new reader to stand on.

Onto our "I-am" origin story is grafted the exoskeleton of the contrarian self-as-nemesis's "I am not who I am." I wasn't born this way. I wasn't meant to be this way. I am not a monster, etc. What belies this self-contestation is that anger always carries the day into night allowing sometimes for a belated reassessment. In the interim, there is the most pertinent extra-human sense that "I am not *not* who I am," the sum of these things I have done were done by me and this tautological tightness clings to me like a skin-suit of my own design. I have sewn on the chest emblem, fashioned the mask, devised the props and accessories. I have put in the time to be this person whose actions cannot be washed clean by purer intentions I am only rumored by myself to have had when I started out, in the *first* beginning, when I was still an original. When people speak of living a life that is not their own, third-person-like in a writerly or cinematic fashion, they are seeing the "not" but reaching for the "not-not-ness" that knots self-realization into complication, complicity, guilt, anxiety, and dread. "I am my own worst enemy" is something more than a platitude and less than a reasoned truth.

Uncanny Resemblance

I wonder whether in picking through other people's writings, I am talent-spotting for family resemblances in my own life so as to expand who I am in relation to a wider "we." But don't you have to determine who this "we" is before subjecting it to measurement? Is this the stuff of small-family origin or an excess of self and is the latter a function of the former? Probably not, as my sister doesn't suffer from this condition any more than she suffers the myriad physical and psychological ailments I appear to have inherited. Then again, excessive self-consciousness encourages self-analysis to a hyperbolic and hypochondriacal degree. All I know is that I am searching for something that is missing, like Howard Jacobson's Julian Treslove who awakens each morning to "a sense of loss...and underachievement." Also, a sense of guilt. And he's not even Jewish. But his friend Samuel Finkler is, and since their school days together the two of them "entwined [a] play around their friendship." That play, *Hamlet*, contemplates the fluidity of meaning and display, language and reality, is and is not, was and was not, beginnings (origins) and beginnings again like in a postmodern novel or in a recurring dream.

Treslove, for whom physical alikeness and "rational coincidence" go not so much hand-in-hand as hand-to-painted-face, manifesting its fictional allowance. There is an almost-ness to all of this that says not what it is, only that I can't get *it* right.[11] Perhaps because I am self-doubling more than mirroring to establish empathy with others. Or am I unknowingly appropriating Wittgenstein's idea of family resemblance as being comprised of what may or may not be recognizably common traits, the relation of a plurality of things rather than insistence upon one or two essential ones? Is the practice of plurality fundamentally diasporic? Can one simply affect diaspora as a performance mode or style? Do I curtail argument in favor of framing relation of image to image, idea to idea, and even word to word to collage meaning *as* plurality? Or more simply, in my surfeit of de/self-ing do I strangely (or not strangely) lack self-discipline? Do I receive credit for asking the question of myself? You don't have to be Jewish to ask these questions, but it couldn't hurt.

Everywhere, non-observant Jewish writers speak not so much of being attuned to Jewish culture as to possessing a "Jewish mind." By this they generally mean they are (stereotypically): anxious, neurotic ("I think, therefore I fear [who] I am."), self-deprecatingly joking (see neurotic), obsessive, catastrophic, self-conscious (see also secret, secretive), self-critical, intellectual (see self-conscious + self-critical), paranoid/guilty (see self-conscious + self-critical), fatalistic (see catastrophic), paranoid (see anxious + neurotic), overly attuned to bodily functions (see anxious + neurotic + paranoid), and relativist—weighing possible options and meanings, truths and untruths (see all of the preceding characteristics). Identity driven in ways that individual non-Jews could be but non-Jews generally are not, mostly because they are eclectically, majoritarian-ly, non-racially, non-Jewish. Aware of their Jewishness and of other people's awareness of their Jewishness, for good and ill. That is to say, aware that the world at large is *not* Jewish, putting your mind at odds with the world as a socially structured and determined reality. Is the Jewish uncanny a pejorative co-opted as a positive or the reverse?

Jacobson is especially good at getting this, at getting me, and, it turns out, getting that "I" am "we" after all. (The joke might begin: "A Jew walks into a room...," with the singular subject always already

---

[11] Howard Jacobson, *The Finkler Question* (New York: Bloomsbury, 2010), 47, 48, 51, and 53.

being plural.[12]) Treslove regards all Jews as being a number of distinctly recurring characteristics that make them all "Finklers" and "Finklerish" in his somewhat limited imagination and despite the fact that the original Samuel Finkler does not possess all of the aforementioned characteristics—but the wannabe-Jew Treslove does. Treslove lives in the realm of the uncanny, romantically fatalistic, a divining rod for chaos in mind and body, the sort of person (like me) who utters "Ouch!" in anticipation of something hurting. ("His shins ached with the imagined collision.") On the street, "a tree reared up at him" and he imagined being one of the homeless. He is menaced by road and pavement. He sees others in the reflected chiaroscuro light of his own "saddism," a Jacobson coinage from another novel, making the case that the so-called atypicality of the self (-conscious) is, in fact, typical. He is a real character only in the sense that he is "a story waiting for a plot." As a double, a role he sometimes plays for profit, Treslove is noted not for his verisimilitude but for his versatility: his ability to be *so many other people*. A woman leaves him when "he became the double of no one in particular," that is to say, when she gets to know the real him who is not all that interesting.[13]

At the same time, Treslove's "passing himself off as someone he wasn't, a universal lookalike who didn't feel as others felt," may be a double fake. He recalls at school Finkler "mak[ing] him feel like someone he wasn't," "false to a self he didn't know he had." Finkler, Treslove says, never dreamed, but he (Treslove) did, specifically of something he misplaced "between the pages of a book even when what he was looking for was bigger than the book." Does this denote a healthy awareness that there is something bigger than the self, or is it the self's dream of overflowing the borders consciousness (mis)places upon it (i.e., self-containment), freeing itself to metastasize into everybody else, or into another ilk, or to no one in particular?[14] Can this overflow compensate the non-Jewish reader for not being one of the people of the book? Is Treslove searching for a "we" to which he cannot belong, no matter

---

[12] Howard Jacobson, *Shylock Is My Name* (New York: Hogarth Shakespeare, 2016), 65.

[13] Ibid., 10 and 24.

[14] "Maybe self didn't enter into it, maybe it was actually a freedom from self—a timid awareness of one's small place in a universe ringed by a barbed-wire fence of rights and limits." Note that even here Treslove is appropriating the physical terms of internment familiar to concentration camp survivors. Jacobson, *The Finkler Question*, 7, 9, 10, 18, 24, 26, and 29; *In A Lonely Place* (dir. Nicholas Ray, 1950).

how much he schools himself in them? Do we seek to measure ourselves against the community into which we were born or to escape it, and, if the latter, do we find that even if we can leave the neighborhood of cultural lookalikes behind, we double them in the world at large? I ask these questions not on Treslove's behalf but for myself *as* Treslove.

The World at Large, Writ Small

Living in London during my college years, I was followed cross town by a young man older than I. No matter where I went, ducking into and out of one pub and another, there he was, until I found a way out the back of one and lost him. I never understood what this meant and since my follower spoke no English (what language does a shadow speak?), I never found out. Following is never innocent, always intentional. Following so as to be seen being unseen. We worked in the same hotel kitchen, where the only other English speaker was a young Englishman my age named David, who when he wasn't working as a sous chef, was an amateur thief. He stole everything—food from stores and the workplace (the gigantic Dickensian baker hung him on a meat hook in the frozen storage locker for stealing one of his meticulously crafted desserts), books, his neighbors' cars, an ambulance from outside a hospital emergency room. He may have lied about this last bit to make himself sound more interesting as he did about a long abdominal scar he claimed to have received when someone came up to him out of the blue and stabbed him in a parking garage. When I returned to London many years later, he told me the truth that the scar was the result of an operation performed shortly after birth. I did not ask him about the ambulance, but it seems like it might have issued from the thought of the operation had it not been successful. On this return trip, David gifted me with a small book called *Mind Games*, whose second entry, "Listen to my Voice," concerns sleep and hypnosis. I mention this because while writing I read about all of this following business in a novel by Joseph McElroy called *A Smuggler's Bible*. The book was published in 1966, so it just preceded my trip to England by one year, but I have come to understand that chronology is not to be trusted.

In the novel, there is a character named David Brooke whom the narrator (presumably McElroy, but maybe not) claims to have penetrated with his memories and his voice. "I put it into David's mind, and he writes it down," writes the anonymous narrator, leaving unclear as to whether we are reading the book of David or not. The voice instructs David to "analyze, synthesize, assimilate; project yourself," by which the voice means itself or itself as David. Still, someone, the narrator perhaps hastens to add, "But there were other origins."[15] David in turn insinuates himself into the life of the English antique bookseller Peter St. John who is interested in genealogy, that is, in translating Bouchet's *Genealogies* into English, and who is himself followed across Brooklyn Heights by a young boy bouncing a rubber ball named Walter Roy (rhymes with "Boy"). Roy thinks that Peter might be his recently deceased father, because he looks like him in profile, but when Peter tells him, "I should *like* to have been your father," as if the "*like-ness*" makes comparison not so much flattering as sincere, Walt quickly responds, "I'd rather...have him dead and have *him* than have him back and have him *you!*"[16] After my father died, I followed a man in Cambridge (Boston), who I thought might be him. For years after this event, I have dreamed that my father had a second family, which I only now realize was my attempt to keep him alive. That is, the second family did not represent the betrayal of simultaneity but the hopefulness of a post-death chronology that I know to be false. This is on the order of Moore's Paradox in which the thing you know to be factually untrue can be true in your view as stated via attention to grammatical tense change and the viewing position of the subjective "I." One might also call this, as opposed to knowing, belief.

Consider the following:

> **Question**: A man and his son are in a terrible accident and are rushed to the hospital in critical care. The doctor looks at the boy and exclaims "I can't operate on this boy, he's my son!" How could this be?
> **Answer**: It's the boy's mother.

The foregoing riddle is often cited as an example of systemic gender bias, namely the failure to consider the possibility that the doctor could be the injured boy's mother. But in relation to Moore's Paradox, there is a more basic and profound riddle at work having to do with how the pronoun "I" (rather than "he" or "she") can be attributed to statements that are not of one person's making. So, Moore's famous paradox—"It's

[15] Joseph McElroy, *A Smuggler's Bible* (Woodstock, NY: The Overlook Press, 1966), 5.
[16] Ibid., 28.

raining but I don't believe it"—may only appear to attribute the agency of dis/belief to the event on which it is commenting, "It's raining." Without knowing where "It's raining" comes from we cannot know when it was said either as we have lost the capacity to bracket together the ideas of implicit and explicit subject statements. The only way to heal this split is to do what we do in error, to assume that the "I" floats from the end of the sentence back to the beginning as being my observation which is seen to be contradicted by my disbelief in this observation. ["But (say "I") what about the generous paranoia of those who pursue themselves?"[17]] This is the primary error that attaches to the doctor-son riddle—not the failure to assume that the son has two parents, one of whom may be female but that the tendency is to scan the subject as an indivisible entity back and forth through the two-headed statement of in/capacity. It's not so much a matter of not knowing who the subject is as that the subject is inherently divided.

Put in a slightly different way, the "fact" that it is raining in Moore's statement is authenticated by an "I" that is missing. It is this absence that enables disbelief—either because the "I"-witness does not appear or because there is no evidence that there even is an "I" different from the second "I" or identical to it, to the one that speaks of disbelief, because that would not so much contest the statement that it is raining but the possibility that there is even a single "I" that can be trusted as being real. In Wittgenstein's treatment of Moore's Paradox, his famous "Slab!" passage, he treats the "I" as being parenthetical, as in the implicit command, "I want you to bring me that slab," silently shortened to "Bring me that slab," and then again to "Slab!," the request having become more commanding as the subject pronoun disappears and the action-qua-action asserts itself as if it had no point of origin. As the Moore-Wittgenstein tandem illustrates, the "I" is a slippery slope. What keeps us from sliding down it or from the "I" slipping away is Moore's so-called common sense argument in his "Proof of an External World," that says: "By holding up my two hands, and saying, as I make a certain gesture with the right hand, 'Here is one hand', and adding, as I make a certain gesture with the left, 'and here is another.' I *knew* that there was one hand in the place indicated by combining a certain gesture with my first utterance of 'here' and that there was another in the different place indicated by combining a certain gesture with my second utterance of 'here'.

---

[17] Joseph McElroy, *Ancient History: A Paraphase* (Ann Arbor: Dzanc Books, 2014), 16.

How absurd it would be to suggest that I did not know it, but only believed it, and that perhaps it was not the case! You might as well suggest that I do not know that I am now standing up and talking—that perhaps after all I'm not, and that it's not quite certain that I am!"[18]

If Moore's "I" is parenthetical in his object lesson, it is grammatical in Wittgenstein's adaptation of the same. One can say "I do this. I do that." or even, "I do this. I do this." in Wittgenstein's construction with the two "I'"s serving the same grammatical function while standing in for two different subjects. The real, surface confusion in the latter case, though, lies in the apparent sameness of the two predicates. (The puzzle regarding the doctor and son is here revealed not to be about family relationship but about what Wittgenstein called "family resemblance"—in which commonality is more complicated, more variegated than it may at first appear—in this case between an articulated and un-articulated "I." Wittgenstein argues—in paraphrase—that, "There is no essence to language, but only different phenomena related in various ways." This underlies Wittgenstein's notion of a language game, which he likens to the "complex network of overlapping and criss-crossing similarities" shared by family members.[19]) The ability to see difference in the subject-predicate negotiation in the two sentences—"I do this. I do this."—speaks to the *poetic* aspect that Wittgenstein ascribed to the best philosophy (to which I here attend), which his own philosophy demonstrated could only be achieved with some measure of failure. The reason for such "failure" is the absence of proof, which pertains to fact not to view. Then again, "there are more things in heaven and earth, Horatio,/ Than are dreamt of in your philosophy." These words were, of course, spoken by the son of a father who had appeared to him as a ghost, an abstraction (*Hamlet*, 1.5.167–8).

That David Brooke's Walter Roy bounced a rubber ball while shadowing his father's life-like ghost recalls for me the origin scene (to which I will return) of me as a boy bouncing a succession of Spalding brand pink rubber balls off a door in my father's parents' apartment which featured a multiplicity of locks to keep my paranoid aunt in and the ghosts, her and possibly their demons out. The rubber balls were given to me not

---

[18] G.E. Moore, "Proof of an External World" (1939), cited in https://plato.stanford. edu/entries/moore/StanfordEncyclopediaofPhilosophy.

[19] Hans-Johann Glock, *A Wittgenstein Dictionary* (Malden, MA: Blackwell, 2005), 120 and 121, paraphrasing Wittgenstein, *Philosophical Investigations*, §§ 65–67.

by my father, whose home it no longer was but by my grandfather. They were handed (down) to me in a wrinkled brown paper bag that looked like it could have been brought with them over from Russia, which they fled, thereupon entering a state of a chronological fear and paranoia, the feeling that they had somehow been followed not so much across space but across time.

Trauma is a great dis/locator. Childhood brokers these elements into a formula for troubled forgetting and remembrance. Aging teaches you that childhood reinvention is a mother. It toys with your past, present, and future. We were all schooled by assassination, in grade school for it, kept out of school to watch how its aftermath played out in more, even more televised assassinations. The sky was falling too or was threatening to. Kill-re-kill-overkill, like in some Witkiewicz play. We were in school for that too, kneeling at our hallway lockers, hiding under our desks in absurd postures, as if we, personally, were the targets and not just part of some larger abstraction. Drinking out of our non-dishwasher-safe mugs and bowls hand-painted with our childhood nicknames, the latter invented to suggest a sociability, even popularity we did not, in fact, possess. How could we, when they (these names), were aliases? The ceramic shards lying on my dormitory room floor my freshman year in college, having collided with a hard rubber ball that flashed down the hall like it was wearing a homing device and through my door, which was uncharacteristically open. The ball now bounces away off different doors' locks in directions conspiring to form paranoid patterns of behavior that roughly model diaspora. There were other grandchildren, but I was the only one who "knew" this, the only one given the balls to bounce and follow wherever they might lead. There are more things in wrinkled brown paper bags, Horatio, than are dreamt of in your philosophy. Can there even *be* a post-Holocaust Horatio?

"Time is unreal" is true insofar as the statement "Time is real" does not capture the truth of what time is. It is merely descriptive in a grammatical sense. It is not an empirical proposition.[20] But then, what is? It's like me or McElroy saying that I or Peter or David was walking and was followed (shadowed). Zeno claimed that motion (e.g., walking and so also shadowing or following) was impossible (see Zeno's arrow which moves in not through space). In response, Diogenes stood up

---

[20]Wittgenstein extracts from Moore's common-sense propositions the thread of their would-be empiricism and finds the latter to be more a matter of seeming than being.

and walked back and forth across the room with Zeno watching unimpressed. Diogenes's action could not disprove Zeno's statement because it represented his view and not a factual proposition.[21] This, of course, does not prevent philosophers or us from accepting Moore's Paradox not as a structural demonstration but as a functional truth about writing as it does about speaking. The fact is, there was a shadow, and a boy following another boy, a shoplifting friend named David (McElroy's David steals a book, and "a smuggler's bible" conceals something stolen—a physical item in the case of the actual object, a life or lives in the case of a novel that bears the smuggler's object's name), a rubber ball, a locked door with perhaps each one of the several locks concealing a different story, a dead father who may have been cheating (only on) death (an obvious fiction), and a need to discover origin and alternate stories in other people's lives in order to "analyze, synthesize, assimilate; project yourself"—that is, "myself" as a concept, a proposition.

David Brooke's origin story as a "smuggler" dates from when his mother invited a blind ventriloquist of their acquaintance named Mr. Jones to perform first at her son's tenth birthday party and then again, when he graduated from Dartmouth College by which time David had achieved some distance from the act and his childhood memory. This aligned with the "royal distance" that blindness imposed between David and Mr. Jones, despite the fact that the ventriloquist looked him right in the eyes. It was on this occasion that David, an earnest reader of the *ABC'S of Ventriloquism*, "witnessed that horrifying moment of mechanical failure" in which Jones "lost his timing so his voice was no longer synchronized with [his dummy's] trap-mouth." At the moment, Dartmouth-educated David knew "that he must someday come back to that childhood self now spinning deeper and deeper within him, and project into someone else, project not his own voice but himself—so his own voice would become that of the self temporarily housing him." For a time, this was for David a group project, in the sense that he would enter into the minds of numerous denizens of a certain Kodak Hotel, as he did with his own mother, "as if it were an apartment with furniture." As he matured, David found this to be unsatisfactory and instructed his own mind to "Simplify. Forget the denizens of Kodak [mere shallow, photorealistic reproductions]. Get one person. Set the voice back in its shadowy flesh."[22]

[21] Moore, *The Philosophy of G.E. Moore*, 380–81 and 386–87.
[22] McElroy, *A Smuggler's Bible*, 96, 97, 98, and 100.

The degree to which you can do this and still retain something of yourself is the paradox but also the problem that can resolve itself as loss, as self-identity theft. When the pale Strangers from a dying world create the neo-noir science fiction metropolis *Dark City* (dir. Alex Proyas, 1998) from extracted human memories in the hope of learning how to grow new life from the example of the human soul, they mistakenly forgo the heart. Analysis, synthesis, and assimilation fail them despite or because of their own superior intelligence (their bookishness) and that of their scientific technician who shares his name with Daniel P. Schreber, the real-life judge and schizophrenic author of *Memoirs of My Nervous Illness* (1903), which fascinated both Freud and Jung. The Strangers, whose generic names include Mr. Book (their leader), Mr. Wall, Mr. Sleep, Mr. Rain, and Mr. Quick could be characters in the multitasking acting repertoire of Peter Sellers, master dialectician and impersonator, the Great Ventriloquist, who lived in and through other people's characters, having no character of his own.[23] Lacking his quintessentially generic character résumé, I recognize that the inception of self-knowledge through other people may result in unrecoverable loss of self to a mind that bears the brunt of its beating (he)art. I don't know whether to expect a convergence of my (there will be) three David's and whether the functions they serve individually parallel those of McElroy's two—the dreamer and the interpreter of the dream, both David's having been engineered and monitored by some author, perhaps me, perhaps not I. When McElroy or his unnamed surrogate says, "I speak as much to the reader as to my David," I am either listening to or for the ventriloquist's voice. But which one of us is the ventriloquist and which the reader?[24]

ENTER SANDMAN

The gist of McElroy's *The Letter Left to Me* (1988) is not what the letter tells the son about his father and his hopes and feelings for him but the distribution of the letter that opens up the unknown parts of the father's life for the son. More than this, it is a measure of the son's projection of

---

[23] Sellers often played two or more characters in one film. The role he most valued was that of abstract life-observer Chauncey the Gardner in *Being There* (dir. Hal Ashby, 1979), adapted from self-mythologizer Jerzy Kozinski's 1970 novel of the same name. Roger Lewis, *The Life and Death of Peter Sellers* (New York: Applause, 1997), 79.

[24] McElroy, *A Smuggler's Bible*, 132.

the father's letter into other hands that makes its and his (the father's) meaning unlocatable to him once it left the desk drawer, the room, the house in which the son had tracked it. "Family," always in quotation marks, is an information source and hub so that whoever has the information is, in a sense, part of an extended family of auditors, knowing something of your life and something of the lives closest to you that perhaps you haven't known. But distribution of letters is also the writer's task and the letter readers read his words as well, or more properly, project themselves into his words with their own selves. ("The letter moved before my eyes with each person who laid eyes on it...I had made them speak."[25]) There is no escaping this interpenetration, no matter how solipsistic the writing appears to be or the philosophy behind the writing affects. We are always and only made meaningful in human hands. This is what the testing of the subject tells us. Wittgenstein was right in asserting that the limit of his language was not only the limit of meaning but of his (self in relation to the) world. (At the same time, the fact that "language is essentially *placed*," contextual in/as to its meaning, shadows the doing of language with mise en scène, like one "I" following another, and also "another."[26])

We are always sending one another letters that we cannot help but read. And so, the protagonist in *The Letter Left to Me* reads a postcard on which "the stamp [is] upside down, the message *knew you'd look* palpably beneath the half-licked stamp."[27] But this sharing of the father, made palpable after his death, is painful for the son who feels he is losing the father's memory to the world at large, across which it is scattered like the dead man's ashes, the dead letter(s). If the immediate aftermath of the father's death is to follow his likeness around corners that turn into blind alleys, the distribution of his memory in letter form sets off in too many directions to follow "him" at all. How are you supposed to follow in his footsteps, to be a better man than he, as his letter prompts you to be, when you have lost track of who he was? The more widely distributed his letter is, the more secret(ed) his identity becomes until you ask (in the trickster-ness of time) whether he was really your father at all. Maybe he was someone who had been contracted to play your father, the role you

[25] Joseph McElroy, *The Letter Left to Me* (New York: Alfred A. Knopf, 1988), 38.

[26] Danièle Moyal-Sharrock, *Understanding Wittgenstein's On Certainty* (New York: Palgrave Macmillan, 2004), 12.

[27] Ibid., 114 and 128.

are now playing for your son, although he will not see this until after you are gone. ("Keeping his costume should we need to become him one day. When the time came. When my father's space was hollow enough for another body, possibly one of our own, to fit into it."[28]) And so on. Mortality counts on this sleight-of-man to keep us all in our place, to not see beyond our lives until our father's death gives us our first glimpse of the unreality of it all. And once you see this, it cannot be unseen. We become more distracted by pretending we can look away.

But there's more. The self-copying letter (or so it appears) is likened to cells that reproduce themselves.[29] My father died from cancer. I have had two rehearsals of my own, nineteen years part, nineteen being the age of a young man living in London where *he* was followed by a cancer that was still more than nineteen years away and which, upon its initial arrival, made him old. I was older than McElroy who was fifteen when he lost his father. Let's focus on that word, "lost," a euphemism for "dead" or "died," but also "lost" as in misplaced, like a letter that you forgot or neglected to send. Was my father's letter to me misplaced in my first old man's cancer (cell reproduction) in a relatively young man's body? *Misplaced*, as in did not fit, did not belong. Did said letter reproduce itself as if it were being sent to someone else, an extended family member in my second cancer that had wandered off for nineteen years, only to return to me, an older man who had finally caught up with the now more age-appropriate disease? (Cancer returning after nineteen years is a lie told not by causality but by continuity. It only retrospectively suggests a hiatus.) To the letter, cancer signed its name to physical recollection, a reminder of sorts from the brain in my body that reads: "Now is the time when you *should* be getting this, your father's cancer." Heeding Paul Auster's words, "and that is where the story begins, in your body, and everything will end in the body as well," my mindful body is telling me: "Now you know what you're about, what your story is."[30] It is, of course, the continuation of your father's story just as his was the continuation of *his* father's, your grandfather's story.

You will never be (cancer-) free. There's a rhythm to this, as McElroy suggests, that captures our memory at a certain age. When the father's

[28] Ben Marcus, "The Father Costume," in *Leaving the Sea: Stories* (New York: Vintage, 2014), 180.

[29] Joseph McElroy, *The Letter Left to Me* (New York: Alfred A. Knopf, 1988), 119.

[30] Paul Auster, *Winter Journal* (New York: Picador, 2012), 12.

letter said it hoped the son would be a better man than he, did this mean "better" in the sense of "healthier," non-cancerous? Was my father trying to extend my life through the healing power of words? Surely, he knew this to be an impossible task, but it's a father's job to be aspirational for his children, a tragedy when he stops being so. Did I begin writing in my own true voice in response to his death because I intuited his message as having been written to save my life? Was I writing then in my father's voice? My dedication in an earlier book reads not "In memory of my father" but "*In my father's memory*," an enlargement of *his* memory rather than a recollection of mine.[31] My father gave me not his death but *his death consciousness*. I remember this all my life. McElroy's protagonist wonders whether someone other than his father could have typed the letter left to him, then immediately recalls his father giving him a typewriter for his eighth birthday. The implication, at least for me, is that the son is the someone other than his father who typed the letter in the sense that he has within him the cellular message his father left for him in so many words, words like "family" ("he left my mother"), like "friend" ("he left friends who I believed care for me"), and like "cancer" (a blank goes here).[32]

Speaking as a father of how catastrophe, trauma changes you, singer-songwriter Nick Cave says that it alters your ability to identify people who were or were not your friends. (Cave's catastrophe was his twin son Arthur falling to his death in 2015.) When one of these "friends" asks "how are you doing," the new "you," the changed "you" does not know how to react.[33] But what if you're not conscious that the catastrophe has happened, has befallen "you"? What if the misrecognition of a "friend" is the first clue you have that the catastrophe, the trauma has already happened and perhaps is still happening and also is going to happen again, is immanent and imminent? We speak of wisdom being the consolation prize of aging, but wisdom is not knowledge, because we have difficulty understanding what objects of knowledge are. Wittgenstein questioned whether the propositions that constitute Moore's Paradox "are *neither*

---

[31] Ibid., 38; Spencer Golub, *Infinity (Stage)* (Ann Arbor: University of Michigan Press, 1999).

[32] McElroy, *The Letter Left to Me*, 120.

[33] Nick Cave speaking in the film *One More Time with Feeling* (dir. Andrew Dominik, 2016).

known *nor* open to doubt."[34] Name your episteme, pick your poison. I do not necessarily know what I assert I know. Where's the proof beyond the fact that I have picked out a frame to put around those things I hold either to be real or true? It's all a loop anyway. That's what trauma teaches us. There is the one time that redirects everything so that people, places, and things return, even when you can't see it happening and especially when you do.

Recently, I went to see my friend David's show. This is a different David, someone with whom I've co-written a novel long distance, whom my wife believed for some time was really just me speaking in two voices about my own writing that would not come. "It's frustrating that David is not writing to me," I would say aloud when no new electronic writing arrived on my computer for long periods of time. She naturally assumed that this was my writer's block speaking, this assumption becoming in her mind a certainty when after handing her the phone to talk to David to prove his independent existence, there was no one on the line. We later invited David to our home for dinner and despite enjoying a perfectly cordial evening together, my wife could not be persuaded that I had not hired someone to impersonate "David" as part of my self-delusion. This history is what made what happened recently so disturbing. While waiting outside the theater to be admitted to a show David had written, I saw him walking toward me down the street. I did what I almost never do. I hailed him by his name, in the process walking up to him. "David" walked right past me, without changing his gait or facial expression. How could he not have seen me? Alternatively, how could this not be David? I was shaken both by my uncharacteristic forwardness and the catastrophe that naturally attends behaviors that I do not recognize as being my own. As the event continued to torment me long after "David" had disappeared from sight (at least I didn't follow *him*), I found that I could not unsee him, and so I had to build a new vision around him. The "David" I think I saw, I saw, but was it a "David" he had discarded that no longer recognized me because we were not inhabiting the same time, only the same place? Or, more likely (?), did David not recognize the "I" performing the uncharacteristic behavior of interpellation? "I should have known you would be the last one to

[34] The references are to Wittgenstein, *On Certainty* (1969), which, philosophically speaking, constituted his dying words, and appear in Andy Hamilton, *The Routledge Guidebook to Wittgenstein and On Certainty* (New York: Routledge, 2014), 179–80.

exit," David said upon seeing me for the first (?) time after the show. He looked no more or less like himself than he had before, but I apparently looked just like myself only after. A third party brokered a phone call between myself and an earlier David to bridge the gap that had opened between us. As the conversation preceded with some difficulty and with some heavily veiled intimation on the other end of the line that there was something this David had to tell me but was withholding about myself, I began to suspect that "David" was actually *the voice of* my telephobia. The story of the three David's may link to this telephobia's origin story in which I mentally misidentified a caller's voice three times, responding to a different "she" with a different "I" each time. I later found this reiterative mental habit to extend from names to words and their meanings with me straining to switch tracks and trains of thought so as to stay in conversations where the speaker thought he/she was talking to a stable "I." Robert Pinsky says that "(Jewish king) David's gestures of affliction subsume their unflaunted paradoxes—purposeful grief, cunning madness—with additional levels of perspective and reservation, where *is* and *is not* occupy the same space. David attains the simultaneous engagement and calculation of art."[35] Maybe my wife was right after all. Maybe I *am* David.

Sandy is trying to pick up Susan at their first college mixer (he's at Amherst, she at Smith) in *Carnal Knowledge* (dir. Mike Nichols, 1971), each bemoaning and discussing the finer points of people not exhibiting who they really are at such events. Susan tries to distinguish between the person and the act.

> *Susan*: I think people only like to think they're putting on an act. But it's not an act. It's really them. If they think it's an act, they feel better because they think they could always change it.
> *Sandy*: You mean, they're kidding themselves because it's not really an act.
> *Susan*: Yes, it is an act, but they're the act. The act is them.
> *Sandy*: But if it's them, how can it be an act?
> *Susan*: 'Cause they're an act.
> *Sandy*: But they're also real.
> *Susan*: No.
> *Sandy*: You mean, I'm not real?

[35] Pinsky, *The Life of David*, 67.

Susan: No.
Sandy: I'm an act.
Susan: It's all right. I'm an act too.[36]

Sandy later says to Jonathan, who has secretly slept with his now girl-friend, Susan, "Sometimes I think I'm a better friend to you then you are to me." In the next scene, the three "friends" are seen laughing at Sandy's mondegreen, "I've been myzled" for "I've been misled." "Sensitive" Sandy, as his unfaithful future ex-wife Susan calls him, is tone deaf to the irony of how perfectly this mishearing captures his present situation. The inadvertent Yiddish-ness of the misheard word ("myzled"), not intentionally comic or profane as are the Yiddish words that are generally inserted into American English conversations, is ironic too given the fact that both Sandy and Jonathan were written as Jews. Jonathan is played by non-Jewish Jack Nicholson and Sandy by Jewish but faux-Yiddishly speaking Art Garfunkel. My mother and Jonathan both went to (the majority female) Evander Childs High School in the Bronx (misheard as Evander "Chiles" in the film's English subtitles for the hearing impaired), although fortunately not at the same time or in the same reality. My father and the film's writer, cartoonist Jules Feiffer were both at James Monroe High School, also in the Bronx, but again Feiffer was younger. In my generation's novel *Slaughterhouse-Five*, Billy Pilgrim affects an intergenerational passage, walking "through a door in 1955 and [coming] out another one in 1941. He has gone back through that door to find himself in 1963…He says." Or, as they say on the closed-circuit TV news of the self-broadcasting self: "Back to me." If it really *is* me. Here Billy bounces us back to the performance premise of Susan and Sandy's conversation *two years later*: "He is in a constant state of stage fright, he says, because he never knows what part of his life he is going to have to act next."[37] Or what part *in* his life, for that matter.

---

[36] And in Philip Roth's novel *Sabbath's Theater* (New York: Vintage, 1995), 290:
   Everything feels acted.
   Everything *is* acted.
   Whatever. With me there's some glue missing, something fundamental to every-one else that I don't have. My life never seems real to me.

[37] Kurt Vonnegut, Jr., *Slaughterhouse-Five* (New York: Dial Press, 2009; orig. pub. 1969), 29.

For David Norris (another David) in the film *The Adjustment Bureau* (dir. George Nolfi, 2011) doors that unlock and scramble times in space can only be breached by wearing one of the older generation's fedora hats (like older Jews wear in shul)—as if David, like Billy, is jumping between World War II generation and its later posts. David dons the hat to reengineer fate to synch up with his heart's desire, even at the risk of losing his identity and his memory. The men in hats make mental adjustments to the life-plan each of us has set out for us, which perhaps accounts for Moore's Paradox being possible. Also, for me misrecognizing David and David mishearing me when I called him by name on the street outside the theater in which his play was being performed. The way I remember it, the David I saw on the street was wearing a hat. I know that I was not. I was not, after all (I think), playing a role.

Late in *A Smuggler's Bible*, David Brooke, whose practice of projecting himself into others may have left him in a fugue state, receives letters of consolation that speak mainly of the letters' authors themselves and their disbelief that his amnesia (his forgetting them) is real. These are a series of chain letters that David worked out in advance. One of these letter writers, a fraudulent historian named Duke Amerchrome, instructs David to "get well properly." This invokes an earlier passage in which David asked himself, "What's the hardest thing in the world?" and answered himself, "To be *properly* selfish." Duke instructs David to make of his fugue state "a designed truth built grain by grain out of your own self: be your own sandman."[38] David's wife Ellen, who does not read her husband's writing, has also objected to what appears to be his permanent (pre-fugue) distraction, and despite herself, feels herself to be full of him. "I'm sorry: I don't understand, said David, who hadn't been listening but could tell that even if he had been he wouldn't understand." So maybe it's "David" who has put me up to this solipsism. Am I anymore in control of what "David" says than McElroy's unnamed narrator/McElroy the author is of his "David," despite "David" believing that it is he who is projecting into the minds and lives of other people whom he casts as characters that contribute to his writing and to his authorial identity? David claims to want to be hypnotized outside of himself and yet when the hypnotist he consults advises him, "Do it yourself! Do it yourself!" the author (David himself? Duke later to David in the latter's fugue state) adds, "Or did David put that construction on whatever the

[38] McElroy, *A Smuggler's Bible*, 307 and 345.

man said?" Perhaps David is speaking in the third person throughout the book, speaking of his own authorship *as if he were* Joseph McElroy. David is not comfortable in his own skin (thus his third personhood), which is why he ignored my approach on the street outside his show and why he waited for me outside his show later as well. Despite his recurring use of the Italian word *invertito* ("It means 'turned inward,'" said David.) there is no "inside" to David, only to the characters he projects into as "David." Am I projecting myself into him or him into me? Am *I* one of *his* characters? ("I gave David his independent existence; I guess I'm a fool to expect him to let me have my say.")

Is that me smiling into the camera while three young Italian women form shapes behind me on a beach outside of Rome or is that McElroy's David? I know he took his wife Ellen there, where she was variously memory-shaped.[39] I thought at the time that it was an uncharacteristic pose for me (Why was I smiling? This seemed too suggestive to me *in the moment I was smiling.*), despite my having set it up so that the background action would be in frame at just the right angle to my foreground image. My wife is not in the picture or is that her multi-shaping behind me? Why and for whom is she showing off like that behind my back? What is her agency or complicity in this non-recognition? Is she a shape-shifting "I" as well, or is it me, the three David's transformed in gender but not in function?

Strange things happen on sandy beaches. In a previous book, an airplane grew smaller as it passed overhead with me on a beach.[40] In *Inception* (dir. Christopher Nolan, 2010), the protagonist Cobb and his dead wife Mal, the memory he cannot bring himself to lose, build skyscrapers in limbo. Dom even reclaims Mal's original house, transporting it from her memory to their shared memory space as if there were a real origin story at work here and not just an obsessive idea that the real world only exists on the beach where we first discover them (*From Here to Eternity?*) amid the architecture of their own making.[41] I didn't take the picture on the beach but I posed for it as the agent and subject of self-projection. So, was this an instance of trick photography? It can take a lifetime to realize that you have been trying to trick your solipsism

---

[39] Ibid., 273, 295, 308, 318, and 325.

[40] Spencer Golub, *The Baroque Night* (Evanston: Northwestern University Press, 2018).

[41] *From Here to Eternity* (dir. Fred Zinnemann, 1953) features the movies' most famous romantic beach scene.

without really trying to strip it away. You monitor your heartbeat as you nominally try to outrun it, while watching solipsism backpedaling ahead of you waiting for you to catch up with some measure of self-awareness that puts you back on the clock.

Cancer is the most solipsistic of diseases and possibly the most clock-worthy. It makes you clock-watch rather than just making your ticker stop or your brain burst. Is that *cancer* presenting as three reconfiguring Italian women, happily metastasizing in the background even as I in a pre-conscious state smile in the foreground for the camera to indicate that I feel well, even optimistic, on holiday (prolonged remission), free from care. It's as if two parallel films were being shot that impossibly intersect, this impossibility derived from my not knowing or believing that cancer can wait nineteen years to recur. Still, I chose to frame the figures in the shot; they did not just happen into it. So, did intuition precede consciousness? "Bring me back a memory," filmmaker Cartwright's daughter Jenny in McElroy's *Lookout Cartridge* asks him whenever he goes on location. "I" went to Italy and all I have to show for it is this photographic pre-memory of my cancer. That is, until cancer returned, after me.

For years, I had a childlike image of a cancer as being a small, pink, hardball, much like David Brooke's father Halsey did.[42] Maybe, though, this has always been Halsey's image (he's about my age), which means that it was David's (my writer-friend "David" also had cancer), not mine. I just took up the pink ball and ricocheted it off of multiple surfaces. David and I have co-written a novel called *Hemispheres*. We wrote it via email correspondence and it's about spies and surveillance. David (Brooke) gave Halsey *Atoms and People* for Christmas and scribbled in the margins of the book:

(HEMISPHERES) Unite = Disperse
Heart of Matter = Heart of Person
Atomic Bomb = Discovery of Apartness, Epistemological Impotence[43]

"I believe in Union, of course—All Worlds are One World," David's father Halsey says, which makes me think momentarily that maybe that

[42] Joseph McElroy, *Lookout Cartridge* (Woodstock and New York: The Overlook Press, 2003; orig. pub. 1974), 423.

[43] Ibid., 429.

was my alma mater Union College's motto, only in the latter case translated into Latin. There must be something to this. R. E. Lapp's *Atoms and People* (1956) does not say whether radiation causes hair loss, as it does in cancer treatments. "Only that with his trusty screwdriver he moved the hemispheres of bomb stuff too close and the neutron counter screamed and he tore the reacting mass apart. Hospitalization. Blood counts."[44] "David" and "I"—we were destined for this, writing cancer into ourselves as a joint project. Our minds, our cells have subdivided within an apparent unity. "It's raining inside, but David does not believe it...and it does not believe in 'David'."

The pivotal case of misrecognition was that of a childhood friend (a non-David) whom I contacted by email after a chance encounter with his name online and his initially not remembering me. He had been (I thought) my *best* friend between the ages of five and twelve. I will return to this for me Moore-like paradox of believing and not knowing, of disbelieving this not-knowing that invented this book, but for now let me posit the thought that maybe friendship, like recognition, is an accident of unrepeatable synchronicity at which time what is perceived as "he" and "I" is working through the essentialism of quotation marks (with which Wittgenstein sometimes frames the word "know" in *On Certainty*).[45] "He," I learned only long after he forgot who I was, was at the time of our friendship in self-denial and did not perceive my own inner experiencing of self-disengagement. We both grew up to be other people who write books, he about other people like himself. I about myself as other people.

Recently, I dreamed that I was sitting for a math exam that had only one question. We were presented with a single sheet of white paper (a one-off bedsheet?) that was completely covered with writing and drawings that I could not decipher as to meaning or even recognize as a form. A typical anxiety dream, but with a difference. I was told by the

[44] Ibid., 392, 412, 415, and 422.

[45] "This is a clear indication that we have here to do with an expression that is being *scrutinized* but not *used*. Wittgenstein is not, however, consistent in this practice...and his inconsistency has led to some grave misunderstandings, such as the interpretation of *On Certainty* as upholding a form of *knowing* or *epistemic* certainty as our basic form of assurance. As a rule of thumb in reading *On Certainty*, I suggest systematically regarding the word 'know' as *under scrutiny*, even where it is neither underlined, nor otherwise emphasized by Wittgenstein." Moyal-Sharrock, *Understanding Wittgenstein's On Certainty*, 25.

teacher that since I did well on the previous exam I did not have to take this one. Still, I was both fascinated and frightened by something that was so manifestly inscrutable that it seemed to demand some completely other way of understanding that I did not possess. I noticed that the girl sitting next to me had completed the exam with no difficulty and so I asked if I could see her paper since I was not taking the test and this would not constitute cheating. I was stunned by what I saw. She had turned the white page with its assorted gnomic signs completely black using only her black-ink pen so nothing was visible anymore save for this total darkness. Noticing my confusion, she turned to me and said, "the answer to the question is New York City."

On the day of this particular night's dream, I was suddenly amazed at realizing that I had lived with the same first name for my entire life. This too suggested the intrusion of some way of understanding that I could not fathom but I imagined it had something to do with identity *as a theme* and that this theme was related to my growing up in and around Gotham. Recently, on two separate occasions two different people, both of whom should have remembered me, forgot my name and forgot ever knowing me as well. It only takes one person forgetting you to make you think. When two people forget you within a relatively short timeframe, you wonder whether there is a certain diminished mindset at work. Both of these people lived in New York, which I no longer do. Both of them would have been there to experience the blackout of 2003, although not those of 1977 and 1965. As with forgetting, though, it only takes one blackout. I think maybe my dream about a blacked-out New York City might have been theirs', not mine, or else my dream about them forgetting who I am. Who am I if I am no longer remembered? If I am redacted? But doesn't redaction imply surveillance? And if I am being surveilled (followed), how can I also be forgotten?

I entertain the paranoid suspicion that neither the inside nor the outside can be trusted.[46] Being alert to such doubt and discomfort risks overlooking one's distrust lapsing into a dependence on betrayal even by the self, especially by the self, which is deferred to articulations of other selves and in the process disarticulated. My fears are great and small— atomic at both extremes of the size spectrum. Keywords that circulate throughout this text include: atom/ic (bomb), cell (cancer), family cell

---

[46] See my book, *The Baroque Night*.

(cancer, betrayal) and friend (betrayal of memory, cancer again). (I take "family" and, above all "friend" as words that, as in a McElroy novel, encompass a fair degree of elasticity and fictionality.) Cancer returned me to my dark cell(f), to paranoid hallucinations of nebulous figures seated on the edge of my hospital bed murmuring to me. Did they expect me to answer their barely legible sounds with something reasonable or is talking to a hallucination at any time an unreasonable thing to do? Is it what we or they call "Philosophy"?

I realized belatedly that the murmuring figures at my hospital bedside were from Chris Marker's *La Jetée* (1963), whose unnamed protagonist was glued to an image from his childhood which he finally comes to understand and experience as being the moment of his death. I likewise feared that if my doctor did not release me from the hospital immediately, I would die from a life-long, age-inappropriate fear of dying that looped through my childhood like a prescient image from the future. Like the man in *La Jetée* (whose eyes were bandaged like mine were in a much earlier hospitalization), I spectated my life through and as film, searching for that one film that would capture the image of me dying. It was not the post-operative pain medication I was given that caused me to hallucinate, but the situation brought on by the cancer itself. My mind needed a reason to frame an image that had been buried in my consciousness from as early as I can remember and likely earlier than that, as memory is so poor a marker.

I had at the time of my hospitalization been reading about the atom bomb, the scare tactic of my early youth without yet thinking directly that I might be thinking about harnessing atomic radiation to bomb my cancer into submission (which I did not) and once and for all end the war. I was by then getting ready to direct a play about Los Alamos's founding father, J. Robert Oppenheimer, who died of cancer (or from the chemotherapy he was given to arrest it; the medical course that I took) and who in the interim was betrayed by a close colleague and sometime friend with the appropriate surname "Teller." At the same time and for some time thereafter, my immediate biological family was being torn apart by an unbearable estrangement of feelings precipitated in part by a shared mental condition that rendered proximity more unbearable than being apart. Also, around this time, I reached out to the aforementioned childhood best friend who my family took in when his family fell apart following his still young mother's untimely death from cancer. He did not remember me. It turns out that he changed his life for his own good reasons late in his twenties and that necessitated in his mind that his previous life, the life in which I knew him had to be blown up and its ashes buried so deep in his subconscious that he now regarded it as belonging to someone else.

Everyone's mother in the neighborhood where we grew up was working on the same sculpted figure of a female nude. I know this because whenever I visited someone's house on my street or around the block, there "She" was in various stages of dis/articulation. Of course, I noticed the breasts as they were set off by the absence of a head, legs below the knees and feet, as if a boy my age needed additional reasons to fixate. At around this time, my mother had a breast cancer scare that proved to be just that. This together with my friend's mother's early death from cancer threw these surgically altered female nudes into bold relief, although otherwise they offered no relief at all. My mother's "fatal cancer" (as I mentally cast it) was as rare and frightening to me as my father's "secret second family." There were times I imagined that those parts-severed nudes were articulating something similar. I expected them to incorporate changes to the health and well-being of their makers/ owners in whose images they were, of course, not made. It was rather the generic representation of womanhood I then identified as maternal that captured my attention until the plastic "visible" man and woman models of junior high school biology took their place. For all their "visibility" the scientific models did not reveal where cancer grows inside the body in the way that the life models could, at least to a child's satisfaction, by gouging out an area or lopping off a limb.

Movie Melancholia

I hadn't seen my father in a long time, not since "the divorce." I didn't know where he lived, maybe Nevada. I set out on a walk and was met along the way by a cousin I did not recognize who practiced law and a young Russian woman whose path I crossed seemingly by happenstance. She began by talking to me about Russian literature—to break the ice, I thought—but soon began asking me about a career in law, a thought of mine since childhood, abandoned in college. I referred her to my "cousin" who joined us, whose advice focused entirely on the protocols of taking meetings so as to honor the status of superiors while affirming your own status as someone who understood how things were done. The important thing he said was to tie meetings to occasions for eating and/or drinking. This announced your sociability, your sense of the ritualistic quality of practice, your serious intent to play the game as it was meant to be played. The Russian woman seemed to understand this better than I allowed myself to given childhood memories of my father telling me about business associates who consumed liquid lunches during long, leisurely blocks of time, making them unable to go back to work for the remainder of the day. As we proceeded down whatever path—common or otherwise—we were on, the Russian woman, lawyer cousin, and I entered some interior space proceeding down corridors offering choices at every turn. My cousin told us to follow him and as he was so confident (much more so than I remembered him being in real life), we followed (the) suit. One time, in particular, he roughly guided me away from a directional choice, despite there being no clear direction in which we were going and with no agreed upon destination in mind. The suddenness of this course correction indicated to me that I had missed my last chance to choose another direction. He told the Russian girl that one should never walk in between a table and a chair in which another lawyer was sitting, even if the latter adamantly refused to move his chair back, which he would since to do otherwise would be read as a concession of status on his part. She said she would keep this in mind. No sooner had the words left her mouth, then we entered a room barely large enough to fit the table that was in it. I proceeded in a straight line as if in a trance, not realizing that I had become trapped between the table and a body in a chair. I pushed against the obstacle, without thinking or even looking up. I was not as "there" as the other body was, the body that refused to move. I looked up to see my father sitting there, perplexed by the vehemence with which I kept pushing against him. The picture was now somehow inverted, me glaring down at my father's face as if he were lying on the floor and he looking up at me, perplexed.

"What is the matter?" he asked.

"What do you mean?"

"You look so angry."

"I'm not angry, not exactly. How long have you been in town?"

"I'd rather not say. Your mother wouldn't like it." He looked around, nervous in a way that I don't ever remember seeing him be.

I continued to glare at him.

"One week," he said.

"One week! You didn't think to contact me?"

His facial expression said that he had thought of it but shared with me the already common knowledge that any chance for genuine communication between us was long gone. Maybe it's because the divorce occurred only after I had reached adulthood, giving me no time to grow into it as a new normal that left me processing where to put him in my life or whether to make a place for him in my life at all. For his part, he seemed content not to have me in his life, and I was convinced that he being in this room when I entered it was purely accidental. He had probably planned on leaving earlier, on my cousin not coming along and leading me here (it's a place I would not have found on my own, as it required some outside consciousness). My father was here like Jesse James sneaking back into town to see his girl while the posse was out searching for him. I think it was that smiling outlaw face of his that set me off. A child grows up thinking of his father as a broad-chested superhero whose outline he will never fill. An adult (thinks he) discovers faultlines in what Ben Marcus calls "the father costume."[47] The costume is no longer a superhero's. How do you know when the story will not let you in, perhaps because it isn't *your* story? After his sunny young wife died from cancer, my "best friend" from childhood's father moved to Nevada, as I recall.

We know from director Christopher Nolan that his *Batman* trilogy was driven by fear (*Batman Begins*), chaos (*The Dark Knight*), and pain (*The Dark Knight Rises*). We know too that fear is the constant and that not overcoming fear but learning to live with it and specifically the fear of death is the only way to live through trying situations and in the condition that is given to us at birth. We know that Bruce Wayne is obsessive and that Batman manifests his compulsion to bring order to chaos in a vain effort to dull the pain of witnessing his parents' murder and the responsibility he feels for not stopping it despite his having been a powerless child at the time. So, he tries to stop it over and over again knowing that this "over and over again" is a compulsion which by definition cannot alleviate pain or its original cause. If he did not have enemies, Batman would have to create them to justify being as obsessive-compulsive as he is and as I am.

---

[47] "Keeping his costume, should we need to become him one day. When the time came. When my father's space was hollow enough for another body, possibly one of our own, to fit into it." Marcus, "The Father Costume," 181.

There is a lesser known Gotham villain, "Melancholia," a name given him by Batman himself because as with Harvey Dent and "Two Face," Batman and "Melancholia" are one and the same. "Melancholia" is an old-fashioned name for an as yet clinically unclassified mood disorder Hippocrates suggested is provoked by lingering grief and fear.[48] Melancholia first appears at the wedding of a young woman named Justine in Lars von Tier's 2011 film that takes for itself the villain's name. Unlike Bruce Wayne, Justine is traumatized by her divorced parents still being alive—the irresponsible father and the catastrophist mother who does not believe in any social institution, least of all marriage. Despite all speeches and vows to the contrary, a wedding is nostalgic, a fact not lost on Melancholia, who crashes the wedding the way Batman villains invariably interrupt high-toned private functions and celebratory public events. The wedding of Justine and Michael quickly goes south from there. "Don't make a scene," Justine's sensible sister Claire instructs her, but how is it in her character to tell another character to not "make a scene"? A condition presents itself, makes itself present, makes a scene, makes itself appear or appear to be present, appear to be. A condition is a form of being, lacking the Kantian mere-ness of a situation. "Don't make the situation worse than it already is" might be a better way of cautioning a character whose penchant is for acting (out and up).

Melancholia is as yet an unnamed, unwanted party guest in a handsome tuxedo, not yet decked out in cape and mask. It is only in the film's second part, named for "Claire" as the first section was for "Justine" (more "saddist" than sadist) that Melancholia spreads its dark wings like a shadow on the moon, announcing its presence as a planet on a collision course with Earth. In the usual narrative, this would be a job for Superman, who would either turn back the errant, possibly malevolent planet or else turn back time itself as to avert the moment of collision. But Melancholia is the superhero's self-same super-villain, his own worst enemy. Claire views Melancholia through the crude wood and wire device her rational husband John has fashioned in an effort to literally reduce her fear and dread. At its nearest point, John quoting scientists tells her, the planet will come close to filling the metal ring, but in the next five days, Melancholia will actually recede from the Earth meaning that it will shrink in size inside the metal circumference. However,

[48] The Journal of the International Institute. https://quod.lib.umich.edu/j/jii/4750 978.0002.205/--history-of-melancholy?rgn=main;view=fulltext.

on what we assume is the fifth day Claire awakens to find John missing and the planet Melancholia grown back to full size within the
child's toy circle that offered her false hope. Can we assume John and
Claire's child knows it's the fifth day and what putting the words "fifth"
and "day" together here (and now) portends? Wittgenstein begins his
Philosophical Investigations with an anecdote about sending someone (we
assume a child) to a store with the written instructions to purchase five
red apples. The philosopher asks, "But how does he know where and
how he is to look up the word 'red' and what he is to do with the word
'five'?" To this, Wittgenstein's interrogative "I" responds (to his narrative "I"), "Well, I assume he *acts* as I have described. Explanations come
to an end somewhere."[49] Yes, they do. But where does understanding begin—in explanations? How does one explain "red" or "five" or
the end of the world? Does the child's mind counterfeit the dialogism
that Wittgenstein's voice here evokes? Claire finds John's dead body.
He has taken all of the pills she bought for herself to take in the event
that Melancholia's presence proved too much for her to live. Justine of
whom little was expected and who expects little of this earth welcomes
Melancholia's presenting humankind with the opportunity to accept its
fatal condition of being self-absorbed. She has embraced Melancholia as
a sort of anti-hero wearing a villain's masked disguise. She has moved
from chaos and pain back to fear as a way of facing the human condition
without a mask. This works well enough until you realize the contracting
and expansion of Melancholia seen through the crude, lens-less telescope
meant for a child's eye/"I" and level of understanding is meant to be
a facsimile microscope and that the dark night rising signals an end to
remission and cancer's inevitable but unwelcome return—a villain wearing the anti-hero's disguise. This is where my story begins again.

GOLUBITSKY

The record may or may not show that my paternal grandfather whose
surname was Golubitsky took a wife whose maiden name was Golub,
which their sons took with them into their American marriages. How
might my life have been different had my father not forfeited the name

[49] Ludwig Wittgenstein, *Philosophical Investigations*, ed. P.M.S. Hacker and Joachim
Schulte and trans. G.E.M. Anscombe, P.M.S. Hacker, and Joachim Schulte (Malden, MA:
Wiley-Blackwell, 2009), §1.

Golubitsky? Orthodox Judaism and orthodox Jewish cultural practice would have guided my life and limited it too. I would have regularly attended synagogue, temple, or as my grandparents called it, *shul*. The only other Golubitsky of record, my maiden aunt Ruth who lived with and shopped for my grandparents would have shopped for me too. And like her, I would have trembled at each knock at the apartment door, not knowing if and when her father, my grandfather left behind when the family came to America, would throw off the reclaimed wood of his sub-floor concealment in the old country and reclaim his rightful place as the family's head. And what manner and measure of chaos would be conveyed in this oddly built Trojan Horse head when it arrived? What fear? What melancholy? Would I have even more directly known the bo(a)rders our family took on as part of this frightful inheritance? Would I be assigned my own foreign tormentor, showing up at all hours of the day or night no matter how many years later? What is the statute of limitations on *someone else's* fear? Did my father's refusal to allow me to change my surname back to Golubitsky after college derive from the fear that to do so would make it easier for uninvited visitors from the old country to find me? Or did he fear it would make it harder for him to find himself in me? As it is, I went looking for "Chaos" on my own and found her, surnamed "Golubitsky," on the web. True story. As far as I can tell, she's no relation, but there are more things in heaven and earth, Horatio, than can be discovered in your Facebook.

Maybe with the practice that living as a Golubitsky would have afforded, I'd have learned how to bounce Spalding rubber balls off the door without them ricocheting off of all the metal security parts into darkened bedrooms with gigantic wardrobes, wreaking havoc with shelves of framed photographs, books, and collected objects, some of which, I am sure, broke what was left of memory. "Spalding," the name, I could not possibly know at the time, was a clue that like the pink ball (used to play stoop and stickball by New York City area kids) I held in the palm of my small hand but could not fully grasp. It was a clue to the accident that severed Spalding Gray's sciatic nerve. The accident I had waited all my life to happen to me and happened to someone else. The accident of full-on consciousness that hits you head on, leaving you with a plate for printing books inside your brain. John V. Canfield, speaking as/for Wittgenstein, says: "Surface grammar tells us certain rules we must follow in producing acceptable sentences. 'I sees the tree' violates a surface grammatical rule. 'I see the tree because I see I am looking toward it' is all right as far as surface grammar goes, but it violates one of the underlying or depth grammatical rules for using 'see.' Similarly, we cannot say 'I weighed his pain on the scale.' This violates the depth grammar of 'pain.' 'Pain' in this regard has a different depth grammar than, say, 'book.'"[50] Certainly, I cannot weigh the pain the late downtown performance artist Spalding Gray felt when, as a result of a head-on car accident with a truck in Ireland while celebrating his sixtieth birthday left him with a broken hip and a metal plate in his head to address a compound fracture of his eye socket and skull. I cannot weigh his pain against what it cost him to write his books, let alone mine. He has written about our first and only meeting in the following passage:

> This past week I performed my *Personal History of the American Theatre* at the University of Virginia and visited an acting class at the invitation of a professor (with whom I share my initials, SG) whose students apparently resented the fact that I called my observing acting. I had in the interim admitted to the professor that I had only shuffled the cards from which my performance is comprised until some time ago I settled on an order I liked enough to retain. It was then I abandoned the chaos of chance for the saving grace of order and called that order "theatre." So, what I was doing in performance was no longer improvisational. My mind could take no more of that level of uncertainty. Did that make me a phony, or did that make me into a real actor and not just a reactor? To quote myself: "I became like an inverted method actor, I was using myself to play myself. I was playing with myself. It was a kind of creative narcissism....more memories came and I began to develop this little cottage industry."[51] The professor seemed to get it and I would not be surprised to hear that he uses this story to say something about what acting is and is not to his students and maybe about what I am and am not. If he knows this about me, then he knows more about me than I do. Maybe I should ask for his notes.

Many of Spalding's narratives are embellished, but this journal entry has been invented by me.

And there, wielding my pink rubber ball, my missile in the brown and gray, cancerous old world of my paternal grandparents' decaying

---

[50] John V. Canfield, *Wittgenstein, Language and World* (Amherst: University of Massachusetts Press, 1981), 5.

[51] Spalding Gray performing in *And Everything Is Going Fine* (dir. Steven Soderbergh, 2010).

apartment, I became a storyteller, although the story would wait a long time to be told. Sometimes it takes a lifetime to discover the voice you have found, in which you speak, is not properly your own, any more than the image reflected and deflected through the three-way mirror inside your grandparents' monumental wardrobe was not yours alone, not a singular "I." The chaotic "Spalding" that bounced off locks and found a watery grave was playing a long game of family resemblance through me and mine. The ball was following me as I was following my family genealogically speaking, bouncing up, and down across the movie screen subtitles, the lyrics we were asked to sing along or at least mouth the words to when we were young.

Saul Bellow's fictional Augie March says: "Everybody knows there is no fineness or accuracy of suppression; if you hold down one thing you hold down the adjoining."[52] My generation did not fight in the war against Hitler or in the prejudicial prologue or epilogue against the containment via quota of our allegedly negative cancerous cultural influence. Whenever we visited my grandparents' apartment, before my maiden aunt Ruth would agree to unlock the series of security devices that protected the Golubitsky family bunker, she would ask who was there. My father, who liked to bait her (she was innocent like a child), would invariably answer, "Hitler." "Hitler" is the "open sesame" command for Jewish anxiety to enter the scene, as in Rupert Pupkin (in Scorsese's *King of Comedy*) telling Jerry Langford that he made a mistake and Langford responding, "So did Hitler." After a pause during which Ruthie was undoubtedly working out in her addled mind the likelihood of a dead Nazi, let alone *the* dead Nazi riding the elevated train to Jerome Avenue in the Bronx and then trudging uphill (trudging like a Jewish peasant) to Davidson, the door slowly opened in stages, as if the spinster guarding it was herself being audibly un-girdled. For this, there was precedent, as they say "in Jewish." Although this precedent was after the fact. "It's Nazis!" thought Philip Roth's young Peter Tarnopol as a child in Philip Roth's 1974 novel, *My Life as a Man*. "I thought they parachuted into Yonkers [where two Golub cousins lived], made their way to our street, and taken everything away. *Taken my mother away.*" Roth's nine-year-old alter-ego self soon realizes that these Nazis were only the house painters working in the apartment to which he and his

---

[52] Saul Bellow, *The Adventures of Augie March* (New York: Penguin Books, 1953; 2006), 1.

family had recently moved. Then again, it must be remembered, that Hitler too was "only a house painter," and for a Jewish builder, no less. Such aspirational concordance feeds a fearful obsession, which is, in the end and from the beginning the only kind of real obsession there is. Thus, young Peter wonders whether the upheaval of his family's recent move from the Bronx to Yonkers might anticipate a pattern of future "Eviction? Confusion, Disorder?"—diaspora and chaos—that might "somehow result in my brother's ship, off in the dangerous North Atlantic, being sunk by a German torpedo?"[53] Back to you Herr Hitler, the Jewish people's closest relation to what "relation" most meaningfully is: fear and the promise of chaos, the people of the book with its cover and table of contents page, its index and its endnotes ripped out. The author's name remains "Anonymous."

[53] Philip Roth, *My Life as a Man* (New York: Viking, 1974), 247.

CHAPTER 4

Cowbird

On my mother's side, there was a cousin named "Zelig," her cousin not mine. Zelig was his first name, not his last like the eponymous human chameleon character Leonard Zelig in Woody Allen's 1983 film. He was a doctor but not the kind that could operate to transform you into someone you weren't. Nor was he a psychiatrist who could talk you out of believing you were someone else, or talk you into believing it either. The fact was I didn't know my family's Zelig well at all, so for all I know he could have been someone else in all the years before I knew him, before I was even me. He may have even made his last name into his first in the same way that people often adopt pseudonyms that include all or part of one of their original names, even if it's only a set of initials. You'd think people would be smarter about this but (at least in the movies) they're not.

Leonard Zelig's family lived over a bowling alley, the son of a Yiddish actor, not to be confused with an uncle on my father's side, a former actor in the Yiddish theater who after marrying my aunt played the role of a real-life Willy Loman, selling door-to-door. Leonard Zelig has a sister Ruth, who was a shoplifter and alcoholic. Ruth, of course, was part of my father's family, not my mother's, and my father's family lived down the street from my father's older brother's pharmacy (the new, shorter family name debuting on the storefront window), where my uncle lay unconscious inside on more than one occasion after being robbed. In the fictional Zelig's scenario, his half sister Ruth is his (the doctor's) guardian rather than the other way around.

I am reminded of Gertrude Stein's *Everybody's Autobiography* (1937) with its succession of "possibly but probably not then's," its rapid narrative shifts, and above all her statement: "I used to think the name of anybody was very important and the name made you and I often said so. Perhaps I still think so but still there are so many names and anybody nowadays can call anybody any name they like."[1] Stein published her book in 1917, the year of the Russian Revolution that would shortly send my father's family packing in the middle of the night and fleeing their shtetl with the lights still on—all save for my paternal grandfather who hid under the floorboards of some shack or another in Russia or Poland, perhaps. The rest of the family made it to and through Ellis Island with their unwieldy surname "Golubitsky" somehow intact. When the New York City census was taken sometime later, the family's place of origin was marked down as "Poland," perhaps because the family feared being branded "Communists," as in "Bolsheviks." Or maybe it was because the storied but I am assured not fictional shtetl where they lived was in a part of Belorussia that traveled back and forth between Russia and Poland, depending upon shifts in geopolitics. Two forms of assimilation, a form of impersonation by a different name.

Leonard continues to insist he is a doctor, which as "Zelig," of course, he was, but only on *my* mother's side. Perhaps not a psychiatrist but a pharmacist, not quite a doctor—a pharmacologist perhaps? In my uncle's (not my mother's uncle Zelig's) drugstore, he also sold toys, specifically painted tin toys. The one I remember best was a circus artiste who repeatedly spun around a metal bar, sometimes pausing with arms fully outstretched in a handstand, his slippered feet pointed at the ceiling, as if waiting in suspense for the inevitable fall.

Voiceover narration: "Zelig has sold his life story to Hollywood for a large sum of money. [Following a personal scandal—Zelig married a woman and fathered a child while he was someone else.] The scandal breaks. The studio demands its money back. Zelig can only return half as the rest has already been spent. Outraged, the studio gives him half his life back. They keep the best moments and he is left with only his sleeping hours and mealtimes."

Sometimes, "I" feel this way too.

---

[1] Gertrude Stein, *Everybody's Autobiography* (Cambridge: Exact Chance, 1991), 10.

"I've chosen to become my own primary research subject."[2] So says Cynthia Hopkins in her solo performance piece, *Accidental Nostalgia* (2004), or rather so says the person she is playing, Cameron Seymour, who is described as being a 1970s pop sensation who descended into drug addiction and disappeared. The "Cameron" we see performing suffers from psychogenic amnesia and has nominally authored the book *How to Change Your Mind: A Self-Help Manual for Psychogenic Amnesiacs*. So, this "Cameron" is "in fact" her (own) daughter Henrietta performing (perhaps unconsciously) her mother's identity. Henrietta is either the actual author of the book, which as Caroline she is quoting, or she is herself a person of the book, or neither (if Caroline really is amnesiac and is so now performing as "Henrietta") or both (if Henrietta is both "Caroline" and amnestically herself). We are told that the "real" Caroline Seymour is living in an insane asylum. But who is telling us this—Henrietta or Caroline? Henrietta as Caroline or Caroline as Henrietta? You begin to feel like the protagonist of David Markson's *Wittgenstein's Mistress* (1988), who may or may not be the last living person on earth or at least is that person in her own mind. That book's opening sentence, "In the beginning I left messages in the street," reimagines the *Tractatus*'s famous first line, "The world is everything that is the case," that is less an epistemological claim than it is intuitive— and in the case of Markson's self-doubting "I," perhaps falsely so. "Was it really some other person I was so anxious to discover, when I did all that looking, or was it only my own solitude I could not abide?" the narrative voice somewhat rhetorically asks itself amidst its character sightings/citings. Some other person not to be with but to be me, to lend credence to my being (t)here. Some external proof that my first-person (Markson's "sole person") intuition is real.[3]

In his pseudonymous novel *Hocus Bogus* (2010), Romain Gary describes how the "real" author of his novel, "Emile Ajar," brought himself into being by repeatedly, obsessively signing his assumed name. The name brought the person to life (left the door to alterity "ajar"), while reinscribing with each usage the original author Gary's fear of dying. Romain Gary committed suicide on December 2, 1980, an actual event on the date when his fear of death as a literary debt to his contested self

---

[2]Performed at St. Anne's Warehouse, New York City, January 2005. A DVD of this performance was provided to me by the author, who is my former student.

[3]David Markson, *Wittgenstein's Mistress* (Normal: Dalkey Archive Press, 1997), 7 and 32.

came due.[4] The narrator did it. Killed Gary-as-Ajar/Ajar-as Gary, that is. The narrator always "does it" where writers are concerned. What is the psychological condition of an authorial pseudonym, of a name that pretends to a physical and mental independence it does not, in fact, possess? Emile Ajar claims to have stolen cards from his own medical file in which his psychiatrist diagnosed him as follows:

> Simulation taken to such an extreme and pursued without interruption or slip over such a long period of time clearly constitutes obsessive-compulsive behavior and betokens an authentic personality disorder.[5]

Might not we ask, though, what is "authentic personality disorder" where a "dupe" is concerned, when the grounds for authenticity and of personality per force contain the very real possibility of disorder as part of what defines them? Ajar himself considers this in light of the vexed authenticity claim for "life itself," as an absolute that names no other subject. "I don't want to have any connection to context," Ajar (nominally) writes, taking up life's claim to be self-defining and self-sustaining. But vacating context is in some sense, as Ajar states, also an attempt to vacate the self. To what end? One cannot simply discard the self and at the same time or alternatively embrace life itself, unless "self" is vacated from the expression and life is defined (only) as an "it" minus any human subject-value. In which case, who did "it"? And yet Ajar acknowledges, "I knew I was fictional," as borne out, by his psychiatrist's note that the patient "takes on the physical appearance of various objects (pocketknife, paperweight, chains, key ring)," and as a further means of escaping from "his human predicament," a python. The self-obsessive, paranoid determinism the author presents (he fears not only death but logic and even future chronology—e.g., "I don't know what I've done next.") leads him into periodic double feints. "I don't speak Danish, but not well enough," he says, instantiating language's apparent suiciding of meaning so as to trouble meaning further, part of an overall self-incriminating narrative strategy.[6] The narrator did it, but did he do it *in name only*

---

[4] Romain Gary, writing as Emile Ajar, *Hocus Bogus*, trans. David Bellos (New Haven: Yale University Press, 2010), 57 and 58.

[5] Gary, *Hocus Bogus*, 3, 33, 46, and 47.

[6] To a hotel clerk's checking-in question, "Is this your first time staying with us?" in *The Memory of a Killer* (dir. Erik Van Looy, 2003), a hitman who is losing his self to Alzheimer's Disease responds, "I speak Dutch."

and if so does writing under a fake name abnegate the person behind the name and not the narrative strategy from any and all responsibility? "Inexistentialism," he calls it—the absence of authorship in the presence and name of writing. Does ghost writing assume a self when it is written by a ghost of the very self here being invoked? "If there's one thing I can't stand," the ghost writer says, "it's lies. They're much too plain."[7]

In Roth's *Sabbath's Theater* (1995), puppeteer Mickey Sabbath tells his Croatian mistress Drenka Balich, "I am not by nature a monogamous being. Period. You wish to impose a condition that either deforms me or turns me into a dishonest man with you. But like all other living creatures I suffer when I am deformed." For Roth, adultery is a representation of "non-monagamous being." This may have something to do with the author's belief in each person's duality, if not multiplicity. "You are not yourself, Drenka," says Mickey, to which Drenka, who Sabbath elsewhere describes as having "a mind whose core was all clarity," responds, "*This is myself.*" This notably contrasts with the resistant selfhood of the actor who insists on being addressed at all times as her character and specifically of Sabbath's obsessing over his actress-first wife Nikki's inability to follow his stage directions to the letter. This is what led Sabbath back to puppets, who have no "self" and are not who they are, only *what* they are and who they become in his hands, which despite his insistence that they are not metaphors become just that as an author's subject(s). Satyric (derived from a licentious *wood*land creature) Sabbath's reverie has him thinking of "wood" in relation not only to puppets and to the play in which Nikki performed. Roth's choice of Chekhov's *The Cherry Orchard* in this instance acknowledges his way with a metaphor, even where his character says there is not one. Sabbath's nickname for his ex-wife, who embodied a "pervasive sense of crisis," "A-Crisis-A-Day," suggests another possible nickname—"Chaos."[8]

[7] Gary, *Hocus Bogus*, 5, 7, 8, 10, 16, 27, and 55.

[8] "Rabbi Yohanan ben Zakkhi said: Once I was walking along the road and I encountered a man who was gathering wood. I spoke to him, but he did not reply. Then he came up to me and said: 'Rabbi, I am not alive. I am dead.' I said to him: 'If you are dead, then what need have you of wood?'" Thus, begins a story that tells of the invention of the mourner's kaddish, ending as it does with the wood-man, in life a great sinner who is burning in hell, being saved by the son he abandoned when the latter (once schooled in reading Scripture) proclaims, 'Bless God, who is blessed!'" It is tempting to read the wood-man of this story as being a possible prototype for the perpetual mourner Mickey Sabbath who sees himself as unable to be released from his personal hell of being dead but unable to

As little as I know about my family's origins and as little as they care to know about a past in which they directly played a part, I am fairly confident that I am not of the Golubitskys whose daughter's middle name is "Chaos." I am not her father who lectures on chaos theory, nor its nominal appropriation. But I know a butterfly effect when I obsessively see one in the larger order of personal, catastrophic determinism. My mind melds things into new entities that carry with them their own larger causality. As family histories predict and families present, cancer is both causal *and* chaotic, physical, and metaphysical. For those of us who infuse the physical world with metaphysical significance, cancer is a rough reminder of how physical we primarily and ultimately are. Leon Wieseltier says that "the choice between the physical and the metaphysical is the choice between air and water."[9] Damned if you are, damned if you are not who you are, especially when who you are is what you get.

AND NOW A WORD FROM MY CANCER...

"My cancer," it wants you to know, has an origin story too. It started with my paternal grandfather, moved through my father and then to me when I was in my forties. Then it went away for nineteen years, less a remission than what appeared to be a total eclipse. Stress, I believe less than imagine, brought it back, gave it new life, and fittingly it was the stress visited by a child upon a parent, a stress the child modeled after her parent that made the unwelcome visitor appear as darkly as had Melancholia. To experience cancer is to rediscover the body with organs as both a physical fact and an expressive mode. (More elementally, it reasserts a-propositionally, "I have a body.") Organs express fluids and cells, along with the correspondences, analogies, and metaphors that

die, to give up on the life he hates. Philosophically, there is Schrödinger's cat in a box (see Chapter 6) which may be alive or dead or both until we know by opening the box. Psychologically, there are Capgras and Cotard's syndromes in which the lives of others and of the self are regarded as forms of imposture. In Cotard's, the individual believes that he, the self, is really dead. (See my discussion of Charlie Kaufman's *Synechdoche, New York* in Chapter 6 in which both of these conditions present). More mundanely, Roth adapted *The Cherry Orchard* for a production at the Chichester Festival in England in which his then wife Claire Bloom played the role of Madame Ranevskaya. Leon Wieseltier, *Kaddish* (New York: Vintage, 2000), 130; Claudia Roth Pierpont, *Philip Roth: A Writer and His Books* (New York: Farrar, Staus and Giroux, 2013), 142; Roth, *Sabbath's Theater*, 9, 20, and 21.

[9]Wieseltier, 27.

adhere and inhere. Organs likewise articulate expressive limits—in my case, a kidney that had lost some of its self-expression as a healthily functioning organ that puts out and takes in necessary fluids. Transitional cell cancer, which is what I had this time, expresses itself in various organs, places, and ways. It navigates a territory that chemotherapy re-navigates to skirmish with cells that tumorous organs cast off, send off like castaways in search of another host organ in which to plant the black flag of their renewed intrusion and resistance. Cancer wants to express itself as a fugitive desire that is independent of and resistant to what the body wants and needs (and perhaps of what the body *is*). And yet cancer is likewise interdependent with what we want and need to be told about our death and dying, our vexing relationship with interiority as a dark realm of conceit and conscious enclosure, a vibration not quite a voice lost inside its own resonance as if it were itself a body, a space, or a room. The cancer in our body expresses death as a fugitive desire about which we are un/surprisingly ambiguous and ambivalent as a form and function of self-expression. This cancer that is and can never entirely be "*my* cancer" (as Kant would have it) and so n/either expands n/or explodes the domain of self-expression will be the death of me.

Cancer turns the "I" into exhibit A with such numbingly self-referential exhibit cards as "I am scared," "I am unlucky," "I am doomed," "I am dissociated from myself," "I don't know what to think," and "I am numb" (or I wish I were). Meanwhile other, more knowledgeable exhibit cards were being written for me by the professional tumorists (from Witkiewicz's play *Tumor Brainiowicz*, perhaps?) who discussed and adjudicated my cancer in my absence, as a body absent an "I." My doctor petitioned to go before "the tumor board," acceptance turning on my tumor being judged in mock-personhood to be interesting enough to warrant the attention of other medical specialists. I was informed by my doctor that my tumor passed the test, which was a bit like getting into a college that I didn't know existed let alone applied to for admission. Or rather it was like *my doctor* gaining admission to such a college on the basis of *my* credentials. He got to discuss the particularity of my tumor with other doctors, to solicit and record their opinions and perhaps discover publishable data for which the research subject (me) now writes in some strange simulation of their discussion, self-abstractedly. It is, perhaps not ironically the same position in which David Mamet places the apostate Jew, "the Wicked Son" who asks in the voice of belatedness, "Why me?" and "What does it mean *to me*?"

and whose constant mode of performance is confession. I do not confess, though, to gain entrance to the majoritarian culture, within which I would seek to become anonymous, but rather to the much smaller, more particular Jewish one into which I was admitted at birth. I have quite literally at the end of the day, much to my surprise and on the evidence of what my personal and some say cultural history does and does not present, a strong "desire to belong."[10] Which I now do, twice over, but only as a survivor of another sort of holocaust.

Chaos pilots our cellular journey to parts that have become unknown to us by self-replicating, that disabuse us of who we are in service to what we always have been and will become. How can there be self-replication independent of a self that replicates? Cancer is a riot of motiveless self-destruction un-rooted in the brain even in its most censorious imag(in)ings, even as we look for causes in who we have been and what we have done, in what we have said and left unsaid, held, and withheld. What are we to make of what has been made in our own image but inside apart from where we imagine our interiority as being?

Cancer speaks not only to mass but to border and not only to breach but to border's interiority. A cancerous cell is a deeper, darker interiority of what is already inside you—the unseen room, the secret annex. It is the Leibnizian monad inside the monad that replicates minus relationship. In this regard, cancer acknowledges no outside. And yet we may not only look outside for signs of chaos, we tend to locate chaos as something we encounter "out there." Brett Zehner writes, "At any given time on the earth's surface, there is a vortex in motion, whether that be in a fluid dynamic like the Pacific trash gyre, the trade wind circuits connected directly to ocean temperature currents, or the cyclonic motion of the hurricane eye, there is perpetually a vortex spinning."[11] Chaos is always somewhere, doing its decreative work in the world. Is

---

[10] "Belonging was never what we were good at anyway. Being a stranger is what we do. It's the diaspora, they are at pains to assure me, that brings out the best in us." Note here the speaker's (the modern Jew Strulovitch seeking counsel from Shylock) attributing this belief to "they," meaning to the Christian world who view Jews in this way. Jacobson, *Shylock Is My Name*, 62. Contrast this with Mamet speaking for himself as a Jew: "To me, real life consists in belonging." Mamet includes in this the "hermetic groups" in theater and film to which he has belonged. David Mamet, *The Wicked Son: Anti-semitism, Self-Hatred, and the Jews* (New York: Schocken Books, 2006), 110, 112, 13, 114, 115–16, and 135.

[11] Brett Zehner, unpublished essay, Brown University, Department of Theatre Arts and Performance Studies, November 14, 2016.

it any wonder that in the course of a human life of troubles we are said to weather the storm? Indeed, life-threatening diseases and neuroses make us the storm's eye/"I" in the "weathering." This chaos is part of my identity theft, a self-enacting de-selfing, of which cancer is a bemused but ruthless cohort. Cancer makes me less me and more "them," or as Edward Teller says in his Hungarian-inflected English in Carson Kreitzer's *The Love Song of J. Robert Oppenheimer* (2006), "All the thems...out there," the aliens (foreigners, communists, cancer patients) of my alien (self), as if I am replicating them from a singular cellular self, born of my diseased condition. What, then, do "they" call *their* cancer?[12]

Cancer allows the patient to indulge on a serious note the phenomenon of what Laurence A. Rickels (writing on another subject) labels "foreign body switching, becoming over and again who (or what) one isn't."[13] The science fiction writer Philip K. Dick, whom Rickels is describing, sounds like a Philip Roth erotonymic invention, and given Dick's schizophrenia, his self-doubling, perhaps he was. Then again, perhaps he wasn't and by virtue of the same condition—the Dionysian, schizophrenic mind presents as a form of "unity of multiplicity." Like Dionysus, after Avital Ronell, "he rules a force that affirms multiplicity and is affirmed of it."[14] Mental illness here proves superior to mental discipline in making the uncanniness of authorial self-contestation seem real because it *is* real. Psychosis and neurosis are form-seeking entities, much as creative writing is, but whereas the latter gestures at the form that madness can take, the former are the very thing they set out to find. In the temporary madness brought on by my own drug-induced hallucinations, I found that contrary to a lifelong romance with mental illness that cracking up is not all I had cracked it up to be. With cancer, though, there exists the very real possibility of a sort of naturally programed non-existence that no longer resembles the writer's post-adolescent romancing of death as self-othering. What once were regarded as instances of unhealthy self-absorption have now become the illness this prior mostly writerly condition named, *actual* self-absorption by way of a

[12]Carson Kreitzer, *The Love Song of J. Robert Oppenheimer* (Woodstock, IL: Dramatic Publishing, 2006), 61.

[13]Laurence A. Rickels, *I Think I Am Philip K. Dick* (Minneapolis: University of Minnesota Press, 2010), 3.

[14]Avital Ronell, *The Test Drive* (Urbana and Chicago: University of Illinois Press, 2005), 10 and 13.

closing down of the physical plant to which mere metaphor until recently attended. Now reality, *that* reality, the one that advertises and supports a body that *is* presses down upon the mind with its limits (of self-knowing) that are now requirements, no longer imaginative requests.

Rickels, who is a psychoanalytic theorist, writes,

> The onset and career of identification requires that you not recognize your own provenance as host to guests or ghosts. But in time you do finally see the brand name attached to what you assumed was properly your own in flashback or as insight always accompanied by a groan or yelp. I refer to those moments of catching up with identification, like all those other moments of recall of extreme embarrassment, as "scream memories." But these are the identifications that can be assigned. This after-the-fact predicament of never quite undoing your assignment [to be "Woody Allen" or "Philip Roth" or "Philip K. Dick" or "the neurotic," "the schizophrenic," "the obsessive-compulsive"] leads you once again into assuming wrongfully that identification is a contact sport. That "first contact" is what identification, beside itself, can be shown to commemorate holds true in cases of mourning or unmourning. But what about the world of no difference out there that organizes itself in circumvention of mourning?

Are we host to our own disfigured ghosts as Roth seems to suggest we are vis-à-vis Moishe Pipik (a stunted monument to performative self-regard) in *Operation Shylock*, the other, "fake" Philip Roth? Roth's most consistent counternarrative is penned and enacted by his alter ego Nathan Zuckerman, who is both a writer and a *ghost* writer. Rickels, writing as a psychiatrist who speaks his mind and not like Portnoy's "Harpo," who does not, calls the feeling of being large with other selves as being "the situation of adolescence, the new frontier that artists and thinkers, for example, attempt to invest with staying power." Rickels, though, goes on to argue that, "the onset and career of identification requires that you not recognize your own provenance as host to guests or ghosts," and that "the traumatizing 'energy' of adolescence [is] the building block of an oeuvre that is here to stay."[15] Who am I to say that this and the other is who I am not? Why "me"?—Why *not* "me"? I invented death. I wrote the death sentence. Now I am death, destroyer of cells. I was Hamlet. The atom bomb was the apple of my "I," a *Hamletmachine*-like new subjectivity born from reverse engineering

[15] Rickels, 3.

destruction as being unnatural—the provenance of man rather than of Nature. I killed representation to bring my death about (about what?). In the shadow cloud of exteriority's demise, I am ex-interiority. I am Hedda Gabler, Doc Holliday, and all the other dead dressed up as characters, as if they had somewhere to be, somewhere to go. They sit in Kantor's *Dead Class* with nothing more to learn. When called upon to speak, they say only "I was," or else say nothing at all.

I wonder whether what Roth called "sardonic and satiric cancer turning to carrion the…body" was already reading me in secret as if my body was the book.[16] Despite his own heart attack, it is cancer that takes pride of place in Roth's novels. A heart attack is brought on suddenly. Cancer initiates an at first subtle then manifest war of attrition in the body, which easily presents as metaphoric changes in time, duration, and point of view. Cancer is philosophical in all the ways that a heart attack is not. For Roth, cancer is a way of tracking characters and their secrets, their own metastasizing identities visible on his figurative CAT scan screens like the cancerous shadow of imminent and immanent mortality, a humbling with the religious, spiritual, carnal, and cultural forces (read: Judaism) that shaped them/him.[17] Even without the example of the Shoah, the Jewish faith is traditionally (beginning in the Talmud), particularly horrified at the body's unnatural violation, which is why autopsy and cremation are forbidden (although there has been some movement among non-Orthodox Jews regarding the latter). Above all, Roth sees cancer as being repellent and as such he makes use of it in service to his stated goal: "I wanted to bring the repellent in…because we try so hard not to see it."[18] The futile attempt to render the elemental body as annexed to and not commensurate with who I am. E. M. Cioran suggests that, "those who possess good health [also known as just "health"] have been denied the opportunity of realizing it, for self-conscious health is either compromised or about to be."[19] In Cioran's

[16] Roth, *Sabbath's Theater*, 424.

[17] Jackie Stacey, *Teratologies: A Cultural Study of Cancer* (New York: Routledge, 1997), 238; Louise Hay, *Heal Your Body: The Mental Causes for Physical Illness and the Metaphysical Way to Overcome Them* (London: Eden Grove, 1989), 22.

[18] Pierpont, *Roth Unbound: A Writer and His Books*, 198.

[19] E.M. Cioran, *The Trouble with Being Born*, trans. Richard Howard (New York: Arcade Publishing, 2012), 13.

formulation, self-consciousness cancerously gnaws at health by infusing it with thought about itself. Where then does the author's primary repulsion lie—in thinking or not thinking about his ailment, when "thinking about" *is* the ailment?

Roth wants to make cancer seem no less tragic by being ordinary, in the sense of being a part of real life. Cancer is, at the same time, an unnatural violation of the body *in life*, while the body is still alive. It opens the mind to what Cioran calls "posthumous knowledge," which "functions as if the knower were alive and not alive, a being and the memory of a being." "For such knowledge," Cioran affirms, "everything is without basis except itself."[20] There is a Poe-esque quality to this particular horror, as if the body were being buried alive, which in effect it is in cancer in which replicant cells steal oxygen and smother the healthy body on the inside. In *Exit Ghost* (2007), Nathan Zuckerman has been rendered incontinent by his prostate cancer treatment. (A previous novel, 1987s *The Counterlife*, ceded Nathan's impotence from the same prostatectomy to his brother Henry, the operation to correct which presumably causing the heart attack that killed him within the force field of Nathan's reverse-engineered imagination.)[21] In *Exit Ghost*, Zuckerman's only friend, his neighbor Larry Hollis, who as an only child watched his parents die painfully in close succession from cancer, commits suicide while in the hospital to spare his children his childhood ordeal. As a boy, he laid out his causal plans for his life to come in a "Things to Do" diary, with growing a cancer not being one of them. Everything else he got right, or thought he did, including changing his name to "Larry Hollis" as soon as he graduated from college so that he could join the air force without a trace of his Jewishness. His birth name, the name he consigned to a now self-denied past was "Irwin *Golub*" (true story, that is as far as fiction allows). He was sixty-eight years old when he chose death by sleeping pills overdose, which is ironic to this Golub (Me) who cannot sleep and is of a similar age. Is there a predictive quality to the relationship between authorship and readership? Is/Was Roth reading my body or my mind? Did I write *myself* into his novel under the pseudonym "Larry Hollis"? No, "Larry" was my father's name. Although it was not his original *given* name.

---

[20] Ibid., 3.

[21] Philip Roth, *Exit Ghost* (New York: Viking, 2008); Philip Roth, *The Counterlife* (New York: Viking, 1996).

There is, of course, never a good time to contact cancer. When you are young, it is tragic but when you are old(er) it is ironic. The former needs no explanation, but perhaps the latter does. When you are older, you (should) have settled upon who you are and may, if you are a writer, even have entered into an experimental retrospectivism that posits yourself passing through the several selves you have been with an eye toward fictionalizing the past or entertaining the idea that the past and its operative memory are fiction. You test the mastery with which you are able to perform versions of who you are in the now nearer awareness of whom you will sooner rather than later forever cease to be. You are self-montaging in tribute to the versions of your life you either played or never got to play. You are testing your freedom to be and not to be who you and the world have said you are. And then, without warning, you have cancer and it takes over the replication and othering of self as a merely physical process. "The self has turned against itself."[22] And this self is, perhaps for the first and only time unitary, saying as it does that you have only one body and it is breaking "you," an absolute "you" down *on the inside*, where it goes about its work ferociously, with an animalistic repetition, like a dog that keeps biting you without a thought as to why. There is no "why." "The cancer is not thinking of the consequences. It is thinking only of blossoming, growing," Kreitzer writes in her play about Oppenheimer, the father of the atom bomb, who died perhaps not of his cancer but of its cure.[23] With cancer, mitosis recasts your multi-self-ing as embodied multiplicity. Cancer cells are dumb, "simply misguided replicants," science without the fiction.[24] I must recast them as colonizers from a dying planet in a science fiction movie who arrive on Earth to take, by force if necessary, much-needed supplies so that their planet can survive. My body is planet Earth; my cells and possibly my organs, are the supplies. But oddly enough, I am self-colonizing. My body is depleting itself of the resources it needs to survive as if it has no care as to its future, sees itself enacting a self-programed process

[22] Stacey, *Teratologies*, 177.

[23] "It also seemed [from the autopsy report] that the radiation treatment had completely eradicated Oppenheimer's throat cancer—in which case he died as a result of the chemotherapy." Kai Bird and Martin J. Sherwin, *American Prometheus: The Triumph and Tragedy of J. Robert Oppenheimer* (New York: Vintage, 2006), 683, n. 587; Kreitzer, *The Love Song of J. Robert Oppenheimer*, 92.

[24] Stacey, 178.

of planned obsolescence, or is simply too dumb to see that what it is doing is self-defeating. "I" and my body are the twin authors in Charlie Kaufman's film *Adaptation* (dir. Spike Jonze, 2002), only one of whom can write, the other being psychologically blocked. The one who can write cannot write about the one who cannot, unless the former composed the narrative that contains them both, which is writing that does not produce a cure for not writing, for being blocked, being ill.

Cancer is a "good" Rothian disease, allied as it is historically with guilt. There is the sense that in some (mythic) way, likely owing to emotional repression, you have brought it upon yourself. It is not simply a matter of how stupid of me to expose myself to asbestos so much as how stupid of me to expose myself to myself and not recognize the damage of which "I" (as author) am capable. Why didn't I do something about myself? Like what, psychoanalysis? But that has always felt to me like a cure that is working in tandem with the propagation of the illness. If chemotherapy makes cancer seem real and true, so too does psychoanalysis make what is really getting (to) "you" so abundantly manifest as to be sustainable from session to session. The psychiatrist wants to know what's troubling you and "you" (alternatively, "you" and you, or "you" and "you") are there to talk about it. An embarrassed discomfort fills the silence in which she awaits your testimony as to how bad it's been since your last session. This is how and where the work begins. If the trauma (to which cancer physically analogizes or else to which neuroses and psychosomatic conditions analogize in turn) is concealed, cure must be manifest by rendering trauma unconcealed. "I recognize you," the cancerous body says to the trauma of concealment. "Here you are. And here. And here too. I am your disease, the disease of 'you' and also 'your' cure. I am 'you' acting upon 'you.' I am both manifold and reductive in that way."

In *Cracking Up* (dir. Jerry Lewis, 1983), the "Jerry Lewis" character (who here goes by the quasi-pharmaceutical name 'Warren *Nefron*') spends the entirety of his session with his psychiatrist sliding to the floor from the doctor's vinyl furniture. The healing room has been designed to continuously and permanently disable the patient who as a result of his performance/work suffered (as does Philip Roth) from a very bad back. It is in fact what led Lewis to Percodan and near drug-assisted-suicide. The same drug led me into full-scale hallucination and a similarly dark place wherein I came to believe that if I were not released from the hospital where I was recovering from my cancer surgery, I too would die and not of the disease but of the cure. Why would a hospital try to kill the patient it has nominally cured? Why would a psychiatrist make it impossible for his patient to sit comfortably without fear of painful humiliation and just plain pain? Why require the self to perform the impossibility of its own encoded demands? Is psychoanalysis the writer's self-fulfilling fantasy of failure at being (able to locate as in retrieve) an integrated self? Does the mind not so much slip the body as represent embodiment as slippage? This drama of unconcealment is in itself a neurotic operation. Cancer, like tuberculosis in the nineteenth century, and other medical conditions since, has on occasion been regarded as a personality disorder (a form of autopathogeny), a theme against which Susan Sontag argues powerfully in *Illness as Metaphor*. Cancer nominally removes self-authorship from our grasp, even as it enables our complicit subsuming of preexisting identity with that of "cancer survivor," the disease's recasting of us as its narrative's neurotic character, as an ongoing condition.[25]

One line of discourse regarding "the cancer personality type" (a myth I wish neither to propagate nor regenerate) is that it has broken away from the *Urself*, the Jungian "original or 'primitive' self" which knows how to be in the world. In the tunnel-visioned efforts of the amnestic, superficial self to become who or what it aspires to be (often seen as being a condition associated with "the excesses of modernity and late capitalism"), it no longer knows how to become itself. In this narrative, self-recovery is literally *self*-recovery. It may be why I have (as of this moment) taken to calling my cancer "Chaos Golubitsky," it being the original self that in my life I have un-become to my peril but also because in this point of origin abides a generative undoing that resists my conscious control, my self-help. This Ur-self is the gist of "Portnoy's Complaint" and *Portnoy's Complaint* (1969): "But don't you see—my right mind is just another name for my fears! My right mind is simply that inheritance of terror that I bring with me out of my ridiculous past!" This from Roth's eponymous onanistic (self-redundant) character who confuses as in frustrates his right mind with his right hand, the one he also uses for writing. No one but a philosopher would say "I know that I have two hands..." It's elementary, pre-epistemic, says

---

[25] Ibid., 195, 196, and 197.

Wittgenstein to G. E. Moore.[26] Repellent, says Roth, of this earthiness that makes the neurotic mind run riot. "Chaos" is my kin. I lied when "I" said that she wasn't.

Ever since the opiate-induced hallucinations experienced during my recovery from my most recent cancer operation, I have been reading and rereading Philip Roth and "Philip Roth," all of the counterlifes led by the author's fictional surrogates that invert fiction's true lies going this way and that until there is no demonstrably clear "way" or one to be at all. Perhaps my bedside visitors, glowing amorphously as if radiated by some (to me) unknown atomic energy and structure were telling me to return to Roth, or maybe to a comic book Roth in which the author like Batman, like an immune system fights off such fearful adversaries as Neurosis, Self-Hatred, Egotism, Priapism, Cancer, and Inadequacy. This is a man, after all, who turned one of his fictional alter egos, David Kepesh, into a giant breast (the novella *The Breast*, 1972) and rendered his most consistent character mask Nathan Zuckerman impotent. Perhaps the glowing figures at my bedside were actually exchanging bits of dialogue from Roth's books in order to inoculate me against potential madness with the saving pseudo-psychosis of well-wrought metafictional play. The wife of the recurring Kepesh character in Roth's *The Dying Animal* tells him that his stroked out friend "seems to enjoy the voices."[27] Newark, New Jersey's fraternal (i.e., non-identical) twin sons, forming for me the team of Philip Roth and Jerry Lewis speak to me of Jewishness and tumorhood replacing selfhood as diasporic conditions, and warn me ironically (Roth) and un-ironically (Lewis) of the danger of becoming consumed by bathetic anxiety bordering on self-abuse.

"Rhoda" in Richard Foreman's film *Strong Medicine* (1981) cries out: "I've got aftershock. I've got aftershock" but quickly reminds herself, "Everybody was trying to be helpful but in the back of my head a voice kept whispering that everybody else felt just as bad as I did and I didn't want to believe it."[28] There are tests for these things, reality tests that appear to establish a new identity or else to reaffirm an old one. Alexander Portnoy, the bad boy of modern Jewish American literature,

[26]Philip Roth, *Portnoy's Complaint* (New York: Vintage, 1994), 160; Ludwig Wittgenstein, *Zettel*, ed. G.E.M. Anscombe and G.H. von Wright and trans. G.E.M. Anscombe (Berkeley: University of California Press, 1970), 405.

[27]Philip Roth, *The Dying Animal* (New York: Vintage, 2002), 118.

[28]Richard Foreman, *Strong Medicine*. https://www.youtube.com/watch?v=42zRkya9yn4.

refers to "Thereal <sic> McCoy, which is the name I attach to the slut-tiest-looking slut in the chorus line."[29] "You," the conditional you, the "you" that is your condition is given a name and proceeds toward having a career of its own as an experimental subject, a manifold subject whose conditional state perpetuates multiplicity, counternarratives to the iden-tity with which you entered therapy. Avital Ronell has noted, "as dis-appropriating forms of experience, testing and experimentation [drugs included] are related inextricably to acts of negating and affirming."[30] I was such an eager patient that they needed to keep piling on the diag-noses and the pills so that I could perpetuate the pleasures of my own authorial self-othering. Mine is a repetition compulsion/condition, like Roth who keeps returning to drink from the same sweetly poisoned well of art as counterlife. Roth's protagonists all manifest what he calls "the ambiguities of prudence and the anxieties of disorder, about life-hunger, life-bargains, and life-terror in their most elementary manifestations," which I would further broadly divide under the subheadings of mar-riage and divorce, parent-child relationships, illness and death, guilt and shame, imagination *as* experience, all of which are tied up for Roth and "I" with the self-authorial questions of how and why to be Jewish.

The fictional writer E. I. Lonoff in Roth's *The Ghost Writer* (1979), characteristically of Roth, has authored a short story entitled "Life is Embarassing" and a short story collection entitled *It's Your Funeral.* Roth links what he calls "our relentless household obsession with the status of the Jews" as a theme in Lonoff's stories (and by extension his own) with Lonoff's belief (which his wife, the counteractively named Hope contests) that "only my 'self,' as you like to call it, ["the baby-ish, preening, insatiable self"] happens not to exist in the everyday sense of the word." For Roth, the self is a constructed thing, which is why at one point Nathan Zuckerman muses, "I could not remember having *myself* ever felt like such a round character before," and why Zuckerman can imagine and for a while believe that Lonoff's young mistress Amy Bellette is the real Anne Frank and yet make her sound like she herself knows that she is a fictional character. ("I can't live anywhere. I can't *live*." Amy's oxymoronically posthumous survivor "Anne Frank" recog-nizes that "I have to be dead to everyone.") Amy only begins to believe

[29] Roth, *Portnoy's Complaint*, 131.
[30] Ronell, *The Test Drive*, 10.

herself that she is Anne Frank (and that Lonoff is "Pim," the pseudo-nym the real Anne gave her actual father in her writing) after watching the play *The Diary of Anne Frank*, adapted from the memoir which itself exists in several slightly different variants. Amy Bellette is then a fictional self twice over (like a cousin twice-removed, like Zelig), as she realizes when she speaks of her own delusional self-authorship, which is actually a product of Zuckerman's imagining of her, which is in turn the prod-uct of Roth's authorship of both of them and his fascination with Anne Frank as a way of protecting himself through Zuckerman (who fantasizes that he marries Amy *as* Anne Frank) against the charges of anti-Semitism that have dogged him since his earliest published writings. Roth even has Anne Frank pre-imagine that she is or will become Amy Bellette. Amy wants to be Lonoff's "Anne" (she tells him), his fictional charac-ter, while also unknowingly being Zuckerman's and Roth's. Each rep-resents the other's counterlife. "You've got to be somebody, don't you? There's no way around it," she tells *her* author (Lonoff) who is not her real author (Lonoff refuses her offer to be him) any more than the fic-tional Zuckerman is.

All of this is characteristic of an invasion fever that metastasizes cells of fear and the cancerous condition of anxiety into metaphors of self-on-self-affliction and into excesses of naming and meaning.[31] Metaphors constitute a renaming process, a transposition of the name that "rush[es] to the rescue of the subject whose terror is otherwise uncontainable… provid[ing] the necessary balm for the psychic pain of the unbeara-ble knowledge." Jackie Stacey could be speaking of Roth, especially the Roth and the "Roth" of *Operation Shylock* when she warns that "the experimental disposition cannot count on impassable borders to rein it in but runs on excess, trespass, and essential instability."[32] Roth's chasing of his own corporeal shadow in Israel, first thought to be the extended aftermath of his having been administered the drug Halcion following heart surgery, slips the borders of even that drug-induced delusion to live within the contested borders of Israel and Palestine, of the assimi-lated and unassimilated Jew, to occupy the occupiers and in turn to be occupied by an occupier of his own, who claims credit for having written

[31] Philip Roth, *The Ghost Writer* (New York: Vintage, 1979), 11, 14, 25, 41, 56, 64, 118, 124, 135, and 154; Sontag, *Aids and Its Metaphors*, 100.

[32] Paul Ricoeur, *The Rule of Metaphor: Multi-disciplinary Studies in the Creation of Meaning* (Toronto: University of Toronto Press, 1977), 4; Stacey, 63.

his books, including the one in which the two Philip Roth's convene, *Operation Shylock*.[33]

The "real" Philip Roth regards each new branching of his identity-formation and identity theft as being a test. "The one register of testing offers results—certitudes—by which to calculate and count on the other, including the self as other, as tested others. Another register consistently detaches from its rootedness in truth: self-dissolving and ever probing, it depends on boundary-crossing feats [where better than in Jerusalem, a divided city at the root] and the collapse of horizon." This is not Roth speaking but Ronell speaking as if for him, as if for the "as-if-ness" of his self-un/making as a test that in whichever of the two registers she proposes threatens to vacate the presence of the real and the real as presence, to dissolve into "an instantaneous dissociation from the present," into what Derrida calls "a *différance* in being-with-itself."[34] Roth is not free of anyone, lest he be free of himself which paraphrases the formula *writing = death* and also <u>not</u> writing = death. The collapsed horizon that Ronell cites recalls Deleuze's description of haptic vision, in which "there is neither horizon nor background nor perspective nor limit nor outline or form nor center."[35] Roth's counter—"Roth," his ignominiously named (and so self-shamed) Moishe Pipik (or *pupik*, meaning belly-button in Yiddish) constantly oversteps what for Roth is his own and in his mind, his impostor's limits. The fake Roth is freer than the real Roth and yet anchored by a cancer that is the source of this apparent freedom to do and be whatever and whoever he wants. "Phillip Roth" betrays vision, which is to say his author's script, his writing, his signature, the name he puts to the tale he tells on himself, the metaphorically many-branched menorah of personal remembrance by proxy/ies.

"If I hadn't been analyzed I wouldn't have written *Portnoy's Complaint* as I wrote it, or *My Life as a Man* as I wrote it, nor would *The Breast* resemble itself," stated the author who calls himself "Philip Roth." "Nor would I resemble myself. The experience of psychoanalysis was probably more useful to me as a writer than as a neurotic, although there may be a false distinction there." The writer as psychoanalytic subject says, in essence, "'I' have only 'myself' to blame (for not being

[33] Roth, *Operation Shylock: A Confession* (New York: Vintage, 1994).

[34] Ronell, *The Test Drive*, 10 and 18.

[35] Gilles Deleuze, "Nomad Art: Space," in Constantin V. Boundas, ed., *The Deleuze Reader* (New York: Columbia University Press, 1993), 170.

'cured')" and proceeds to tell his psychiatrist about his next book. The psychological subject is provisional, not absolute, open to its own fiction. "You have to become your doctor's doctor, even if only to write about patienthood," says "Roth," and I know that I am both the anxious patient of an even more anxious doctor and the author of said doctor's anxiety. We feed off of what we can make and have made of me. We are a creative team, like Charlie Kaufman's fictional selves recast as twin writers negotiating between them authorship of an un/blocked consciousness that is novel, "not like everybody else" (as neurosis calls it and which is what we call "neurosis"). Of this writing, this writing, as Julia Kristeva says of Marguerite Duras's, is and has been "complicit with illness," forever "faithful to discomfort," making cancer itself, which starts as an "invisible malady" into "an excess of fascination."[36] The newly minted cancer patient's question "why me?" is, at least in my case, rhetorical: "Because you have been a bad liar, an untrustworthy liar." Lying as concealment and truth as unconcealment after Heidegger constitute two versions of counternarrative in "the universe of fear," as Susan Sontag calls it, this "it" relocating the fight to inside the body.[37] "Gentlemen, you can't fight in here. This is the War Room," the US president famously announced in Kubrick's "absurdist" nuclear holocaust satire, *Dr. Strangelove* (1964). There is a certain fearful, paranoid redundancy at work here, a performance of self-consumption that is being fought on an atomic level.

The atomic bomb introduced my post-World War II generation of unintentionally ironically nicknamed "baby *boomers*" (after a boom in population growth) to the universe of fear. The bomb left us vulnerable, unconcealed to the possibility of alien invasion in the form of hyperbolic metaphor. Sontag regarded "illness as metaphor" as being synonymous with "metaphor as illness," the interpretive elaboration of our condition as an alarmist and even fascistic condition of language use.[38] Duras views each of us as bearing within us "the malady of death" triggered by the first atomic bomb blast, what Kristeva calls in characterizing Duras's

[36]Julia Kristeva, *Black Sun: Depression and Melancholia*, trans. Leon C. Roudiez (New York: Columbia University Press, 1989), 227 and 229–30.

[37]Susan Sontag, *Illness as Metaphor and AIDS and Its Metaphors* (New York: Picador, 1989), 15 and 161.

[38]"Language is a virus." William S. Burroughs quoted in Sontag, *AIDS and Its Metaphors*, 156.

perspective, "the conniving, voluptuous, bewitching contemplation of death...of the wound's constancy." This explosion into "voluptuous" inwardness, what Heiner Müller calls, "explosion of a memory," is "the remembrance...of a crucial fear." Kristeva's chilling summary assessment of what Duras says the bomb has wrought is that, "we are survivors, living dead corpses on furlough, sheltering personal Hiroshimas in the bosom of our private world."[39] We are, each of us, an unstable compound. Having been raised a Conservative Jew in the shadow of my immigrant grandparents' Orthodoxy, that compound was further engendered by the near-legacy of another compound, the death camps that during my formative years demanded concentration in my mind's struggle with patrimony. As a child, I was exposed to the "monstrosity of images" and "the new rhetoric of apocalypse" that eventually led me to this point, the "de-monstration" of the real by tacitly, fictively recording my disapproval.[40] Not that I would say as much out loud. In childhood, to paraphrase the motion picture *Alien* (dir. Ridley Scott, 1979), which scared the life out of me, no one can hear you scream.

FALLOUT

HE and SHE meet in the atomic ruin of Margarite Duras's *Hiroshima Mon Amour* (1959), which ended my late father's war. HE is a native of Japan who denies SHE the seeing or remembering of the ruined city, and SHE a citizen of France, originally from "Nevers," which is, on the surface an affirmation of the "Nothing" HE ascribes to SHE. "You made it *all* up," HE insists. "I didn't make anything up," SHE says. "Nothing."[41] Cancer reinvents your identity and by extension the identities you give to others as fictions. "This is the true value of the trauma: the chance to find yourself." The trauma itself can no longer be remembered as an event. (But does this mean that it cannot be ritualized?) Thus, HE's "Nothing" and SHE's "Nevers."[42] A septuagenarian Nathan Zuckerman speaks of an age-old rekindled desire, "life's obstinacy," as she (i.e., Duras) calls it. It is akin to SHE's hair growing back as if after

---

[39] Kristeva, *Black Sun*, 234, 235, 236, and 238.

[40] Ibid., 223.

[41] Marguerite Duras, *Hiroshima Mon Amour* (New York: Grove Press, 1961), 19.

[42] Stacey, 13.

chemotherapy and/or radiation treatment for cancer.[43] Cancer joins that short list of traumas, like Hiroshima and the Holocaust where the body and a culture (a body culture, the culture of embodiment, or just "culture") may metaphorically be said to be of the same scale. ("SHE: How could I have known that the city was made to the size of love? How could I have known that you were made to the size of my body?"[44]) The impossibility of the trauma's originary moment being captured (and here my thought is linking family history to genetics) means that one lives multiply and manifestly with its repercussions. Psychiatry says that those of us whose relatives either directly or indirectly experienced the Holocaust carry the pain of its memory inside us where it creates an array of anxiety disorders, or, for that matter, cancers that are these suppressed anxieties' physical expressions. These cancers are our "cells in chaos," these "cells" being our biological and ancestral families.[45] Is it any wonder that my family no longer remembers what it was or is? The ancient Greeks called displacement Metastasis, which is, I think, another good character name for a villain.

Cancer, specifically mitosis, "makes too much of the self," if the self is not considered to be abstract but instead visualizable as an integrated system of mind and body as some cancer therapists/theorists argue. In this way, I am well-suited to my disease as an ongoing condition. Cancer tops off my interior dialogue with un/certainty. Mine is not the hero's linear journey from chaos to control but rather the obsessive-compulsive's circular orbit around chaos-*as*-control in which no self is authentic and excessive self-monitoring produces not so much clarity as fiction. In this, I find much to my surprise, my thinking is at least superficially in line with alternative approaches to cancer treatment that say "the authentic self is the one that is in the process of transformation; we are required to be involved in actively 'working on ourselves'."[46] I say "superficially" because I find that I am not so much working *on* myself (becoming more in touch with myself) as working *up* myself as an assortment of selves drawn from other authors' fictional models (often for *themselves*). As a writer, I have my own system of boundless reference, which unlike those

[43] Duras, 98.
[44] Ibid., 25.
[45] Stacey, 11.
[46] Ibid., 174, 176, and 192.

who flip the script of cancer as othering to that of "selfing," is unclassifiable as "self" and "other." There is always only the new book. The writer's instinct, like the Brown-headed Cowbird's, is to move into the nest of another, making her biography his own reality, replacing her eggs with its own without the involuntary host's knowledge. Cuckoos do something similar but their eggs perfectly mimic the eggs of the host bird. Unsurprisingly then, Cuckoos metaphorically make better writers.[47] In discussing Thomas De Quincey's fascination with young Thomas Chatterton and his literary creation "Thomas Rowley" Frances Wilson writes, "De Quincey was destined to be a ghost crab inhabiting another's shell." The book you are reading is an expression of multiple such habitations, of being less the perpetrator of such fictions but the fiction itself, as De Quincey was said to be less like Chatterton than like "Rowley."[48]

FALLING/FALLEN-AWAY

Spalding Gray, who called a book he was writing *Monster in a Box* (1991) as a sort of catastrophic Schrödinger's Cat reimagining, was a strange Cowbirdman, depositing his neurotic self-effusion/self-effacement, in a nest that was but appeared not to be his own. In his *A Personal History of the American Theatre* (1985), in which he played himself and again in his novel *Impossible Vacation* (1992), in which he played someone else playing him, Gray spoke of wanting to play Chekhov's young dramatist Konstantin Treplev in *The Seagull* because he "gets to commit suicide—every night! over and over again!"[49] It may not have been the suicide that fascinated Spalding so much as the character's inability to be himself. To be able to play *that* might have set him free. Simon Axler, the 66-year-old actor in Philip Roth's *The Humbling* (2010) is unable to act because he has become "conscious of

---

[47] http://nestwatch.org/learn/general-bird-nest-info/brown-headed-cowbirds/; Alasdair Wilkins, "Nest Stealing Cuckoo Birds Are Locked in Evolutionary War with Their Would-Be Victims." io9.gizmodo.com/5785233/nest-stealing-cuckoo-birds-are-locked-in-evolutionary-war-with-their-would-be-victims.

[48] Frances Wilson, *Guilty One: A Life of Thomas De Quincey* (New York: Farrar, Straus and Giroux, 2016), 50.

[49] Spalding Gray, *Impossible Vacation* (New York: Vintage, 1992), 47; Interview with Edward Vilga, in Vilga, *Acting Now: Conversations on Craft and Career* (New Brunswick: Rutgers University Press, 1997).

every moment he was on the stage in the worst possible way." He could no longer forget who he was so as to be able to play someone else. He suffers a nervous breakdown and even here notes: "When you're playing the part of somebody coming apart, it has organization and order; when you're observing yourself coming apart, playing the role of your own demise, that's something awash with terror and fear." His condition gives new meaning to stage fright, what the British call "corpsing." And so, "the only role available to him was the role of someone playing a role...a man who wanted to live playing a man who wanted to die." In effect, Simon Axler ends up where Spalding Gray began, and yet both choose to go out like and as Treplev—somewhat indirectly suicided, undercover. Simon actually goes so far as to make a list of "plays in which a character commits suicide," something like as a Wooster Group adaptation of Spalding's work might call it, *A Personal History of the American Theatre: Just the Low Points*.[50] Simon's list is heavy on Ibsen, Shakespeare, Miller, and O'Neill, the last achieving a two-fer in *Mourning Becomes Electra*, but then that was based on *The Oresteia*, a trilogy.[51] This list-making with an option to perform was more of a Spalding Gray strategy than a Philip Roth one, as characters in the latter's novels, like Mickey Sabbath in *Sabbath's Theatre* would sooner torment themselves "to death" at someone else's gravesite than actually do themselves in when it comes right down to it. They are not looking to cash in early on all the misery that life has to offer—the aches and pains, the loss, the heartbreak. Simon Axler is the exception. No longer able to play anyone other than himself, he leaves as his suicide note, *The Seagull*'s final line spoken sotto voce by Doctor Dorn: "The fact is, Konstantin Gavrilovich has shot himself" (*The Seagull*, Act IV). In this, as in Spalding Gray's final act—a lingering head injury robbed him of focus and memory—it was almost as if the suicide was not speaking for him but as itself, as if the self could now say, "I have never felt more like a self than in the moment of my disappearance." This is in turn my book's subtitle speaking.

As he finishes Jaques's "Seven Ages of Man" speech in *As You Like It*, which appears to be hollowing him out like master of

---

[50]The reference here is to the Wooster Group's treatment of Arthur Miller's *The Crucible*, L.S.D. (*...Just the High Points...*), 1984. By this point, Gray had already left the company.

[51]Philip Roth, *The Humbling* (New York: Vintage, 2010), 2, 5, 7, 38–39, and 140.

mulit-pseudonymity Peter Sellers without a self to play, Axler spreads his arms out to both sides as if they were wings, like a birdman, like the stage writ wide, and flies as in falls face down into the empty orchestra pit below. A flightless bird, he is already extinct. Roth gives him a writer's death, specifically Hemingway's shotgun suicide, an idea which Axler himself advances in the plot. This is precipitated by his inability to return to the stage in the role of James Tryone, Sr., O'Neill's thinly disguised version of his actor-father in *Long Day's Journey into Night*, a title that in effect sets the stage. The film version of *The Humbling* flips the script to King Lear, a change of which stunted Shakespearean James O'Neill would have approved. This, he would say, calls for "real acting," although Axler no longer knows what that is. As he is being wheeled on a hospital gurney following his off-the-stage accident, Simon asks the attending nurse whether the moans of pain he has been emitting are convincing.

Thereafter, Simon's discourse with life asks variations on the same question, "am I delusional?" His phone's eerie ringtone projects the dehumanized frequency of "a shell of a man," as he is called. "I have these lunatics showing up at my front door. I think they know I'm here. They smell me," Simon tells his Skype-iatrist. One of these lunatics brings her cat, whom Simon accidentally backs over in his car, resulting in a trip to the vet who injects Simon's bad back with a dog and horse tranquilizer as an uncaged cockatoo disinterestedly observes. "There's a buzz about you. They want to see you," Simon's agent tells him trying to coax his client back to the stage. "They want to see if you'll jump again. You know like *Spider-Man*. People just went to see when they're flying around on all the cables if somebody would fall."[52] One way or the other, they want to see the actor propped up. Simon has taken up with the much younger daughter of a family friend and fellow actor whom he played opposite in Chekhov's *The Seagull*. Chekhov took his friend Potapenko's shooting of a woodcock for no reason, cutting the cables as it were of empathy as his own play's reversal of reasonable expectation. "It's not dementia," Simon tells his Skype-iatrist. "It's something else…The abandonment [of the work] is so severe, it causes such pain, and causes confusion, fear, because I don't know where to go." When Axler's lover "Pegeen Mike" (named after O'Casey's

---

[52] Publication of *The Humbling* actually antedated the accident-prone 2010 Broadway musical, *Spider-Man: Turn off the Dark* by one year.

intemperate fictional heroine) (allegedly) leaves him on the day of the night of *Lear*'s opening night, Simon cries out to her (believably): "Come back, come back Shane! Come back, *Shane*!" He has regressed at this point to the primordial cowboy Western's scene of abandonment (*Shane*, dir. George Stevens, 1953), as the fair-haired child chases the idealized white knight-like rider off into the irrevocable sunset and onset of dolor's youth that Shane sees in an ill-advised backward glance that I can only imagine.

CELEBRITY/SKIN

Early in *Birdman, or The Unexpected Virtue of Ignorance* (dir. Alejandro G. Iñárritu, 2014), there's a dress rehearsal of a kitchen-sink realism scene from a play, during which a lighting instrument suddenly falls from the flies and hits one of the actors squarely on the head, giving new meaning to the theatrical direction: "find your light." "It was no accident. I made it happen," says actor Michael Keaton playing Hollywood actor Riggan (and his superhero alter-ego "Birdman") as assertively as he did ("I'm Batman") in Tim Burton's two Batman films in which he starred. Riggan is looking for an authentic experience of the self, by which he means counter-intuitively (except to him) "real acting," unlike what he did as the movies' "Birdman." A sign posted in the lower corner of his dressing room mirror reads: "A THING IS A THING, NOT WHAT IS SAID OF THAT THING." The actor misreads (as in mirror-reads, backward) the message in his own posting, which does not concern authenticity, the real. The sign invokes Wittgenstein's response to Moore's "There are external objects" common-sense argument. Wittgenstein writes in *On Certainty* (36) that a statement like, "'A is a physical object' is a piece of instruction which we give only to someone who doesn't yet understand either what 'A' means, or what 'physical object' means." The statement in itself is pre-etymological. It is just something that we know. To say that "a thing is a thing" is to say nothing in a philosophical sense. And, as Wittgenstein famously stated at the conclusion to the *Tractatus*, "Whereof one cannot speak, thereof one must be silent" (§7). Riggan has posted this sign because of an unacknowledged ignorance (previewed in the film's subtitle) that makes it meaningful to him not because it *is* meaningful only on this level but because he thinks it has a deeper meaning. So even though Riggan quickly loses patience with a talented but insufferable Method actor in the cast, the former "Birdman" has likewise sought a deeper alternative to acting as mere simulation. Riggan would like to think he can strive to intuit a philosophical method of acting that does not know or will not acknowledge its name. With this in mind, the title of the production that Riggan hopes will make him a legitimate actor—*What We Talk About When We Talk About Love* (adapted from Raymond Carver's influential 1981 short story collection)—is a psycho-philosophical joke which Riggan and his fellow actors cannot understand as being one. Hospitalized for rhinoplasty after (allegedly) shooting off his own nose in the pursuit of his art (i.e., to spite his face), Riggan wears a white half-mask composed of surgical tape turning him into the recumbent ghost of Keaton's Batman, a celebrity sighting and a citing, an advertising of what celebrity is: THE THING *IS* WHAT IS SAID OF THE THING—e.g., "I'm Batman."[53]

At the time he shot *Birdman*, Iñárritu would certainly have been familiar with the work of fellow Mexican artist, Jorge Marín who sculpts birdman statues of all sizes, all of them wearing long-beaked masks like they emerged from a painting by Hieronymus Bosch. (Iñárritu and Marín, who are the same age, even look like they could be twin brothers.) *Birdman*'s director would likewise have been familiar with Marín's series of giant sculpted metal wings that any man or woman can pose their bodies between to transform them instantaneously and for a moment into Birdmen or Birdwomen. Among the one hundred or more winged things I have in my house, other than a multitude of bird drawings and sculptures, are members of this hybrid species—flying pigs (of course) and cats, mermaids and mermen, saints and spirits. I've named my winged pig "Ulysses" after the Circe episode in *The Odyssey*, who, along with my crow "Murder One," welcomes visitors and fellow obsessive counters of things that speak for themselves into the house's first stor(e)y. Maybe I'll invite Michael Keaton for a visit, and if he refuses I could kidnap him like Rupert Pupkin did Jerry Lewis in Scorsese's *The King of Comedy* (1982). It seems only fitting as Riggan's agent lured him into coming back from the dead (drunk) to perform his play by telling

---

[53]When Batman voluntarily unmasks himself to Catwoman at the end of *Batman Returns* (dir. Tim Burton, 1992) and villain Max Shreck wonders aloud, "Why is Bruce Wayne dressed as Batman?" this "dressed as" speaks to a transference of celebrity of one fiction to that of another, and of the mock-surprise at the lack of authenticity that attends to only one.

him that Martin Scorsese was in the audience looking for actors to cast in his next film.

I kidnap Jerry Lewis in that "next" film (time being immaterially relative), Scorsese's *The King of Comedy* having already come out in 1982 without Riggan in it (I having assumed his role). When we first see the non-up-and-coming stand-up comic, Rupert Pupkin (sounding like a joint Philip Roth-Jerry Lewis production), he is dressed identically to his idol, comic talk show host Jerry Langford (who looks just like the real Jerry Lewis, because he is). Pupkin is the dummy who is made to look like a miniature version of the ventriloquist who gives him life. ("This is not my whole life," Rupert tells an equally delusional fan hoping to get Jerry's autograph or to tear off an article of his clothing. *The* jacket? *The* shirt?) Pupkin, though, is wearing white shoes, a one-off of Langford who is wearing Lewis's signature white cotton socks. "My name is Rupert Pupkin. I know the name doesn't mean much to you, but it means an awful lot to me," Rupert tells Jerry, unconsciously restating Wittgenstein's assertion that the name is meaningful only to the un-instructed. The joke, told by a desperately name-checking nobody unaware that he is saying nothing to an idol he reimagines as a personal friend, does not land. The name of the would-be comic not in on the joke (that the name tells on itself) is forever being misremembered, unremembered, mispronounced. He can't *give* his name away. ("Take my name," please to paraphrase "no-respect" comedian Rodney Dangerfield of 1980s vintage and before.) After later taking Jerry captive to assure him a guest spot on that night's show, Rupert lectures the talk-show host, who is fittingly tied to a chair, on the rules and *bonds* of friendship: "Even though this is a kind of strange situation, there are moments of friendship, and moments of, I don't know, what you call sharing or whatever.... You know, Jerry, I'm gonna tell you something. Friendship is a two-way street. You know that?" In the relationship of ventriloquist and dummy, it is in fact the delusional fan who is the former and the celebrity he holds captive the latter. Jerry Lewis/Jerry Langford, who is aptly mouth-fitted with a gag, bemoans the celebrity life that is not his own, that is intruded upon as violently as a hand stuck up a dummy's ass in equal measure to Pupkin's desire to be there, to be him. "A THING IS A THING, NOT WHAT IS SAID OF THAT THING." Keaton, i.e., Riggan, would have *killed* in this role.

"Jerry Langford, right?" an enthusiastic fan shouts to the comedian on the street prior to his kidnaping and after telling the person she is speaking to on the payphone that he won't believe whom she just saw. "You should only get *cancer*! I *hope* you get cancer!" she yells at Langford for being too busy to talk to her name-checked sick nephew on the phone (in a film that name-checks mental illness as extreme comic behavior). It is not so much the *hope* as the *you* that should be emphasized here? I hope that *you*, "Jerry Langford" get cancer (this "you" being both apt and paradoxical as "Jerry" is playing himself with only a surname change). The woman's not knowing what to say to celebrity is a variation on the person who does not know what to say to the celebrity of cancer when confronted with it unexpectedly. "Is that him?" a thinly disguised Rupert later asks his crazy non-friend Masha as they wait to kidnap Jerry. "No, it looks too much like him. When it's him, it doesn't look like him," she remarks with a Capgras syndrome-like delusional certainty that is nevertheless true. Celebrity confronts us with its illusionary remoteness whose liveness reveals the thinness of its (celebrity's) masked mortality. Metonymically speaking, the fake pistol Rupert has brought with him to take Jerry hostage looks real (Masha says), because (Rupert says) "that's the whole point" of the weapon's celebrity—that it appears real enough to wound, to discover the wound of celebrity's own mortal being, its groundlessness in meaning. Celebrity is an episteme only in the sense of feeling like we know what we don't know. It is a counter-metaphysical sense that feels almost physical to the enthralled, to those who believe in it, who take it as an article of faith (thus the "reality" of a celebrity friend, like the "Jerry Lewis" kidnaped by Pupkin and in my dreams). When Jerry phones his office to inform his staff that he has been kidnaped, no one believes it's really him. They all think it's a prank caller pretending to be him. (Which, in effect, Rupert is, although it's Jerry, now "Rupert's Jerry," the ventriloquist's dummy on the phone.) Mimesis enables mitosis, spins off the non-actor's ability to co-opt the celebrity-skin that holds the actor captive (Birdman syndrome). Rupert first gave voice to a life-size photo mock-up of "Jerry Langford" on a basement talk-show facsimile set in his mother's house across the river in West New York, New Jersey from where you can see the mock-up Manhattan skyline that breaks Rupert's heart with its unreachable proximity. I almost took an apartment there once but knew that I would never be able to live with or as myself if I did.

I am standing across the street from where Scorsese is shooting the film's opening scene. This is really happening, really happened. I can just make out Jerry Lewis, who looks very much like himself, coming through the stage door and the mock crowd mock assaulting him. I expect to see Robert De Niro, who I know is starring in the film, but I see only Rupert Pupkin. It was him and not me who grabbed Jerry out of the car in which crazy Masha accosted him, peering back through the window as if he (Rupert) were inside the television set and screen. I did not kidnap Jerry Lewis even in my wildest dreams, but my dreams have kidnaped him on recurring occasions. In my defense, if dreams need one, I kidnaped Jerry's friendship for the purpose not of furthering my own ambitions but fulfilling a need that I (okay, here perhaps like Rupert) think we might share—the need for friendship to testify on our behalf that we are really who we say we are, that we are saying *something* rather than nothing. Wittgenstein's speech take on Leibniz's "Why is there something rather than nothing?" brings his predecessor's cosmological question down to earth, with Rupert, a messenger who tells people he works "in communications," Wittgenstein's odd relation.

Movies require darkness, but (why) does darkness require movies? A movie theater owner blacks out London by sabotaging the city's central power station in Alfred Hitchcock's *Sabotage* (1936). When customers at the saboteur's cinema demand their money back, the theater's spokes-man refuses, calling the blackout "an Act of God," and goes on to define an "act" in tortured philosophical quasi-speak as "any activity actuated by actual action." Verloc, the cinema proprietor with the power to turn off the dark, articulates a similar redundancy, steadily staring at a bare lightbulb as if he were contemplating inventing it. Verloc is being shadowed by Detective Spencer (his real fictional name) from Scotland Yard, whose presence makes the movies Verloc is showing at his cinema themselves seem suspect. Verloc's bomb-maker is another small shop proprietor. He sells birds, creating another cinema-birdman scenario. A birdcage is used to deliver the bomb, along with a bird to young Stevie, whom Verloc charges to deliver the package with the bomb while also delivering two canisters of film (which he is told by a streetcar conductor are themselves flammable). Verloc's casual instruction—"You know, kill two birds with one stone."—sounds especially ominous spoken in actor Oskar Homolka's Austrian accent. Coming as it does right after Stevie says how funny it would be if his new pet canaries laid eggs, the cow-bird's practice of killing another bird's young before they hatch and sup-planting them with her own eggs seems to invent neurotic behavior for another animal species.

Stevie is effectively "killed" by youthful curiosity. Distracted en route to his destination by a snake oil salesman whose performance (along with a military parade) co-opts his fragile attention, the time bomb puts an end to innocence by running out of time. Trying to recover from Stevie's death, his sister, Verloc's wife, enters into Verloc's theater and watches Disney's *Who Killed Cock Robin?* She stabs Verloc with the knife she uses to carve the dinner roast, noticing after she does Stevie's two canaries in their cage, *not* singing. Seventy-five years later (three years prior to Batman's seventy-fifth anniversary), the graphic novel *A Death in the Family* depicts the death by bomb explosion of the caped crusader's sidekick, "Robin." Some years after that, a student's project in my *Mise en scène* class rewrote part of the picture panels' story, substituting words from my book *Infinity (Stage)* that was precipitated by a death in *my* family. "I am Batman," "I" say, though I know I am not a man pretending to be a bat, but a cowbird pretending to be someone or something else.[54]

[54] Austin Campion was the student who did the project. Jim Starlin, Mary Wolfman, Jim Aparo, and George Perez, *BATMAN: A Death in the Family* (New York: D.C. Comics, 2011).

CHAPTER 5

Generational Loss

My mother's fear of escalators began, as such things do, with a fall. No fear of elevators, though, especially since the handsome young man with the penetrating blue eyes rode it regularly in the Queens apartment building my parents lived in before I was born. I don't recall the building in which I spent my first years as having one—neither an elevator nor the handsome young man in question. By then, Paul Newman had achieved a career breakthrough playing Brooklyn-born boxer Rocky Graziano in *Somebody Up There Likes Me* (dir. Robert Wise), another film from my movie-magic year, 1956. My mother could not have known that she was staring across the narrow space of an elevator in an apartment building in Flushing, Queens, at the actor who would play so prominent a role in the depiction of Israel's founding in 1948, the year of my birth. She might not even have known that in 1948, Flushing, Queens, was the epicenter of the world, the site of the United Nations where the vote giving the Jews a homeland was taken. Chronology being what it is, she would not know to ask Paul Newman what he disliked about his role as fictional Haganah (Jewish Defense Force) officer Ari Ben Canaan and the film *Exodus* (dir. Otto Preminger), which was not released until 1960, one month after my Bar Mitzvah at the age of thirteen credentialed me as a mannish Jew. She does not see me now re-watching this film for the first time since its release and the attainment of my Jewish majority, measuring myself against the events and spirit depicted in it, recalling my father's, her late husband's unwavering support of the state of Israel, owing to the reasons for and circumstances of its origin, notwithstanding (from my, not his perspective)

© The Author(s) 2019
S. Golub, *A Philosophical Autofiction*, Performance Philosophy,
https://doi.org/10.1007/978-3-030-05612-4_5

its policies as a nation-state. My mother, whose blood makes me Jewish, might have wondered whether the fair-haired, blue-eyed young man with the perfect nose in the elevator with her was even a Jew. (Newman, an actor who *did not* change his family name, was half-Jewish, on his father's side, and so lacking the maternal Jewish imprimatur.) Much would be made of this in *Exodus* when the anti-Semitic British Major Caldwell tells Ari, who is disguised as a British officer that he can tell a Jew just by looking at him. "They [Jews] look funny too. I could spot one a mile away... You know, a lot of them try to hide under gentile names, but one look at their face you just know." That Newman-as-Ari-as-a-British-officer affects an awful English accent underscores the fact that the bigot's blindness extends (even) to a transparency as blue as Newman's dreamy eyes, as blue as the Israeli sky of which my father dreamed, as blue as my movie memories of my mother and father's past imagining of my future life. As in movies, my previewed, pre-viewed life.

The first thing my parents did after I was born was to move into an apartment building located around the corner from a movie theater (The Meadows) named after the affordable housing neighborhood (Fresh Meadows) built to accommodate GI's, like my father, who were back from service in World War II with little money to their name. I don't recall Paul Newman's films being shown there but I would have been too young to process (them) if they were. Besides, I was too busy playing the kind of roles (cowboy, baseball player, superhero) that came naturally to a preschooler's imagination being shaped by television. Other than the costumed photographs what has mostly stayed with me from those years is a youth made anxious by a mother's memories of it. I do recall the neighborhood Horn & Hardart cafeteria/(self-serve) Automat (which accepted only special coins and where my mother and older cousin, who lived locally, ordered the vegetable plate with its vivid orange carrots) down one block from the Meadows Theatre. But what I took away from the Automat experience was not the bland food but the mumps or rather my mother's vivid recollection of my cheeks visibly swelling and her carrying me in her arms, frantically running back to our apartment on the same road where a large collie knocked me down initiating my fear of dogs that I also "remember" but only from my mother telling me that it happened. Did she also pick me up and run away from the dog that may have only wanted to befriend me? Did the dog follow? So, hard to say whether my mother and I were outrunning her fear of dogs or mine. Was I only following her lead?

In my mind, the Meadows Theatre marquee shouts in capital letters, COMING SOON: BOOK OF DREAMS, while John Murdoch, amnesiac protagonist of the film *Dark City* (dir. Alex Proyas, 1998) searches for the wallet he left inside the Automat (not necessarily in Fresh Meadows, possibly in Manhattan) to lend credence to his being who he says he is even though his memories are not really his own either. He is a subject being acted upon, acting in a movie. A psychiatrist named after real-life author and psychological subject Daniel Schreber tells him, "The only place home exists is in your head."[1] Who better than a paranoid schizophrenic's namesake to recognize film as being the only known reality? Who better than an obsessive-compulsive like myself to make this film into a time-loop, a circle or circuit of spooling cells causing me to experience both my mother's memories as my own and my father's cancer too early while he is already well-past being too late? Cancer looped back on me like an older self does on its future younger self (both killers) in Rian Johnson's 2012 science fiction film *Looper*. "Closing the loop," they call it—one's identity being a loose costume beneath the ostensibly tight fit your life appears to make of it. The future must kill the old looper to save a telekinetic child's mother who alone can control the destructive power of his imagination. The dog who jumped me in my mother's oversight had vividly colored blue eyes like Newman's own, I imagine. Outside the *Auto*mat, where I too appear in my mother's memory to lose self-control, to need her not just to save me but to tell me I have been saved. The Meadows marquee now advertises CANCER: THE MOVIE. The film is in 3-D, the line for tickets is long, because its potential audience is pre-sold on the possibility that the special glasses they hand out in the theater lobby (I still have mine somewhere inside me) may allow the wearer to see something that perhaps is not even there, namely film as an organizing cure for its own errant animated cells. The red and green lenses alter the color of the star's piercing blue eyes. It is not Paul Newman but Conan Doyle's uncanny beast, the Hound of the Baskervilles. And like the Mona Lisa, its eyes seem to follow me wherever I go.

The glowing dog passed through a fog so thick it makes a man blind and a woman hear things like, "like me, you have in your head things you may not have exactly seen." And with this, Katherine "Kit"

---

[1] Judge Daniel Paul Schreber's paranoid-schizophrenic *Memoirs of My Nervous Illness* (1903) influenced both Freud and Jung.

Preston quickly discovers that hearing voices is no walk in the park.[2] She is being followed. The voice in *Midnight Lace* (dir. David Miller, 1960) informs her, without giving any reason, that "it" is going to kill her. It's the "it-ness" of the disembodied voice that terrorizes the body that holds the voice it houses within itself to be a phantom that may come and go as it pleases. What if the tenor of that voice became unfamiliar—"unreal" as Mrs. Preston tells Scotland Yard's police inspector Byrnes it is—estranged from its putative owner's failing ear? What if others say they cannot understand your words? Are you merely speaking too low or in another voice not quite your own? Why would "your" voice do this to you? Or is it not your voice, but "theirs'" trying to drive you mad? The unreality of the voice threatening Mrs. Preston derives from it being misapplied to the embodied mouth of the ominous-looking character "Ash," whose impersonator, rat-faced actor Anthony Dawson (it's the quality of atypical physical impersonation that most frightens me) likewise tried to kill Grace Kelly in Hitchcock's *Dial "M" for Murder* (1954) in an act/scene engineered by her husband (as Doris Day's is by her spouse in *Midnight Lace*).[3] The suture is completed by casting mellow-voiced, avuncular John Williams as the investigating police inspector in both films.

The Inspector has Mrs. Preston listen to a tape of known "telephone talkers" voices (as they euphemistically call such phone terrorists), dipping into Scotland Yard's casting pool of known suspects. Do you recognize any of these voices? Does any one of them fit the role of the voice-actor you heard? Are these even real voices, or have we created them in-house to test your mental acuity—your mental state rather than power of recall? My anxious hearing, subject to loss of meaning and misinterpretation, says that the Inspector (what else would my anxiety call him?) is talking to me. This unhinges me or rather makes me aware of my lack of hinges, the name Wittgenstein gives to certainties so elemental they can be stated only as pseudopropositions. These certainties "cannot be falsified by experience." OCD represents unhinging: the need for every thought and action to be specially and repeatedly tested. No one sounds like himself, nothing looks like itself, nothing is itself.

---

[2] McElroy, *Lookout Cartridge*, 6.

[3] The nefarious husband in both films is also named "Tony." Both want to dispose of their heiress wives and inherit their disposable incomes.

Life is interrogation meant as in the case of Stanley in Pinter's *The Birthday Party* (1957) to make us confess to the "groundlessness of our believing" in it.[4] My telephobia now asks me, "Is one of these a Jewish voice?" prompting me to ask in turn with something like my grandmother's anxious rhetoricity when hearing JFK had been assassinated, "It wasn't a Jewish man?" It wasn't *Paul Newman*? I hear my mother ask with/in similar dis/belief. How are such questions made possible by what other people mistake for "experience"?

When Mrs. Preston (her three-month marriage coincides with the length of time her husband has been planning to kill her for her money) fails to pick one of the voice actors as the culprit, Inspector Byrne tells her there's nothing they can do until the next time "he" calls—meaning implicitly when his call and her recall sync up without her imagination, her self-invention intervening. But anxiety muffles sound, stops thinking in its tracks and diverts it onto another road, or rather to another road-block. In this vein, a doctor suggests (inaccurately) the possibility that Kit suffers from dissociative personality disorder as a result of some childhood trauma. Because we are living within Kit's anxiety, we do not hear the voice on the phone until the end, when her catastrophic thinking is rewarded by its imminent fulfillment. (Tony's revealing himself to be her killer.) Kit is saved from falling to her death (her husband's original plan) by *Psycho*'s John Gavin, a poor man's Paul Newman made claustrophobic by the memory of his own wartime trauma, who rides up the apartment building's scaffolding in an open-air elevator that would have traumatized my mother, and, in turn me had "I" not intervened.[5]

The rats in the wall have eaten through the phone line producing a ringing I can't get out of my mind and a call I cannot take. This is not Schreber-speak for madness, despite Philip Roth's observation that, "People come apart. And aging doesn't help...Some shock just undoes them around sixty—the plates shift and the earth starts shaking and all the pictures fall off the wall."[6] And the rats gnaw through the wires in the interior walls? The rat episode really happened to me and my brother-in-law in his house in tectonic L.A.—rats ringing the front doorbell from

---

[4] Wittgenstein, *On Certainty*, §136, §166; Moyal-Sharrock, *Understanding Wittgenstein's On Certainty*, 83, 91, and 92.

[5] Alfred Hitchcock's *Psycho* was released in 1960, six years *After Midnight Lace*.

[6] A character says this to Mickey Sabbath, age sixty-four. Roth, *Sabbath's Theater*, 17 and 81.

inside the walls.[7] I have since extrapolated this telephobically to be a contamination on the line that wants to speak only to me, to keep me in the dark while holding me responsible and demanding I pay for the call. They intend to lodge a complaint but I know that they deal only in false memory. They are ringing the bells not just to get my attention but to deflect it from themselves. Now, with caller ID, I don't pick up or else disconnect my phone when I see whose obsessive-compulsiveness I can hear chewing through the line hoping to find my own fully activated and at home. They call and call and I recall and recall, but as always, only in sounds and images remembered from film, like from someone else's memory. Does this false memory template genetically encoded in my own child account for her generational loss, inheriting the symptoms without actually having seen the films that produced them in me?

In an uncanny valley at the turnoff to TWIN PEAKS in a film (*Experiment in Terror*, dir. Blake Edwards, 1962) that arrived decades earlier, a young woman is accosted in the dark, then later in the fog of sleep by an anonymous, asthmatic voice. *"Am I waking you up?"* it rhetorically asks, the asthmatic's own heavy breathing self-awarely marking its own death-time. We are in this together, the voice tells her. Do not scream. And I don't, even though as an asthmatic with sleep apnea, I am the potential victim and self-murderer, potentially killed by my inability to stop myself from *not* breathing in my sleep. This doubled breathing, breathing through and as a double is another kind of nesting with which we cowbirdmen are familiar. I am playing the film's three key roles of "subject"/"victim" (as FBI surveillance labels the film's protagonist, Kelly Sherwood), lead agent John "Rip" Ripley, and the asthmatic villain Garland "Red" Lynch, who likes movies. I am re-watching this movie, which scared me to death at age fourteen, as an experiment involving one particular scene in which Lynch appears in a ladies' restroom disguised as an old woman, triggering my earliest movie terror. The precipitating image of the witch in Disney's *Snow White and the Seven Dwarfs* (1937) coincides with that of the Night Hag, disabler of sleep, bringer of sleep paralysis. As in McElroy's *Lookout Cartridge*, my parents thoughtfully but erroneously tried to make a film coincide with a book (*Snow White*) that my fear consigned to fire, as if we were burning the witch in the corridor outside our modest two-bedroom apartment in Queens.

---

[7] The oil-burner man tells Billy Pilgrim, whose house is cold: "Mouse ate through a wire from the thermostat." Vonnegut, *Slaughterhouse-Five*, 171.

(You always bring terror home with you.) At that moment, I indirectly, to my shame, became a book-burning fear Nazi.

The asexuality of the Night Hag image is enhanced in Lynch's "experiment," by his mouth breathing which is easily mistaken (especially over the phone by my telephobia) for sexual arousal, an auditory image that would have terrified me in my early teens when there was still much I did not want to know, despite my father telling the ladies stag-talking at the restaurant table next to ours I so wanted to learn. "How about a movie tonight?" Kelly's boyfriend Dick pops up through Kelly's bank teller's window right after she has stolen the $100,000 demanded by Lynch in return for her and her sister Toby's safety in a film devoid of parents. Suddenly, a formerly innocent question pertaining to movie-going and movie-watching is no longer just a guilty pleasure. It just makes you *feel guilty*. Perhaps that's the experiment that is being conducted. Can I keep from feeling guilty watching this movie, or must I implicate myself and my own unwanted thoughts in it to make it *move me*, to sequence it with my intent, whatever that might be? Is it the atypicality of *my* thoughts that sets my mind on edge while watching? How am I meant to react when innocent young Dick responds to Kelly's refusal of a night at the movies because she "promised Toby" with the self-incriminating "I'm gonna *drown* that kid"? As if, *he*, in loco parentis, were a surrogate murderer of youth. At film's end, Lynch is forced to run for his life to escape the police and FBI agents, so that when he is shot, his heavy breathing just prior to dying sounds like what it is, asthmatic.

I wake up to the realization that the women running from the voice(s) threatening to kill them in *Midnight Lace* and *Experiment in Terror* are both my mother, or rather my memory of her telling me about her fears (of dogs and cats, of falling down an escalator). My self-absorption is a borrowed state of fear. The voices that are figuratively heavy breathing down her neck are the invisible hand at her back that occasioned her fall and is always with her, like "the escalator ...in my pocket in red ink," to which Cartwright, the protagonist in *Lookout Cartridge*, who believes he (too) was pushed while on an escalator, refers. Cartwright's escalator was stopped, though, a fact that only he among the others in the subway station failed to acknowledge, perhaps because of an imprecise parallel memory that only his mind rehearsed of his childhood friends and he "[taking] stairs three, four at a go and here again now years later no hands." We continue to fulfill as in fall in step with childhood mandates.

Following a repeated reference to his narrative's inciting event of the escalator push from behind and fall, Cartwright speaks of seeing someone *ahead* of him on the street as "someone I should have been seeking but was not yet someone who did not act as if she might be in danger but was trailing two people I thought would be willing to harm her."[8] The subject confusion in this sentence implicitly suggests that any moment we designate as an event collapses time, (con)fuses collision *and* montage, destroying the *distance between* that is necessary to follow someone or to be followed. Cartwright speaks obsessively throughout the novel as being *in between* the forces of order and chaos that are and are not under what sometimes feels to be his god-like control. ("Unfortunately, to be between does not necessitate being constantly connected with what one is between.") McElroy writes: "I am trying to find a way which can use unsatirically the very styles of abstraction that are part of processes we are right to fear. What I am after is some sequence of contemplation that will use and transmute certain sources of our fears without merely rejecting them."[9] We take our fear two steps at a time, stepping over the cracks in our façade, watching ourselves perform this ritual as if it were self-contained and not being otherwise, in frame.

I experienced World War II, my father's war (as he called it) through Hollywood movies and oddly, experienced Viet Nam, my generation's war through World War II movies as well. I was fighting my own internal war between order and chaos and Viet Nam gave me too much of the latter. I was, with the dull force of public school education at my back, holding off the thrall to abstraction, which kept showing up in my thoughts as aberrations I did not yet recognize as being communiqués sent to me from the future by the person I would become. I proceeded passively, detached from distance and difference, not fully assimilated to being here or there. I identified with fire-bombed-in-Dresden, electro-shocked-in-post-World War II-America Billy Pilgrim, the soldier protagonist of Kurt Vonnegut's *Slaughterhouse-Five*. The novel came out in 1969, the year those of us born between 1944 and 1950 learned whether or not we had won (i.e., lost) the Viet Nam war draft lottery. (Although Billy is drafted into World War II, his son Robert volunteers for the War

---

[8] McElroy, *Lookout Cartridge*, 4 and 425.

[9] McElroy, ibid., 59; Joseph McElroy, "Neural Neighborhoods and Other Concrete Abstracts" (1974), 8, *DocSlide*. https://documents.tips/documents/joseph-mcelroy-neural-neighborhoods.html.

in Viet Nam and rises to my father's former rank of Sergeant.) We felt "unstuck in time," moving involuntarily back and forth through different parts of our lives like Billy, looping, not yet who we would become and in-between who we were. Abstract. Abstraction, though, as Billy's (fictional) example attests, may be a precognitive vision or sense of what is real—the trauma of what life predicts and abides. Billy's pilgrimage sees him being involuntarily transported to the planet Tralfamadore (i.e., being drafted again), where he learns that "the world is just a collection of moments all strung together in beautiful, random order." Order and chaos are one. So, to the question, "Why does the actor playing 'Billy' in the movie version of *Slaughterhouse-Five* have a gap between his two front teeth like me?" I counter, "Why wouldn't he?"

Looking back on a phobic, hyper-allergic, pre-asthmatic childhood (my tonsils were removed to postpone asthma's onset until adulthood), I may have feared the future (i.e., growing up) more than anything (which has become my own child's legacy). Having recently entered the teenage years separating childhood from young adulthood when I viewed *Experiment in Terror*, I might have been experiencing not so much conscious fear as a hypnic jerk that left me agog at seeing the imaginatively extended moment between waking and sleeping (hypnagogia) screened for anybody who cared to see the self-exposure of the guilt underlying and undermining my innocence, which, as a teenager abandoned by childhood friends, was already waning. I am still plagued by these hypnic twitches on an almost nightly basis, as I find my mind reverse engineering my life passages along the lines of "should" and "would" in mortal combat with the forever self-undermined "could." I think myself awake without falling asleep. Here I am visited by the hypnagogic auditory hallucination of a man's heavy breathing. It could be the Night Hag, a man dressed as an old woman, an old woman who resembles a man—or both. It could be me, as it could have been me all those years ago seeing myself disguised by the present to conceal the future that awaited me, the future that comes to pass in the moment of extended wakefulness before we fall asleep. Before, when pushed, we fall.

There's film of me growing up to the age of thirteen, I think, but I lost it. It has become for me like the obsessively sought-after films in novels by David Foster Wallace and Joseph McElroy. I wonder if I happen upon the film again whether it will prove as fatal as it is in fiction. Is there something on it, perhaps some combination of somethings that when projected will ensnare my life in a pattern or loop from which it cannot escape and within which it will end? Is it seeing all the family ghosts or the unimpeachable images of a youth I actually lived rather than invented? If I need fiction to sustain me, how can I withstand a record of real memory, even if it was staged for the camera? It's the irony that kills you in the end. Suicide *by camera*. The plot of McElroy's *Ancient History* revolves around a writer named Cyrus breaking into the apartment of a famous novelist, Dom, who has committed suicide in which Cyrus did or did not assist. "Suicide's an existential act, right?/It's also an occasion for measurement//...suicide due to Sphinx syndrome, suicide as a time killer," Cy writes, or maybe he's quoting from Dom's fictional book *On Interruption*. Cy is not so much running out of time (although the knob on the apartment's front door is slowly turning) but out of space (he is down to his last sheets of Dom's Sphinx bond paper on which he is writing the book we are reading), although he wants to tell Dom's son Richard who is on the other side of the door "about this space and how it's become mine to become itself." The suicided author's apartment holds the key to Cy's book—"now spread[ing] like an inestimably charged field ever, yet, within the confines of this room, to a mode like time, but solute—a paraphase," to cite *Ancient History*'s subtitle. "The solute, the paraphase, a substance dissolved in another substance," one self entered into another self, a writer's conceit taken for a life.[10] Again, nesting. If I were to watch the film of my early life, would I actually see myself in my parents' apartment, in my visiting grandparents' presence, my grandparents who cannot be thought of apart from their own apartment in which was felt the crush of space and time? The grainy images offer no clear resolution. "Can all that other life I know about subside into some rankless field and lose its poignant fussy orders? Maybe I never knew what you were talking about." (I'm here talking to my "self.")

To Jupiter and Beyond

I grew up in the in-between, crossing bridges in and out of Manhattan: the cantilevered Queensboro completed in 1909, connecting Manhattan and Long Island City; the Bronx-Whitestone opened in 1939, connecting Queens to the Bronx; the Triboro opened in

---

[10] Joseph McElroy, *Ancient History: A Paraphase* (Ann Arbor: Dzanc Books, 2014), 114, 115, 236–37, and 252. http://www.dictionary.com/browse/solute.

1936, connecting Manhattan, Queens and the Bronx (the triad of my American family genealogy); the Throg's Neck, built in 1961 to connect Manhattan and Long Island and ease traffic congestion on the Bronx-Whitestone. Crossing as a child in the back seat of my parent's car, these bridges lulled me to sleep, dreaming not of suspension but of spansion, a word I mistook for it but which refers instead to a memory that had not yet been invented.[11] Perhaps I knew, as they say of cars and bridges, that there was something wrong with the suspension and tried not to let this particular fear enter my subconscious.

In Philip Roth's novel *Indignation* (2008), the story is told through the dying brain of a soldier, *as if he were a writer*, regaining consciousness by imagining his life and death as incidents in a book. The book tells him not just what happened but the reasons why. This "source code" is a fake origin story but it is real enough for us. For a while, every weekday morning when I was in high school, I ate the same special breakfast that my father did—a rare hamburger with a sunny-side-up egg on top. Following breakfast, my father left the house for work in Queens, at the foot of the Queensboro Bridge and across from Manhattan at East 59th Street, near where my parents would later purchase an apartment. Rather than taking the crowded Long Island Railroad into the city, my father drove the congested Southern State Parkway but turned around before he traveled very far and drove home, where I would still be preparing to leave for school. My mother told me it was an anxiety-driven digestive issue (which entered my body as an imitative condition), but what if it wasn't?[12] What if my father returned home after the same amount of time every weekday morning because his traffic-induced anxiety concealed something else? Did he see or foresee, for example, the neighbor's daughter jumping off the bridge that spanned the Southern State Parkway near our exit, after which he saw a succession of her ghosts leaping again and again? Was he racing home to ascertain for himself that I was still safely there? Did he have to stop himself from saying aloud to me, "You are here," which would have

---

[11] Spansion Flash Memory awaited the new millennium.

[12] I grew up believing that regularity was a goal of Jewish-American culture. The Jewish summer camp I attended posted a regularity chart on the wall of each bunk to make sure that each one of us was biologically processing the kosher food we were being fed properly as our parents would presumably want to know, whether they were kosher (which mine were) or not.

registered no meaning for me, other than alarm that something might be wrong with him?

Starting out for the same destination on the same or a different highway (like an unstable premise to an SAT question having to do with train or car departures and arrival times I lacked the mathematical formula to answer) was my father's employee, "Charlie," whose acute fear of crossing bridges and entering tunnels left him on an island of his own making not named Manhattan. "Terminus the god of boundaries and property may be subject to Mercurial delusions because of insecurity arising from the fact that his post was created to take some of the work-load and even responsibility off Jupiter's back...but [his] post-Terminal sense [is that he] is overcommitted and underconnected."[13] My father (Jupiter) chose Charlie to take over the running of his business when he retired, throwing the one-time employee's mind into a tailspin that turned the New York City's bridges and tunnels into a potentially even more lethal vortex than before. Charlie carried a (I assume loaded) handgun in the glove compartment of his car, maybe to protect him against this phobia of his own design or else to shoot his way out of it by ending his life. If he's still alive he would be quite old now, older than my father who is long dead. So, maybe Charlie had the right idea. Charlie's life was a threat to linearity and the connectives (bridge-and-tunnel logic) necessary to preserve it, to a chronology that would not brook a field, and yet that is just what he did—preserve what threatened to destroy him with his as-far-as-I-know-never-fired handgun and those suicide-site bridges whose possibility he refused to entertain. I wonder how Charlie liked his hamburger cooked and whether he topped it with an egg and ate it for breakfast before he departed for work. Which came first—the chicken or the egg— and why did the chicken not cross the bridge? Because it was the bridge that *made him "chicken,"* of course. As we kids would say. What did we know about grown-up angst?

With each reset precipitated by my father's morning return drives home, I got another look at him. Seen from a different angle, my father's repeated returns did not encode my premonition of the onset of my OCD in which I would repeat actions to such an extent that my father could not understand or abide. My real problem was not psychological, although in high school I equated psychiatry with personal

---

[13] McElroy, *Lookout Cartridge*, 512.

embarrassment, so I certainly thought that it was. It was a lack of education. (I was a grind and a slow learner.) I had not yet read the right books or had the life experiences necessary to make sense of the movies, movie listings, reviews, and theaters my brain was cataloging like my older cousin in Queens did baseball statistics. I was unable to see where I was going, despite having created the mental map. (I have never been able to read real maps.) My frustration at not knowing what was happening inside my brain caused my body to rebel, I literally could not stomach it, and so my mind invented a condition that I watched my father enact repeatedly which I then mistakenly thought *I* emulated. I grew up with many serious allergies, which my parents seriously believed I inherited from my uncle, my father's older brother, who, ironically, owned a pharmacy. My mother was allergic but she did not see it. Everyone makes up stories so as not to panic over the things they cannot yet put together, the signs, maps, and systems they cannot read. I have spent my adult life playing catch-up, trying to draw hidden correspondences out of camouflaged pictures by inventing theoretical constructions. I challenge reality to test my theories, not my motives.

In *The Spirit of the Beehive* (dir. Victor Erice, 1973), a father diagrams "teeming bridges and stairways of wax...invading spirals" for his young daughter, whose life is transformed when *Frankenstein* (dir. James Whale, 1931) is screened in their remote Spanish village of the 1940s. "The movie is coming! The movie is coming!" the children gleefully scream, unaware that a monster is also approaching, the cine-monster of their persistent troubling. The children see (our own childhood memory fills in what we are *not* shown) the film's key scene in which the Creature accidentally kills the little girl who befriends him owing to his limited understanding of his incomprehension's strength. Encouraged by her older sister Isabel, a melancholy six-year-old named Ana, whose dark, watchful eyes (as they say) see everything, believes that the Creature who died in the film lives on as a spirit whom only his friends can see by closing their eyes, an action that sutures sleep to cine-dream. Ana—the actress and character's age and name coincide in this film and its figurative successor *Cría Cuervos* (dir. Carlos Saura, 1976)—is caught in a honeycomb of childhood's incomprehensibility and adult desire (her father in one film keeps bees, her father in the other film keeps women). Like the Creature, who resists but succumbs to its paternally modified, stitched-together criminal nature, Ana's sutured families perform an

attraction-repulsion to death that they taunt with sexual desire that trau-
matizes their young.

In *Cría Cuervos*, Ana discovers her second father Anselmo, killed
by sex, in the marriage bed he no longer shares with his wife Maria,
on whom he regularly cheats even as she cheats death by complaining
of illness while repeating "I want to die" but not dying. But then, as
Isabel tells Ana, "Everything in movies [including death] is a fake." The
grown-up Ana, played by her own dead mother, speaks both of childhood's happy innocence and death's serene clarity as being lies. The
sutured "she" knows only that cheaters—like her second father, like her
surrogate mother, Aunt Teresa, like her sisters who hide from her in a
game of hide-and-seek, must figuratively die. She thinks the loaded military pistol that once belonged to her now late Spanish Civil War fascist
father has an empty chamber, like the one in the abandoned farmhouse
in *Beehive*, where she fed and clothed (with her first father's shoes and
overcoat) a Republican fugitive whom the Fascists are seen executing in
her absence. The fugitive's noble, anti-authoritarian stance (and residual
leg wound) opposed the distracted, academic first father's honeycombed
"sadness and horror" at the symbolic bee colony's "relentless yet inef-
fectual toil, the fevered comings and goings, the call to sleep always
ignored, undermining the next day's work. The final repose of death,
far from a place that tolerates neither sickness nor tombs." True to the
blended families' passive-aggressive legacy, the first father crosses out
this morbid, defeatist thought from his diary but not his life, nor those
of his children and their next-generation parents. When the first father
comes to bed following his late-night crossings and crossing-outs, his
wife feigns sleep, as his oldest daughter Isabel feigned death to further
awaken Ana's vexed thanatopic desire. When Ana thought that Isabel
might be dead, she checked *her heart* to see whether she was breathing,
although she learned at school that to associate the heart and not the
lungs with breath is a mistake. Ana knows better. "I love you. I can't
breathe," were the last words Ana overheard a suffocating Amelia gasp
to her (Ana's) second father Anselmo before he died while having sex, a
passive-aggressive act, which adults (the child thinks) euphemistically call
"making love." A father's loss leaves a giant footprint, like the one outside the abandoned farmhouse where Ana went alone to meet her friend,
the Creature's spirit. So too, does a daughter's.

"I can't understand people who say that childhood is the happiest
time of one's life," darkly camera-eyed Ana/Maria tells us, the camera,

watchfully self-watching. "It certainly wasn't for me. Maybe that's why I don't believe in a childlike paradise or that children are innocent or good by nature. I remember my childhood as an interminably long and sad time filled with fear. Fear of the unknown. There are things I can't forget. It's unbelievable how powerful memories can be." What does it mean for Ana's mother to effectively discuss her own death, for the two-way ventriloquism between mother and daughter to negotiate death's border-crossing that the first father's spirit fearfully crosses out? Is self-editing—or suicide, which mother and daughter separately contemplate—a form of self-possession of which they ultimately do not partake? "It's all a lie. There's nothing. Nothing. They lied to me," Maria's wild-eyed animal fear tells watchful Ana (pain's dream of disembodiment resulting cruelly in observation's exacerbation of pain's performance). "I'm afraid. I don't want to die. I'm afraid. I don't want to die! It hurts." Ana, who in the earlier film, closed *her eyes* to make her spirit-friend appear, now with her hands closes *her ears* to drown out her mother-her self's cries.[14] In so doing, she pushes her father's wax bridges deeper inside, impairing her hearing, "a kind of audible projection of the future of those color-visions of children" from which such movies are made.[15]

False Memories of the Son

Set in the near-future-past (New Year's Eve, 1999), *Strange Days* (dir. Kathryn Bigelow, 1995) is a cautionary tale of how appropriating other people's lives as a vocational choice may cost you your own. What if you had the technical capacity to tap directly into their cerebral cortexes, and all you needed was a circuitry crown concealed by a wig? But what if everyone's hair started to look like wigs, and they were possibly all tapped into lives other than their own? What if nobody's life was their own and you could not take anyone at face value? That you ever thought you could is the real fiction here. The murderer in *Strange Days* employs a virtual reality video apparatus (advancing the primitive set-up of the photographer-killer in Michael Powell's *Peeping Tom*, 1960) by not just capturing his victim's fear in the moment of her death but wiring

[14] Geraldine Chaplin, who plays both grown-up Ana and young Ana's mother, played her own grandmother in Richard Attenborough's biopic of her father, *Chaplin* (1992).

[15] McElroy, *Lookout Cartridge*, 194.

her brain so that *his own brain* interferes and interfears <sic> with hers, resulting in a terminal pleasure-plain circuit.

As an only child in his pre- and early teens learning to touch-type, the narrator Cy in McElroy's *Ancient History: A Paraphase*, "keyed a word so it came up 'interfear'," opening up "a real scene of the difference between [his two friends] Al and Bob," both of whom know him but not each other and who Cy spends the entire novel trying to keep apart. In this way, Cy can more closely monitor and control the scene-changes in his own mind, even though the mental exertions this action necessitates undoubtedly change his mind, maybe even about keeping them apart as he records knowledge of them meeting in the novel he is writing as we are reading it. Despite X-ing out "interfear" as a typo, Cy has already been infected by the need to decipher or else determine its meaning and until the age of fifteen or sixteen writes what he calls "Interfear Mysteries." Looking back, he says, "I was ahead of my time," a fact that *Strange Days* speculatively acknowledges as do I as my original dissertation typist suffered a nervous breakdown in mid-assignment, working with a carbon copy of my fear exacerbating her own expressed to me even before she started typing.[16] Once finished by a second typist, this dissertation lived inside a refrigerator to save it from the fire that my fear later summoned as a prophecy self-fulfilled. Where there's smoke, there's carbon, and where there's carbon, there are multiple drafts that fan the flames of self-awareness, of representational doubling, of a combustible interfear that produces carcinogens and deprives you of the being necessary to sustain even one self.

Philo Gant ("Paranoia's just reality on a finer scale."), a former client-now-enemy tells *Strange Days*'s protagonist Lenny Nero his problem is, "You assume there's something where there's nothing. You assume that you have a life when, in fact, you peddle pieces of other people's lives, and the broken parts of your own." Here we stumble upon an adaptation of Leibniz's question, "why is there something rather than nothing?" as a personal plug-into the world at large in both a physical and metaphysical sense. Specifically, the question underlines Leibniz's principle of sufficient reason, "by virtue of which we consider that we can find no true or existent fact, no true assertion, without there being

---

[16] McElroy, *Ancient History*, 227 and 228.

a sufficient reason why it is thus and not otherwise, although most of the time these reasons cannot be known to us" (G VI, 612/L 646).[17] Leibniz's principle of sufficient reason ("that nothing occurs for which it would be impossible for someone who has enough knowledge of things to give a reason adequate to determine why the thing is as it is and not otherwise.") depends upon the assumption that "things must exist, it must be possible to give a reason why they should exist as they do and not otherwise."[18] So, what then do we do with all this virtual "otherwise," the constant self-referrals to the fictional worlds of other people's lives? Do we consign them to dreams, and, if so, to *whose* dreams? Or, should we recall Moore's Paradox in which two seemingly contradictory things can be true, and chalk it up to a philosophical semantic? Might we, you and I together be not *either/or* but *both/and* at our cerebral core? Why wouldn't we be, might be a more logical question, or maybe even who or what benefits from keeping us apart, as Cy sought to do with Al and Bob? *Strange Days* posits through the example of the murderer, who is found to be wearing a wig over a virtual circuit crown *virtually all the time* (what or how much time is *that*?) that there may not be any interruptive acts between one otherwise experience and another. He, like Philo, is "doing way too much playback," although he accuses Lenny of doing the same. It takes one to know an/other. Unlike movies, the yet-to-be-identified circuit-crown-wearing murderer cautions Lenny, virtual reality experiences lack the music and credits to let you know when you've reached the end.

Memory is, after all, a structural problem, which is to say, something to which I can and have turned my hand as if it were in or synonymous with my mind. "I no longer take for granted personality or, almost, even person." The lost film says, "one day I'll put a raft of these intersectional interruptions [these grainy projections and transmissions] together as if they were one life and all the *rest* were interruption." Living in this interruption, this "beside time" ("paraphase"), as McElroy calls it, is

---

[17] Leibniz, https://plato.stanford.edu/entries/sufficient-reason/; G.W. Leibniz, *The Leibniz-Clarke Correspondence*, ed. H.G. Alexander (Manchester: Manchester University Press), 1956.

[18] Leibniz, "The Principles of Nature and Grace, Based on Reason" (1714); G.W. Leibniz, "The Principle of Sufficient Reason and His Argument for the Existence of God." http://spot.colorado.edu/~heathwoo/Phil100/leibniz.html.

what I do.[19] I think this interruption began the summer I went watch-less in Woodstock in the summer of 1969, having lost time up a tree. [When you lose a parent or a child, I later learned, that time stays lost.] Bob Dylan said that Woodstock was where "we stop the clouds, turn time back and inside out, make the sun turn on and off."[20] Dylan was living up in the hills near us at the old artists' colony (since 1903) of Byrdcliffe, and his rumored appearances at the Woodstock Playhouse, where I apprenticed (and Lee Marvin, who would co-star with Marlon Brando as a fellow motorcyclist in 1953's *The Wild One*, got his start in 1947) were nearly as legendary as the legend himself. Dylan was recov-ering from the motorcycle accident (he was said to be a bad driver) in which he was said to have broken his neck and out of which emerged his new *Nashville Skyline* voice. The Band, who were living in a house they called "Big Pink" down the road in West Saugerties, recorded their 1970 album *Stage Fright* on our stage shortly after I departed, but perhaps my anxious voice (so "stage fright proud") still lingered inside the voices of Richard Manuel and Rick Danko, both of whom died "prematurely," although there is no absolute sense when that is, especially when your career has seen better days.[21] The Woodstock Festival (The Woodstock Music and Art Fair) was happening elsewhere (43 miles south in Bethel, New York) but far too many people thought that we were ticketing it from our box office. Many people have inserted themselves into the Festival after the fact (stating non-evidentially, non-informationally, "I was there"), a strategy I have adopted vis-à-vis *fictional* events only. Only one of us got to go to the festival and that's only because she got fired by the theater's producer. She claimed to be a witch (we dubbed her "Necronancy," incorporating her first name "Nancy" into necromancy), which didn't save her from falling violently ill at the festival, a develop-ment she did not foresee. She came back looking like one of *Macbeth*'s weird sisters, much the worse for communing with the dead, or at least with "the Dead."

Referring to the film *Inside Llewyn Davis* (dir. Joel and Ethan Coen, 2013) for which he executively produced the music, T. Bone Burnett says that despite source material relating to the life and music of

---

[19] McElroy, *Ancient History*, 187 and 225.

[20] Barney Hoskyns, *Smalltown Talk* (New York: Da Capo Press, 2016), 43.

[21] Ibid., 21; McElroy, *The Letter Left to Me*, 48.

Dave Van Ronk, "mostly, it's real songs with made-up people." There were those who considered Dylan to be "a complete fake," and others who thought I *was* Dylan (there was a slight Semitic resemblance) and followed me places (this being *outside of* Woodstock), unable to be disabused of this notion, even by me who half-wanted to think that it was true.[22] Dave Van Ronk stomped his way through a rough and profane performance on the Playhouse stage I swept and crossed in character as a stuffed bear and a Nazi prison guard in between hand injuries, technical theater humiliations, romantic frustrations, and midnight acting lessons absorbed osmotically in my sleep at midnight after a show had ended. Other folk singers came through to perform at our Monday night concert series—Tom Paxton, Tim Hardin, Patrick Skye, Happy and Artie Traum. I remember that Skye, who was the face of innocence, brought with him a dwarf whom he mocked. (I don't think I could be making this up. I think that Skye also walked with a fake limp. Or maybe the dwarf did.) Hardin, a heroin addict, was loaded and unpleasant, but then his bad reputation preceded him, so maybe he was just acting out to satisfy our low expectations of high drama.[23] Happy and Artie Traum were local folk heroes, Tom Paxton a straight arrow in a Greek seaman's cap, I think (although I might have taken this image from one of his album covers). It struck me that these Greenwich Village types may have regarded this as a working holiday out in the country. I had haunted the downtown New York City folk clubs they grew out of during my growing up years, never seeing anyone big until they traveled north and found me in the real Woodstock, an epicenter for figures real or imagined. I saw Jimi Hendrix walking into or out of a head shop on Tinker Street, years before a Beatles collage video to accompany their song "Free As A Bird" compiled after the death of John Lennon showed George Harrison emerging from the London home-office of the legendary drug dealer to the pop stars, "Doctor Robert." Both Jimi and George were wearing broad-brimmed floppy hats, a kind of fictional disguise by which they could be stamped in time to serve memory, so far as memory serves.

[22] Ibid., 38. "*Inside 'Inside Llewyn Davis,'*" documentary on the making of the film, directed by David Prior, Criterion Collection, 2013.

[23] The album Dylan recorded in Woodstock, *John Wesley Harding* (1967) was named after the celebrated Texas outlaw John Wesley Hardin, one of whose granddaughter's sons was Tim Hardin, who took her maiden name as his own. http://archiver.rootsweb.ancestry.com/th/read/HARDING/2000-12/0978009103.

Pop stars popping in and out of my very own Jewish kid's Advent Calendar. The Paul Butterfield Blues Band were sitting at the long, wooden dinner table at The Elephant across from me, because, of course, their assemblage signaled community, like the breaking of the freshly made bread in our mountaintop kitchen that ran counter to the unreal community of theater-making in the barn next door at Byrdcliffe, up the winding "mountains of the mind" road with the tree at the curve into which I often fantasized turning my car and crashing.[24] In a dream-like replay that was, however, real, sleep deprivation and pain medication caused me to fall asleep at the wheel of my car on the New York State Thruway en route to Manhattan on theatrical assignment from the Playhouse to purchase trick props from a magic shop.

Where in this sleep-deprived memory of acting the disturbed romantic youth is the loss of an adult child who is *not* me, who bears none of the identifying physical scars that I have from operating on too little sleep—a partially severed thumb (scene-change accident), a second-degree palm burn (a lighting accident), the loss of time (a wristwatch thrown high up into a weeping willow)? How can words not trivialize this loss by attaching it to what seemed at the time like other extraordinary incidents? How could you know pain's future plans for you? That the child (when she *was* a child), opposable like your stitched-together thumb, who would not commiserate with your cancer, could not look at you ill, outlived illness's ability to strip you bare of hope and happiness. "Light of my life. I search for you, my child," intones the overdubbed voice of the mother who has lost a child in Terrence Malick's *The Tree of Life* (2011). (Family is an enormity in a nutshell, not fallen far from the tree, timeless.) It's a cosmic voice, attuned to nature—to waves and currents, planet waves, as Dylan called them.[25] Sometimes, though, the child never finds her light and you being the instrument of her first light, falls from the flies upon your head in the night among the fireflies. You who had such difficulty hanging lights atop the A-frame ladder in the house of the Woodstock Playhouse that they thought you might either be mentally slow or else a savant whose mind could not adapt to rules and particulars. You thought then as you think now that you're playing tragedy but it's someone else's idea of summer stock.

---

[24] Hoskyns, 6.

[25] Dylan's 1974 album *Planet Waves* featured the Band as his backup musicians.

In Christopher Nolan's film *Batman Begins* (2005), Thomas Wayne and his son Bruce have not the same voice but the same mouth. It's how you know they're related. It is ironic, then, that the one part of Bruce's face that is visible when he masks it to become Batman is this identifiable mouth. The film is all about fear and of achieving mastery of it. Thomas Wayne's final words to his son who has just witnessed the murder of his father and mother are "Don't be afraid." Batman's nemesis in the film, Dr. Jonathan Crane, on the other hand, like the murderous photographer in Powell's *Peeping Tom*, is the damaged product of his father's using him as an experimental subject on fear. As a child, my son feared going to sleep at night, which culminated in a scene in which we struggled atop a staircase like Holmes and Moriarty did above the Reichenbach Falls. My son fortunately grew out of his fear and later stepped behind a greasepaint mask to become not a Batman but a Blue Man. I, on the other hand, continue to list fear as my chief allergen. Dr. Crane's alter-ego "The Scarecrow" (under a face-covering rough burlap mask) blows his own experimental fear agent weaponized in powdered form into the bare faces he wants to infect. Sometimes (as you now know), I too forget to breathe. I wrap fiction around me not so much for protection but like the memory cloth from which Batman's cape is made to allow my in-itself shapeless fear to mimic any shape. I haven't a place to go in which to hide from myself and marshal my defenses. My fear continues to say, interruptively, irrationally, "I am here." The Bat Cave in *Batman Begins* differs from others in that it is not a dry space but instead has puddles and even larger pools of water on the (under)ground. Like memory cloth it has assumed the shape of the fear agent's destination, Gotham City's water supply, so that Bruce Wayne can learn to control it as he would his own fear. Batman gives Commissioner Gordon the fear agent's antidote to self-administer by a needle to the thigh, like the Epinephrine injection device (Epipen) I use to forestall anaphylaxis, which is another pretty good name for a Batman super-villain. With her crooked mouth that turns down at one end, Assistant District Attorney Rachel Dawes asks Batman whether Commissioner Gordon is his friend to which Batman responds, "I don't have the luxury of friends."

Coincidentally, I returned to *Batman Begins* after many years only weeks after my lips swelled and one end of my mouth turned down like actress Katie Holmes's Rachel Dawes after ingesting an unidentified allergen. "I'm Batman," I whisper, my mouth now seen in extreme close-up that exaggerates the size of my lips so that I become unrecognizable to myself in the hospital emergency room. Whatever the nametag on the white coat that evaluates me there says, it is "Dr. Crane" who is on call. It is he who speaks for, speaks through this fearful grown-up child as I am wheeled into the room marked "Self-Imaging."

DAUGHTERS OF CHAOS

A man tells a psychiatrist, "I have a friend who has a daughter," remembering the suspect nature of my having a friend. I don't know whether my daughter keeps a "stuttering diary," like Swede Levov's daughter Merry does in Roth's 1997 novel *American Pastoral,* but I effectively do and I publish mine in installments, like the one you are reading now.[26] For daughters like Merry and their fathers, manipulation takes different forms predicated upon their being curative responses to self-perceived and possibly self-generated conditions of which OCD is one and writing (and writing with and about OCD) is another. Stuttering is a form of repetition after all, an over-insistent effect that is an affect of self-consciousness too. What is more manipulative than self-consciousness and the behaviors it promotes, expanding the borders of the self aggressively in the name of defending said borders as insistently as any despot would and does. OCD is a despotic regime as is the stuttering mind that feeds its insatiable hunger to be self-involved with self-concern. It marks the family resemblance that links me to my two children, not in name only. Wittgenstein writes, "I believe...that the people who gave themselves out as my parents really were my parents...This belief may never have been expressed; even the thought that it was so never thought" (*OC,* §159). But my children's OCD has made me think, "I have a daughter," "I have a son," in much the same way that cancer has made me think, "I have a body" and, of course. "I am going to die." Both OCD and cancer are stuttering, tessellating conditions that make you think about things you should and do already know. They are both, in this sense, counter-intuitive, broken hinge propositions that Wittgenstein says go without saying. "I" cannot go without saying. "I" says (a phrase encoding non-agreement) there is no objective certainty, no personhood that is not citational. As the use of this word "citational" suggests, the

---

[26] Philip Roth, *American Pastoral* (New York: Viking, 1998), 98.

pathology at work here is more literary-theoretical or perhaps perform-ative than it is wholly medical. Even though OCD is a medical condi-tion, it is a subjective one. It is determined by behaviors that respond to certain questions of nomenclature rather than to forms of medical tech-nology (CAT-scans and the like). I did not *not* know that I had a body, a daughter, or a son, before. I just did not think knowing that I hadn't a reason to ask the question what makes them so, or more accurately, how I have made them so. This is where the concept of generational loss comes in, an erosion of certainty in the act of asking the question how a thing that you know, that you have always known is made. Can inner experience demand of empirical knowledge that it account for itself as being what it says it is—real? Once the "autobiographical hinge" is bro-ken, the door to where the given circumstances of your life—home, fam-ily, friends, self—reside swings open or at least is left ajar.[27] Something, someone(s) escapes, and you are left in doubt, your past in error.

Roth's Merry Levov decides that "she had wasted enough time on the cause of herself" and instead maps her self-concern onto the world thinking that this marks an abnegation of her previously dedicated course and cause of self-monitoring. When what is really happening is a greater effort to blow up and so collapse the world into her own inter-nal suffering—not to take on responsibility for the world but to have the world take on responsibility for her. Other people suffer the conse-quences of her "exhilarating power of total self-certainty," like her father who hopes that "she will eventually become herself again." Their (non-) relationship has come to be based on the very concept of what self-certainty is. The self has split the concept of relationship as if "relation-ship" means difference and "difference" the unsustainability of "relation-ship" and "family" as ideas.[28]

Speech Contaminants

The autobiographical hinge being broken, Merry Levov acts radically "out of character," bombing the post office in her town as a hyperbol-ically vocal protest of the Vietnam War. The local doctor who delivered

---

[27] "Autobiographical hinge" is Moyal-Sharrock's term, *Understanding Wittgenstein's On Certainty*, 124.

[28] Roth, *American Pastoral*, 101 and 103.

her into her stuttering life is the only physical casualty of the blast. He had to pay the price of which she cannot afford to speak and still stay true to "her/self." The doctor who delivered my younger sister was killed when the car he was driving collided with an oncoming train as he raced to remove a small toy (I imagine a small car or train game piece) that had become lodged in a child's throat. Merry is not the only one, who as Roth describes her, "revel[s] in the dazzling idea of stealing *time*," if it helps to tell your story.

Now she wants back in, into the house where she grew up and out of our image of who she apparently never was and certainly never could be again. "How could we allow the unexpected back into [our] lives?" asks the rhetorical "Swede." With the doctor dead, all that remains is to destroy the parents to finish the job. Even if it were not *her* doctor or the parents she thinks she had. I am not Swede, who Zuckerman calls "the superman of certainties." I never thought for a moment that it or I "add[ed] up," and less so now than ever. So maybe the bomb should not come as such a shock. Maybe it's like the doctor who drove into the train; maybe I am displacing someone else's sense of order and chaos onto my self and surroundings. But how can you blow up what is and has always already been in pieces? There is no compare-and-contrast index to be applied between my daughter and me. We are in one sense two of a kind, each the other's worst-case example of what fearing life can do to a person and his/her family, even though it is "family" that is only the theoretical last defense against a fear that has long ago eaten away at the self.

Merry was an early and intelligent talker. Swede wonders whether this caused a vocabulary overload that precipitated her stutter. It also caused her to say such age-inappropriate things as "I'm lonesome," before she knew what "lonesome" and perhaps even "I" and its verbal agency "am" meant.[29] As a toddler, my daughter spoke in television advertisements. When I told her, "I'll be right back," she added "after these messages." No fort/da here, as an advertised continuity of return-forestalled separation anxiety. She struggled to remember the place where a pair of snow boots she wanted could be purchased before retrieving from television's memory prompt the answer: "at participating stores." The affect of these communications was value and character neutral, communicating some

---

[29] Ibid., 144, 191, and 226.

other agency's desired effect. Such thinking, I reasoned, allowed self-distancing to pass for personal and social adjustment. Beneath the mask, though, lay "the daughter who is chaos itself"—"Chaos Golubitsky," who is not my daughter, although she shares my surname one-generation removed, severed from the branch of my family tree to affect absorption into a social order that displaced, suppressed the originary self. The doctor racing to save a patient kills himself in someone else's life that is somehow part of my contingency, my accidental nature that resides where grounded belief is not otherwise domiciled. The infant he was racing to save, Merry Levov, who had something, had language caught in her throat. At the sound of the distant collision, the ungrateful child releases her word toxins into the air intended for the father surrogate: "Physician, k-k-kill thyself."

Merry's habit of not bathing so as "to do no harm to the water" (a purposeful, at least on Roth's part appropriation of the doctor's Hippocratic Oath) recalls the "there are souls…imprisoned in every form of matter" premise of a *MAD Magazine* "Flash Gordon" parody from my youth. "Flesh Garden," as he is rechristened in the magazine's typically one-off fashion, refuses to step on anything that moves or even lies inertly on the ground.[30] There are related obsessive-compulsive behaviors posed in this faux-ethical stance that invert the usual fear of being contaminated by physical contact with the fear of contaminating another by touch, smell, word, thought, aura. To paraphrase the famous passage from the *Bhagavad Gita* spoken by Oppenheimer at Trinity, "Now I am become death, destroyer of words stuck in the throat of a stuttering mouth, of a child who did not die but who indirectly caused someone else to die in her place."

The first thing you notice is the darkness of the mouth (in Beckett's 1972 monologue *Not I*), inside and around, and the teeth that do not bite the tongue, neither in the literal nor in the figurative sense. The mouth cannot stop talking, almost as if "she" fears being interrupted by a stray thought that might identify her beyond the designation "Mouth" that the quasi-parental monitor bestows upon her from *his* unseen darkness. Maybe she fears the girlhood memories of which she speaks will overwhelm her. Or maybe she's just trying to make her words keep up

---

[30] Ibid., 231 and 232; Wally Wood, "Flesh Garden!" in *MAD Magazine* 11 (May 1954). In one of my few youthful rebellious moments, I had *The Mad Reader* that ran this story confiscated from me in class by my sixth-grade teacher.

with her thoughts. Who *isn't?* (Whose thought is *that?*). Surely, she is attempting to speak as consciousness without a knowable self, anonymous to everyone or else known only to those who wish to remain anonymous. She is, *not I*, despite what she says, except insofar as her identity is semantic. The dark Mouth that re-inks the darkness frightens me, as if it were the darkness of the printer's ink behind which the authorial voice says it cannot stay silent. This, despite Wittgenstein's admonition at the end of the *Tractatus* (§7) that we must do so if we have nothing to say other than "I am here." This writing as a (fictive) female "Not I" (recalling Cixous's characterization of women's writing as being done in *white* ink) that cannot stop itself from speaking, compelled as s/he is to incessantly exfoliate a history as *said* history.

My parents always ended phone calls by saying "That's the story," turning up "story" on a musical note. And what is *her* story? Abandoned by her parents, she would say, bereft of that essential love to grow a proper self. It's *their* fault, then? Her survival keyed to words that come to her in a flash, that overcome her as down the rebirth canal her voice travels out the mouth and lacking relations to call her other than "Mouth," "Mouth" she becomes, having no relation even to a near or former self and "with no idea what she's saying...till she began trying to...delude herself...it was...not her voice at all," as though I was speaking through her without hearing myself speak. But perhaps that's just me reading in what I want to hear—that she doesn't know what she's saying. It is not this Mouth that I remember with its torrent of harsh words, its "mad stuff."[31] But also to have no idea what she's saying allows her to abnegate all responsibility for it, for "her" life, for *her life*. A moving target, that's the ticket—ironic given that Mouth cannot move, cannot *move past* what is being said and so can never fully become "herself."

PRECARITY

Merry Levov's delusional way of respecting water may have been rooted in fear, like Natalie Wood's (nèe Natalya Zakharenko, nèe Natasha Gurdin), the movie star having been taught this by her mother Maria who believed the gypsy fortune teller's prediction that *she* would drown in the darkness. Having taken on another's fear, Natalie likewise took

---

[31] Samuel Beckett, "Not I," in *The Complete Dramatic Works* (London: Faber and Faber, 2006), 379 and 382.

on another's death. Natalie, who was a non-swimmer, drowned in her mother's place under mysterious circumstances in the "dark water" she feared like a curse from a mother's mouth. Natalie's haunted Russianness and the almost overwhelming need of friendship and protection radiating from her attracted me almost as much as did what I mistook to be her compact Jewish beauty. She did play the Jewish muse Marjorie Morningstar (née Morgenstern) in the film adaptation of Herman Wouk's 1950s New York Jewish American novel of the same name and that was good enough for me. Additionally, that is certainly delusional Maria whom Nathan Englander describes in one of his many short stories seen through a Jewish lens as a mental patient "who corresponds with her dead daughter and the drowned star Natalie Wood." "She writes them joint letters—fully aware they never write back."[32] It's a terrible thing to lose a daughter to the mad awareness of generational loss, to write letters to the before-and-after child who does not write back.

Mother Maria, like my relatives, feared that the Communists were dogging the tracks of her and her children in exile, nesting her fearful dreams inside her daughter "Natalie Wood" like a wooden matryoshka doll, who in turn unnested a series of frightening movie mother surrogates against whom she, in character, could rebel, as if against her own nyctophobia—her fear glowing like a movie screen in the dark. Natalie, raised to think that she was a kind of doomed Anastasia Romanova manqué (many manqués actually believed they *were* the still living or else afterlife Grand Duchess), didn't need to be Jewish to buy into a mortal imagination. Still, had Natasha been Jewish it would have been Anne Frank's picture and not the last Russian tsar's youngest daughter's hung upon the wall of her childhood bedroom. (Natalie Wood was offered the film role of Anne Frank but turned it down.)[33] In either case, what does it mean to aspire to be someone who must always be listening for a knock at the door even while looking straight into the camera? What makes Natalie Jewish is this tremulousness over a secret about to be no longer hidden.

---

[32] Nathan Englander, "Reunion," in *For the Relief of Unbearable Urges*, 64.

[33] Legend and wishful thinking on the part of Russian émigrés said that Anastasia escaped her family's murder by the Bolsheviks following the 1917 revolution. This has since been disproved. Anastasia was seventeen years old at the time of her murder, so the chronology is off even in the Zakharenko *fantasy* family history as Natalya was only born in 1938. Suzanne Finsted, *Natasha: The Biography of Natalie Wood* (New York: Three Rivers Press, 2001), 16–17 and 20.

Like Merry Levov, a second or third generation teenage Russian immigrant daughter, Natalie blew up a building or rather her alter-ego did in *Inside Daisy Clover* (dir. Robert Mulligan, 1965), offhandedly remarking, "Someone declared war." Natalie had a lot of alter egos, who were themselves dissociative personalities. Like Merry, she—i.e., Daisy—stuttered, only audio-visually when in a dubbing session inside a sound-proof booth she could not make her voice synch up with the film in which she was watching herself act. The movie studio writes off Daisy's delusional (fortune-telling) mother, killing her off in the teenage star's official biography. Natalie's own mother was barred from sets—or was that only her stage mother surrogate Rose in the semi-fictional musical bio-pic *Gypsy* (dir. Mervyn LeRoy, 1962)? Maria told her children, "they used to call me 'The Gypsy'," referring to her (dubious) Romany origins.[34] How many names, identities, personal histories can be displaced and still keep the picture from breaking apart into so many puzzle-piece Anastasias (or Ashkenazi's for that matter)? How much generational loss can a picture or a memory withstand before it fades away entirely?

The best defense against chronology is anachronism. "As long as we have this act, nobody is over twelve," Mama Rose tells her young charges in *Gypsy*, and my grandmother must have told her children, including my father the same thing. In *Inside Daisy Clover*, Natalie Wood is a 30-year old woman playing a 15–17-year old girl, much like my own delusional aunt Ruth did for all her days. Would playing Natalie Wood playing ingénue roles in the movies have saved Ruthie from being (thought) delusional? Who could say then whether or not she (my aunt) was only *acting*? If trauma stunts inner growth, why would changing birthdays seek to commemorate this, if not for the purpose of saying, "this is how it really is—past, present, and future, all the same." And if times can be switched out, why not people? Natalie Wood for her mother, Mama Rose ("born too soon and started too late") for her daughter Louise/stripper Gypsy Rose Lee played by Natalie Wood who is in turn played by or at least *for* my aunt Ruthie, who had difficulty taking off her clothes even *in private*.

Like a latter-day Pauline enacting her many perils, Natalie Wood performed her stripped-down vulnerability from film to film, picture to picture. There is a moment in *Splendor in the Grass* (dir. Elia Kazan, 1961), in which Natalie appears not as herself, that is not as the character,

[34] Ibid., 5, 12, and 19.

Wilma "Deanie" Loomis she is playing in the film. Although she's uncredited in the second role it must be Natalie because her near double, a rouged club dancer, is intended to be her sexual surrogate with Bud Stamper, her high school obsession whom Deanie under her mother's puritanical stage-management, left wanting. (Deanie's mother says of Bud's profligate sister, "Ginny Stamper is too low for the dogs to bite." My cynophobic "I" supposes there must be some comfort in this.) This broke the couple up and broke Deanie in two in the process. Deanie is that future person hidden in plain sight who only appears to be chaotic in the present because her temporal modes do not yet align. She is not the person who dies tragically young to whom the high school yearbook is dedicated, but life does happen to her early and overwhelmingly. After her sister Baby June leaves the act and burlesque usurps vaudeville in *Gypsy*, Louise plays her first act as headliner Gypsy Rose Lee, emancipated from her stage mother, in Wichita, Kansas where Deanie Loomis nominally went for treatment after her nervous breakdown. I say "nominally," because the Menninger Clinic, where she was almost certainly sent was located *in Topeka*, although either "Wichita" or "Topeka" would make a good stripper's first name.

Trauma searches childhood for someone to haunt. In one of the few recorded instances in fake history, Daisy Clover *and* my aunt got to keep their real surnames. I don't know whether my aunt ever attempted suicide. Natalie Wood did, and so did Daisy Clover. In what sounds like a cruel Jewish joke, the latter tried to gas herself but was interrupted by a phone call from the movie studio inquiring, "Miss Clover, are you disconnected?" (Is that the voice that calls to you at the end, the Studio that has been producing and monitoring your movie-star life? Does it sound to the suicide-in-process like it is speaking in close-up like Mouth, trading in one darkness for another?) Daisy Clover was hidden in this house by her manipulative producer during her (out-of-sync) nervous breakdown to keep her sight- and sound-proof from the public. Instead of committing suicide in the house, she uses the gas to blow it up. In the World War II film *Black Book* (dir. Paul Verhoeven, 2006), the house in which Rachel, a Dutch Jew has been hiding in 1944 is destroyed by a military plane that unloads its explosive cargo on it. Having lost her hiding place, Rachel listens to her own singing voice on a recording she made before the war silenced her and forced her to conceal herself and her identity. There is a grim iconography of female precarity at work here, a survival tale that Merry's explosive act updates to the 1960s.

But are these voices also part of a larger revolutionary intermedial cell functioning under the name "Chaos" that keeps threatening to multiply inside me, exploding my identity by ending my chronological and even my anachronistic time once and for all? Could I return as my own intermedial ghost, or has my daughter already coopted that role?

Can a fictional character suffer from indulging in the protagonistic fallacy of assuming that the self governs what it is, that the idea of a self is commensurate with its content? Merry has apparently abnegated responsibility for thinking for herself (and by extension for communicating with her father) to a "mentor in world revolution," "Miss Rita Cohen," who treats Swede with a kind of disdain that might signal her own or his own self-loathing. "Kid Mayhem," Swede calls her, his very own Chaos Golubitsky, part of an unofficial family tree to which alternate branch realities append.[35] Rita feeds back to Swede his family history with Merry as if he never personally experienced it. "*Here* was the hater—this insurrectionist child!" Swede tells himself (i.e., Zuckerman tells us, reliving dead Swede's family history). The inevitability of Rita's arrival is to Swede programmed by the self's loss of its own past and its impotence regarding its own future. This is engineered by (self-)doubt at the root of parenting and meta-doubt on the part of the one-time super-certain character who is being surrogated in self-authorship by Zuckerman as narrator and by Rita as the keeper of false memory of which Merry is nominally the source. (Is a super-certain character one who rises above and performs outside his authorship? About what else could he really be certain? That his story is real when *he* is not?) "Was she impersonating someone, acting from a script prepared beforehand?" Swede wonders about "the playacting Rita Cohen," who has appeared in his life, she says, "To introduce you to reality."

Five years pass since Swede last saw Rita and when she fails to reappear he sees her apparent agency in the myriad bombings that articulate the "erupted personality" of the 1960s political radicalism across the USA to protest Vietnam and racial inequity. Swede hears of the two unidentified young women who survived the Weathermen's bombing of a Greenwich Village townhouse (it was all over the news) and *knows* that it is Rita and Merry.[36] Every new bombing leaving death and destruction

---

[35] Roth, *American Pastoral*, 117 and 146.
[36] Ibid., 138, 143, 149, 250, and 251.

in its wake is for Swede a sign that Merry's still alive. It's a morbid, and Swede himself would say, perverse trade-off in which someone else's child's death is your child's proof of life. His mind is being held hostage by her pathology, which has corrupted his thinking's innocence. "There was no longer any innocence in what he remembered of his past....He had been admitted into a mystery more bewildering even than Merry's stuttering: there was no fluency anywhere. It was all stuttering...He envisioned his life as a stutterer's thought, wildly out of his control." He has become the bomb, or else the fuse that set it off.

Five years pass. What are the odds of this being true? Not the events that transpired during this timeframe but the thought that this timeframe is anything other than a fictional ploy to contain and transform thought into some other set of facts. Swede manufactures gloves. He knows all about appearance and fit. It's what obsessive-compulsive thinking does—personalizes outer chaos, makes the world's mayhem reflect the mind's own.

Five years pass. Zuckerman says this to introduce successive sections of historical memory that may in fact all overlay in Swede's obsessive mental timekeeping.[37] (Like daughter, like the father who created "her"—recall Roth saying of Merry that she "revel[s] in the dazzling idea of stealing *time*.") Swede is not so much time-traveling as space-traveling in time to meet with the radical political figure Angela Davis, whose hair reminds him of Rita's and whom Swede believes can get him to his daughter, if not get him his daughter back. Swede is divesting himself of his innocence like a bad foreign investment and perhaps even accepting some class responsibility for the world his daughter's and Rita's generation want to destroy. If Swede's "five years pass" signals his reducing everything he sees and hears to "a single significance," the loss of his daughter to the chaos of unworlding, if for Swede "nothing is impersonally perceived," how can he expect his daughter (and Rita) to do anything less? Merry is acting upon the example of his "relentlessly impersonal use of himself," to see and use him impersonally. (Enter Rita with her psychological taunting and abuse of the father as symbolic object.) This isn't a dialogue per se, but it is dialogic, a coming to awareness inside "my friend" the Swede that not only does the acorn not fall far from the tree (a cliché), it *is* the

---

[37] "A gruesome inner life of tyrannical obsessions, stifled conversations, unanswerable questions. Sleeplessness and self-castigation night after night. Enormous loneliness." Roth, *American Pastoral*, 93 and 173.

tree. "The Child is father of the Man," but perhaps not in the holistic way that Wordsworth meant, any more than "five years pass" is generative of anything beyond generational loss—my daughter, myself, b-b-buried alive in the stories that we t-t-tell ourselves about ourselves in relation to or as an expression of one another. "And the daughter who is chaos itself."[38] And despite the fact (or perhaps because of it) that Rita Cohen may be only a figuration of Swede's playing forward the secret phone conversations that Merry had while living in his house, when it comes to family, imagination fails. He cannot get beyond my fear of dispossession as a possible template for his daughter's unworlding. "You protect her and protect her—and she is unprotectable. If you don't protect her it's unendurable, if you do protect her it's unendurable. It's all unendurable. The awfulness of her terrible autonomy."[39] It's a kind of blown-up empty next <sic> syndrome. Bring her home and he would soon be homeless. That would be a quid pro quo. He would be unable to help himself, to stop his mind from going (there). Now he sees homelessness everywhere, even where it perhaps did not exist. And when he sees it, his brain begins to weep, to leak like Nietzsche's.

She pushed me out of the house, once then twice, out of *my* house. This house is a function of her haunting, the murmured behaviors like a dimly heard soundtrack, the things that were always there but not perceived or else not perceived as being real, things that would pass, that would be outgrown but were in fact grown into from an earlier template of supposed childhood temporality. The hardening of the child at an early age overlooked by an adult world that pleads its innocence. The child already resolved to be who she will be once she ages into accountability. The child fearing reaching the age of accountability, being responsible for what she has become. Parent and child moving this way and that, like tectonic plates. The murmuring of children's thoughts that go unheard in *The Tree of Life* that fill the air, like toxins in Ben Marcus's *The Flame Alphabet* (2012), the extreme, murderous thoughts that the adult ear is fortunately not tuned to hear, except in fiction or in what they call memory. To hear inside an adult child's distorting memory would be akin to Macbeth coming upon the mutterings of the weird sisters' predicting *their own fates* as his own and making him responsible for

[38] William Wordsworth, "My Heart Leaps Up When I Behold" (1888); Roth, *American Pastoral*, 206 and 231.

[39] Roth, *American Pastoral*, 167, 202, 253, and 272.

them. These children are air-movers with their unvoiced thoughts, their words that have not yet taken shape, their ragged energies blindly panting after further energies. Their sensitivity to all things prior to the onset of paranoia and neurosis. The loneliness, the unhappiness of the child, though, already in place and experienced with all the inward force a still not fully conscious mind can muster. No defense against Melancholia. No understanding of it either. Look for clues in movies and on television but they oddly speak to the future, more useful to you when you grow up and do not aid communication between parent and the child who would not sit down with him to watch what are for her someone else's useful images. Besides, he, the parent, is only now catching up on what the shows of *his* youth meant. I haunt my own house at night, like my daughter who used to sleep here during the day and wake at night. Not a morning but a mourning person, enraged by something she thought she had missed and yet not curious enough to search for. I could hear her footsteps, refrigerator and cabinet doors opening. I could imagine her avoidance, her charting of overlaid but alternative space-time. Ahab favoring an injured or absent foot on the deck (she said she found it difficult to walk), making us all follow her crazy instructions, a course not charted but obsessively controlled—not wrong-footed when you believe you are stepping upon and contaminating real life.

In an old photograph, she is smiling that cracked smile that little kids have before they know how to pose for the camera. It seemed as though her face would break. Somewhat later in another black-and-white photo, she is sitting, half-shadowed by the corner of a building in which she appears to be waiting to be found and asked what's wrong. Why no smile? Why so sullen, so angry? She knew how to pose now, how to make her true feelings known, her outsider's envy of the world that did not stop and take note of her, hiding, waiting to be seen. We found her but did not see her either, nor, of course, that she would one day be lost. How could we when she was not there yet, nor were we? We did not know that she was in there, not just hiding but waiting for the day when she would reveal to us the cost of our *not* finding her sooner without her having to come forward and announce herself and renounce us in the act, in the bargain. (*"This way of hers of lying in wait behind herself."*[40]) She stuttered out her anger in the same repetitive statement

[40] Ibid., 37.

about how we "kicked her out...k-k-kicked her out." The three "k" rule here being unfunny, however, presented in a humor. We were, to hear her tell it, self-satirizing. Our family in and out of its humor, in and out of *her* humor.

CRIMES AGAINST DOLOR(E)S

"Why me?"—a question/complaint in the public domain.

The ER doctor in *Synecdoche, New York* (dir. Charlie Kaufman, 2008), asks Caden Cotard if there has been any change in his bowel movements and then recommends that Caden see an ophthalmologist. "A urologist?" Caden asks at which point the doctor snaps his fingers in Caden's face and asks him, "Can you hear that?" as if Caden needed to see an audiologist. This series of verbal procedures gives a wider hearing to Caden's hypochondria, or alternatively, given his surname, to the meaninglessness of named complaints for or from a dead man. Caden is now being examined in an ophthalmologist's office. The wall calendar behind him reads 'MARCH 2006.' The doctor tells Caden, "I think we need to get you to a neurologist...a brain expert." "I know what a neurologist is," Caden answers but then offers, "I said urologist," referring back to the discussion he had with the ER doctor. Caden is both living and rehearsing the life we are seeing, as if in a dream whose "as if-ness" models/is modeled after theater. Caden asks why he needs to see a neurologist, to which the doctor responds, "the eyes are part of the brain, right?" whereupon Caden and the doctor contest the use of the word "right" ("morally correct" or as in "accurate"?) that was causally introduced in the doctor's rhetorical question. A rhetorical question, which is designed to rule out the possibility of contestation, is out of place in a story in which every and all aspects of reality, especially language and even more pointedly definition and categorization (the organizing principles of language) are being contested. For Caden, if something doesn't seem right, then it's not true. Caden is directing a stage production of *Death of a Salesman*, a play that deals with the manifold meanings of "what is right?" in truth and in memory. Caden has cast a young actor to play Willy Loman as a predictor of how youth will end up in loneliness and desolation (and, of course, in death). "I think I have blood in my stool," an insomniac, hemophobic and obsessive-compulsive (specifically, a fearer of bodily fluids) Caden tells his wife Adele, who responds from inside sleep,

"That stool in your office?" Homography is cold comfort for obsession. "I fantasized about Caden dying," Adele tells their marriage counselor, "being able to start over without guilt." To dream of escaping from someone else's phobias is not itself phobic. By this time, Caden's daughter from whom he has long been estranged has already grown an internal cancer garden to rival her externally tattooed vines and died.

Jewish bodies reject tattoos as a sign of non-orthodoxy, so I have gone off to live inside of Nathan Zuckerman's wracked but un-tattooed (except in the sense of beaten upon) Jewish writer's body in *The Anatomy Lesson*, which is like running off to join a circus of pain and the only doctor who might be able to help me—an ophthalmologist, not an orthopedist—cannot cure himself. He cannot bury the memory of having killed one of his patients, not in his office or a hospital but in the apartment he paid for, where he often went imagining a life without responsibility. A disaffected or at best disinterested Jew, his diasporic personality makes him too short-sighted to realize that a life unlike your own is still your own, mirrors what you are least reconciled to in yourself. It's as if one of your children told your story in hopes of finding you to be more interesting for keeping secrets. It's like Zuckerman's mother, whom "when he asked if she would write her name for him on a piece of paper [in 1970], she took the pen from his hand and instead of 'Selma' wrote the word 'Holocaust,' perfectly spelled." This from "a woman whose writing otherwise consisted of recipes on index cards, several thousand thank-you notes, and a voluminous file of knitting instructions."[41] Granted, Selma Zuckerman had a brain tumor when she wrote this word down, but it still came from *somewhere*.

As Sander L. Gilman has discussed, the relationship between medical discourse and Jewish discourse is long-standing, with the Jew characterized in societal terms as being either the illness or the cure. A problem arises when "doctor and patient are one," for which "the only real cure is death," the death of the combined subject from the condition of identity confusion that affects every father as a son.[42] Ophthalmologist Judah Rosenthal's mistress's name in *Crimes and Misdemeanors* (dir. Woody Allen, 1989) is "Dolores." That should have told him something.

---

[41] Philip Roth, *The Anatomy Lesson* (New York: Vintage, 1996; orig. pub. 1983), 41.

[42] Sander L. Gilman, *Jewish Self-Hatred: Anti-Semitism and the Hidden Language of the Jews* (Baltimore: The Johns Hopkins University Press, 1990), 215 and 388–89.

The name "Judah" immediately proclaims miraculous salvation to the Jewish listener's ear, the ancient Judah, surnamed "Maccabee" ("The Hammer") being an ancient "muscle Jew," a great liberator whose limited supply of lamp oil stretched for eight days, a story retold as the basis for the Jewish holiday of Hanukah. "By a miracle," the letter Dolores sent to Judah's wife Miriam detailing the illicit relationship, sat on a table for hours in his house without her seeing it. But salvation comes at a price, since, as Judah nervously jokes that his father's insistent lesson to his son that "God sees all" may have led him (self-protectively hiding from faith behind science) to become an eye doctor.

This is the story of a man who has one bad eye and one good eye, the former physicalized in the person of his brother Jack, another muscle Jew, like the biblical Judah for whom *he*, in a play of displaced self-contestation, and not his brother Judah should have been named. Jack's mob connections and moral pragmatism offset *his brother Judah's* moral fluidity. (There is no holiday celebrating this or that "Judah.") These two eyes move together sympathetically in a way that Judah's man of science and his rabbi Ben's man of faith do not.[43] Ben is going blind, either to illustrate God's arbitrary meting out of favor and punishment or more likely because God knows that Ben's faith is strong enough to recognize blindness not as punishment but as a gift. God is watching Ben and Judah from the latter's eye chart where a pyramid of letters topped by "E" reference the possible letters Jews leave blank in G-d's name, where a mere "o" or any other identifiable letter would not suffice. It's a broken language. The broken body of language. Typical of this is the PAINT sign on the store next door to the apartment in which murdered Dolores's broken body lies. The sign is cut off by the film frame to read PAIN.

The actor playing Judah, Martin Landau knew all about this, early in his career having pressed his foot down hard on Cary Grant's hand as the latter desperately hung on to the edge of Mount Rushmore near the end of *North by Northwest* (1959). The look on Grant's face is one of excruciating pain and utter disbelief at what this foot could bring itself to do. Hitchcock shoots Landau's already big foot in extreme close-up at the moment that he is (gun)shot from a distance and we hear painlessly the sound of his last footfall. In the scene where Judah asks for Jack's help in

---

[43] In Hebrew, "Ben" means "son."

dealing with Dolores while protesting that he doesn't really want Jack to "take care of" the problem, Allen sends the two brothers out for a walk so that we can take their full measure. Landau's splayed flat feet, which looked so purposely out of place in Hitchcock's film, in Allen's seems to have goaded his middle-aged, out-of-its-element body to soften and relent. Conversely, Jerry Orbach's (i.e., Jack's) knife's-edged body culminates in a pigeon-toed walk that gives nothing away, is pinched and perhaps outcast. He walks like the childhood best friend I thought I had. Roth and Allen both play uncomfortably with the long-standing anti-Semitic formula that the Jew's physical weakness bespeaks moral weakness, or as David Mamet would have it, the failure of the diasporic Jew to fight for his life, his land, his name, his traditions, his history, his faith.[44]

At film's end, Dolores is dead and Judah has risen above his guilty conscience by spinning his crime into a story he tells (to the film's director, whose character he has only just met) about a fictional someone else who performed his deeds and another real someone else, "a drifter," who took the wrap for them. Judah never heard or if he did was tone deaf to his daughter comparing him to his Aunt May who "rejected the Bible because she said it had a completely unbelievable sense of character." As if in a parable, the ophthalmologist raised in the Jewish faith to believe that God sees everything demonstrates at the blind rabbi's daughter's wedding, that seeing is not always believing. Appearance is in equal measure speculative. I have modeled my various pain behaviors for a spectrum of medical specialists, who readily attest to all they do not know (from whence comes Caden Cotard's sense of always being in the office of the wrong specialist, perhaps), searching not for a cure but for an audience to which to tell my story in the hope of being told I am not responsible for my conditions only for their consequences. There is no clear origin story, only the one from which I have made my life. So why do we go hunting for our fictional origin story in the end? Because by finding it we could prove that it has always really existed? Mel Brooks said that all old people, no matter what their faith, race, or ethnicity, look Jewish. What do these looks betray? That there is no answer, no miracle awaiting us masquerading under the miracle worker's name "Jesus" or "Judah"? Just the wrack of pain on many levels for someone like Nathan

---

[44] See Melvin Konner, *The Jewish Body* (New York: Schocken Books, 2009), ix; Sander L. Gilman, *The Jew's Body* (New York: Routledge, 1991), 38–59.

Zuckerman, whom Judah Rosenthal might have imagined was taking the fall for him.

Dolores was someone's daughter once if not now, if not estranged or cut off from a relationship that is beyond repair. To her, paternal behavior is a crime (Judah having "taken care of her" in two senses) whose punishment her own behavior enacts upon the ophthalmologist, the all-seeing but un-possessable father god with whom she reenacts a secret history of disappointment and betrayal. Her so-called hysteria is seen as being a male prerogative to assess and append to what she says and does and to who she is. "Life is unfair" is in turn an assessment, the monitor behind Mouth suggests, not best left to the individual as a self-referential statement of fact. Dolores tells Judah that her life was a mess before she met him, and heavily suggests that it is *his* mess to clean up now. Her words are there to greet him when he wakes up in the morning and to trouble his mind all through the night so that if he wakes up at any point they are still there committed to a memory that will not let him sleep. He thinks, perhaps, they are lines from a play in which he has been assigned a role to play with which he cannot identify and questions the casting and the agent who cast him. Actors anxiously sit by the phone waiting for the director or a casting agent to call. Judah fears the phone ringing and he being called to account for his double behavior in the miscast role as the aging lothario. But what of Dolores's real father, if he has lived through their rancorous separation. Does he likewise fear his daughter's call, dread the very ringing of the phone, as if it had nothing else to do other than call *him*? The phone, as Hitchcock knew well, was a terrifying implement, intruding upon our lives, interrupting us, calling us back to conversations we have already had and fear having again. The phone knows or does not know our schedule but in either case does not care what we are doing since it will alarm us into stopping whatever it is we're doing and engage with its ring, its call. We can mute it but we cannot shut it up, nor can we live with its silence indefinitely as its voice is manifold—*someone else* may be calling. You can choose whether or not to answer the call, or you can make the call yourself. "We are the sum of our choices," says a philosopher about whom Cliff (the Woody Allen character in *Crimes and Misdemeanors*) is making a documentary. The philosopher who regards choice as being a hopeful act that gives meaning to the universe commits suicide leaving a note that reads only, "I've gone out the window." Well, as one might say then about choice on the downbeat, "there's that."

Chris, the poor Irish former tennis pro who has married very well but not very happily in Allen's *Match Point* (2005), is terrorized by phone calls from his American mistress, an unsuccessful actress Nola who, like the a-biographical Dolores in *Crimes and Misdemeanors*, threatens to upend his perfect life with her emotional, albeit justifiable demands.[45] Chris feels "so terribly guilty," as well he should, having made Nola, (and) not his wife pregnant. Chris's telephone anxiety is unmatched by Nola's eagerness to answer the call. She experiences waiting as anxiety, whereas his anticipation of the call makes him anxious in turn. Do you know what it's like to sit in a darkened room afraid that the phone will ring and that she will be on the other end of the line? You feel vulnerable, paranoid, afraid to be in your own room, in your own skin. There is no easy way to make the phone calls stop. Judah knows this and Chris only had to reach a fraction of Judah's age to know it too. Telephobia bespeaks a relationship that needs no caller, only a receiver that gives your own anxiety a voice, that amplifies that voice (and the dark Mouth from which it comes) into a deafening paranoid imagining of a targeted harmfulness deafening you to reasonable thought and desire. The voice is threatening you within an inch of your inner life. The call is to arms, to do something perfectly rash and "out of character" to be free of it, the fear of what might happen. Better, perhaps, to make it happen first, whatever "it" is. "You can push the guilt under the rug and go on," Chris tells not-yet-dead Nola. "Otherwise it overwhelms you." But, as Nola's ghost confirms, he is wrong about this. Guilt goes looking for a crime to justify itself, a crime to commit to memory so that *anxiety* does not overwhelm you, putting down roots in your psyche and casting you out of your mind. Chris, we know, has read too much Dostoevsky, *Crime and Punishment*, in particular and intimately. The only way to solve the crime is for someone else to dream his way into it and discover its solution. In *Match Point* this almost comes to pass but a detective's dream logic is undone by luck offering a more reasonable solution. A wedding ring (of all things) belonging to Nola's elderly neighbor (whom Chis also killed to create a staged version of the crime in which she was

---

[45] Allen no doubt had *Strangers on a Train* (1951) in mind when he made his protagonist a tennis pro. Hitchcock's (and author Patricia Highsmith's) Guy Haines rejects the wish-fulfillment fantasy presented to him by charming sociopath Bruno Anthony of swapping murders (Bruno's father, Guy's wife). Chris makes a bargain with himself to murder his mistress to "save" his marriage.

the target and Nola an unlucky bystander) is discovered in the pocket of a burglar killed sometime after in another *real* burglary gone wrong. It is both fitting and ironic that the resolution of Chris's telephonic/telephobic guilt and anxiety takes place through the chance agency of a ring.

In Allen's *Cassandra's Dream* (2007), two working-class Londoners, brothers Ian and Terry Blaine murder their Uncle Howard's whistle-blowing business associate as a favor in return for which their rich uncle bankrolls their own business plans. When Terry begins to fall apart, self-medicating with pills and alcohol, his girlfriend Kate tells Ian that Terry suffers from the delusion that "he thinks he's killed someone," like a girl she knew who, in a familiar OCD trope, thought "she had run someone over. She hadn't. You know, but she was obsessed with it for the rest of her life." My interest here resides not in the aftermath of the crime for the brothers, Ian killing soul-destroyed Terry to keep him quiet. It's in the Dolores figure who gave her name to a dog on whom Terry placed a winning bet at the track that allowed the brothers to buy a second-hand boat they named "Cassandra's Dream." It's about madness and prophesy, the killing spirit of one and the other, and what does and does not separate the two—the obsessive-compulsive girl who thought she killed someone but did not; the man who is thought to be delusional because he actually killed someone but thinks he did so in a dream. We do not dream of causes but of consequences, of a compulsion divorced from and forgetful of why we are obsessed. Cassandra's dream is a foretelling turned inward, drowning fear in a melancholy that becomes unvoiced. Cassandra is the original Mouth, grown dark on the inside and relegated to the non-status of Not I. Self-less she has become past caring about by the monitor who no longer sees this as being *his* crime.

"You can talk yourself out of anything" proves not to be the case for huckster Wally, who Mildred Pierce in the film bearing her name (dir. Michael Curtiz, 1945) locks inside her home alone with the corpse of a husband her spoiled daughter Veda so carelessly left for her mother to clear away. Outgoing Wally is briefly trapped inside the dark symbiotic interiority of a mother who wanted to lead her daughter's life for her and the guilt-blame-and-resentment account that came due on the self-destructive anti-life that daughter lived in flashback and return. Here we learn that Veda's demands on her mother's attention resulted in the benign neglect of the younger daughter Kay, who succumbed to pneumonia provoking Mildred to hold Veda even closer to her unrequited affection. This unrequitedness performs a psychological non-acceptance of reciprocity on all levels, including both self-awareness and self-responsibility. "I didn't mean to do it…The gun kept going off over and over again." I didn't do it, the gun did, Veda effectively said. The more general implication being, "It's your fault I'm the way I am. I am who you made me," which the child inadvertently says about an interiority that will not speak her name. I am mind-screening this film while not answering a phone call from my own daughter. In much earlier times, I would have told myself I'll call her back when I stop writing. But that was before I had to pretend I wasn't here, writing about her.

WRITING ABOUT "HER"

I am watching *Dirty Dancing*, which is set in 1963. It is not a movie I would normally watch at all.[46] I think I am watching it to pick up atmospheric background for remembering my own experience as the fair-haired child of a small Jewish family visiting Catskills resorts like the one depicted in the film. It all embarrassed me as a boy—the gaping old (or so they seemed to me at the time) mouths full of lox, herring with onions in cream sauce, and kosher chicken washed down with alcohol or a spritz of seltzer, the self-congratulatory Jewish stand-up comics with their insider jokes that all sounded like they were being told in Yiddish or like their audience heard them that way in any case. The world of white linen tablecloths that spoke of years of use and seasonal damage float-ing in a sea of faces looking so desperately entertained, belonging, I now realize, to a community whose opportunities to be entertained, even whose continuity was far more hard-won than any nostalgia I can now muster.

I am watching this otherwise unimportant film in my study with the door closed. There is no one in the house but me. But there is some-one due to arrive at the door soon, timing out with, as it so happens (and not timed to) the film's ending, when a loving but stern father and rebellious daughter learn to accept one another for who and what they are, each with something to learn from the other. This will not be the case between the visitor at my door, my daughter and myself. I have left the things she had delivered here just outside the house on a small table

---

[46] *Dirty Dancing* (dir. Emile Ardolino, 1987).

that has come to serve this purpose on a semi-regular basis. She will not be allowed in the house owing to a permanently thwarted relationship, vexed by real and perceived to be real issues and intentions, actions and accusations, the usual unusual story of self-imagined unhappy families. She is not allowed inside the door that she once stood inside and pushed me back through, out of my way into my own house. There were police, terrible things said, terrible things still being said. Help has been offered, again and again, but this help appears to her always to have some kind of ulterior motive attached, the motive for her thinking this I cannot understand. I watch the father and daughter in this and so many other films, envying the fiction of their relationship, their ability to pretend to be happy as my daughter once did. I search through books for instances of daughters estranged from their fathers, trying to discover some common trait, some root cause, some origin. I know she has her own origin story for this, but it is not mine. I don't believe in origins.

I am watching this film in my study with the door closed and with my phone blocked because I am hiding from her. At least this time I'm not also sitting in the dark with all of the phones disconnected, wondering if the computer screen itself is watching me (which it is). Now I am hiding inside the film as the father with a daughter raised with supportive experiences and common values that no amount of rebellion or misunderstanding can supplant reconcile what was never a real break, just a momentary break from. Their lives are still hinged, grounded in ways that need not be written or said. I try to enter into the role of the good father, like a good cowbird, but it's no good unless she accepts the tacit invitation to play the good daughter in return. You're only as good as your fellow actor. I need someone to react to and when necessary to feed me my lines.

I am not naïve enough to confuse the reality of actors and the roles they play. Bronx-born (with a Jewish father but raised in his mother's Catholic faith), with extra broad shoulders to hang a father costume on Jerry Orbach, who seemed so at home playing the good father in *Dirty Dancing*, was as comfortable playing a go-between for his good brother in contracting the murder of the latter's mistress Dolores in *Crimes and Misdemeanors*. She was in turn someone else's grown-up daughter disturbed by her unrevealed early life (and also, played by the same actress Anjelica Huston, a very bad mother in Stephen Frears neo-noir, *The Grifters*, 1990). Had this woman, so desperate for a fulfilling fiction in her life met Jerry Orbach instead of Martin Landau, she could only hope it would be in his role as the good father and not as the father surrogate's bloodless right arm.

I have been reading of late a memoir written by a woman from the old neighborhood about her father's descent into dementia. Her parents were intellectuals who encouraged their daughter to think for herself, to be rational to a fault, and so when the father's mind betrayed him, in a sense he betrayed the family and cashed out his seat at the table of Cartesian personhood. I wonder though if the father, whose self-diminishing allows his child to be less aggressively self-assertive and more understanding, is all the while thinking, "I am not losing a mind but regaining a daughter." Cancer didn't bring my daughter any closer. Maybe I can turn my mind to dementia. She is worth losing my mind over. Dolor needs his Dolores, like he needs his youth in the onset of old age.

"Now we're just here to be memories for our kids. Once you're a parent, you're the ghost of your children's future," an astronaut father tells his daughter, repeating his late wife's possibly last words in Christopher Nolan's *Interstellar* (2014). This is actually a wrap-around thought that mirrors the plot. We do not so much haunt our children as memory, their lives eclipse ours' as part of a survivor's biological imperative that plays out through time. The books on time-travel falling off the shelves that lead young Murph's father Cooper on a mission into the fifth dimension have been pushed off by the astronaut himself who is trapped behind the bookcase in a three-dimensional model of his daughter's childhood room. This has been created by an unseen species living in another universe (arrived at through a wormhole) that wants to save our dying planet or at least the dying people on it by transporting them into a dimension in which time is experienced as a physical space. I imagine that some of the books fallen from the shelves were written by me. I know my daughter has at least one such title on the bookshelf in her childhood room which is now off-limits to her. In my own time-traveling dream, she returns to it now, in this same and future "now," and the book she could not touch, my *Infinity (Stage)* (on *my* father's death) and possibly my *Incapacity* (on my OCD), which I only added later, have fallen face-up on the floor and are open to any random pages that she now reads without having to turn. This being also the future "now" she may be reading what I am only now writing as well. She is seeing a different, although not new me, which enables her to make me a ghost, to move past me, and what she imagines her mother and I have and have not done. In this scenario, my daughter realizes that what she thought was real was in fact imagined and not by her but by a female relative trying to insinuate her fictionalized relationship with *her* parents inside my daughter's mind, as if it were the latter's own story. This business of inserting one('s) self inside another is not always benign and without consequences. Sometimes it creates a "family" lineage lost inside the space of compressed time where images and memories are distorted, collaged from stray thoughts and obliquely perceived experiences. There are books, mostly on self-help, recovered memory and trauma psychotherapy, pushed off the shelves by this other source, who is seeking to spirit away my daughter's mind to another dimension through her own mind-reading intervention. My books are fighting against these secondary "expert" sources with direct and indirect personal experiences of my own. I only hope that my daughter can disengage from the fiction that wants her to live inside it and enter into the fiction I have spun around her and my life so that she and I can continue to live in a nuclear "family" minus generational loss *and* fictional elaboration affecting gravity.

And then I remember: I stumbled and nearly fell. I made too much of it. She was there, a child who not only saw me but saw what was possible in terms of hyperbolic behavior. It was a bad example to set, which like many bad examples go unnoticed to the adult who does not see all that he does, all that he is in front of the child he is parenting. Me almost falling. Me failing. A lesson in the possibility of the negative, the impossibility of doing something as basic as walking. I have maintained an unwanted legacy of discontinuity. I am my mother's hyperbolic son. The ground for me was level, not moving. There was no escalator. I carry my own escalator inside me.

CHAPTER 6

Form of Life

Wittgenstein, who parsed language and especially philosophical language so closely and who called attention to the latter's misspeaking, found himself to be misunderstood and was not infrequently the literal and functional source of this misunderstanding. Every system, even of disbelief, as Wittgenstein illustrates, requires self-correction. So, at this point in the book, I will say that its events have all been staged by an impersonator, a Cartesian Great Deceiver of the first order and in the first person. The "I", for example, in "Today I am a man," gave no evidence (at age thirteen) of actually being at the event this statement commemorated and the (Jewish) identity it sought to contain. The tables of celebrants at "my" after-party were all other people's friends. There were middle-aged men working toothpicks and their wives working one-size-fits-none dresses. My father had served with these men on the island of Guam in the Pacific, where, Japanese pilots offloaded trash through their bomb bay doors on their way home. There were also: dead pilots from my father's wartime pilot training school, who could have collectively written *Catch-22* under the assumed name "Joseph Heller" had that book not been set in Italy, although fiction itself constitutes a change of venue; grown-up new-immigrant-tormentors too busy eating the foods of all nations set before them to recognize the irony of their pasts being invited into the present; the deaf and the lame, including a tall, angular man who may have entered my uncle's pharmacy, wielding a glass cane to render him unconscious. He was looking for me and "I" am looking for him.

© The Author(s) 2019
S. Golub, *A Philosophical Autofiction*, Performance Philosophy,
https://doi.org/10.1007/978-3-030-05612-4_6

"I" was being initiated into what Wittgenstein calls a "form of life," a system of beliefs but also a world picture (*Weltbild*). Of course, I had already been thirteen years and multi-generationally in this culture but we were not yet on actual speaking terms, not on a first-name nor even a first-pronoun basis. The bar mitzvah was offered in the spirit of self-correction. I was to have been bar mitzvahed with another boy from school but he and his family opted out as the day approached. I have saved him a seat at a table by himself but have left his outline empty, un(ful)filled, un-self-corrected. My guess is that he lives with himself better than "I", in my undone tuxedo tie and non-alcoholic, unlit cigarette stupor, posing in unconscious imitation of landsman Lenny Bruce's backstage at the strip club, the neighborhood girls in their bouffant hairdos and restructured child's pink party dresses cradling for the camera my faux-boychick's head like they didn't know what it was, let alone what to do with it. The room was being spun by platters of liver sculpted to resemble the actual chickens they once knew. I snapped my fingers so that the camera could make my grandparents disappear, two of them dying not long thereafter so "I" could make the legacy of Jewish guilt my own. Secret agents otherwise identified as family friends approached me with the recognition code, "Don't tell your parents" and made inside jacket pocket-to-pocket exchanges of thin envelopes containing fat checks as if in payment for some terrible thing I had already done (perhaps, the foreknowledge of succession's relation to disappearance). "Whereof one cannot speak, thereof one must be silent" (*TL-P*, §7). "I" read this as a language game in which "checking" could be repurposed as an OCD faux-therapeutic pain-behavior. Stand-ins were hired to act as and like my friends, and they scanned like two identical sentences penned by Wittgenstein that looked the same but differed as to actual function.

"Well, maybe he's Jewish *inside*," director Mike Nichols told Dustin Hoffman when the latter balked at playing Robert Redford-esque (from the novel) Benjamin Braddock in *The Graduate* (1967). "That was certainly in me, in terms of a *cursed* identity," the non-bar mitzvahed Hoffman conceded. The actor, who admitted to concealing his Jewishness while growing up carried it concealed in the film, like Willy Loman did in his sample case in *Death of a Salesman* and unlike the six million loaded on trains whose hastily packed suitcases were later emptied of their Jewish history then piled high and incinerated at the camps where their physical (id)entities were likewise voided.[1] Can you choose another form of life or is it given to you, your name entered in the book of "the chosen" at birth, a book you read from once at age thirteen and thereafter do not practice the faith to which the book attests except as the pain behaviors of the form of life you cannot discard? "USE OTHER DOOR" reads the airport sign at the start of *The Graduate.* There are actually two identical signs on two adjoining doors. What has Wittgenstein to say of this? Do these two doors function in different ways or do only the signs? Are the signs to be read together, their compounding signaling what only appears on the surface to be a nonsensical *self*-exclusion? Hoffman's affective on-the-offbeat line readings, which appear to want to make a show of this self-othering, may have already been unconsciously rehearsing the self-correction manifest in his later choice of roles constituting his own chosen people.

When Hoffman asked Nichols what he thought the older Benjamin Braddock does for a living, he said. "Oh, that's easy. You direct television commercials." In *Barney's Version* (dir. Richard J. Lewis, 2010), a Canadian film adapted from the novel by Mordecai Richler, the title character works as a producer of the low-budget soap opera "O'Malley of the North" for TOTALLY UNNECESSARY PRODUCTIONS, reflecting Barney's self-deprecating sense of humor. Hoffman plays Barney Panofsky's very Jewish father, Israel ("Izzy"). He's a retired Jewish cop, who says he can't get promoted to detective due to anti-Semitism. More than this, though, he's a mensch, who performs all manner of ostentatiously affectionate behavioral mannerisms designed to advertise a newfound affection for the form of life they represent and by inference that life's non-agreement with his chosen profession. I retrace the father's and Richler's own steps through the author's hometown of Montreal, past that special brand of large fur-hatted (the Shabatt *Shtreimel*), dark-suit-over-white-dress-shirt and long-overcoated Hassidim, their somber, dutiful wives in their plain, shoe-length dresses and well-behaved, *payos-ed* (curled side-burned) *boychicks* (there are no

---

[1] "What was in all those empty suitcases piled mountain-high by Nazi murderers and their self-serving collaborators at Auschwitz and other European prison houses for mass extermination? Even more horrifying to contemplate, where are their contents now?" Enoch Brater, "Drama Matters: Suitcases, Sand, and Dry Goods," *Michigan Quarterly Review*, vol. XLVI, 4 (Fall 2007). https://quod.lib.umich.edu/cgi/t/text/text-idx?cc=mqr;c=mqr;c=mqrarchive;idno=act2080.0046.414;g=mqrg;rgn=main;view=text;xc=1.

girlchicks in Yiddish or in Jewish orthodox culture) following behind them. I contemplate the distance to favorite son Leonard Cohen's final resting place in the Jewish Shaar Hashomayim Congregation Cemetery on Mt. Royal Boulevard, buried as per Jewish custom in the requisite unadorned, pine box among his forbears. "Well, maybe he's Jewish *inside*," "I" tells me, as if it were not me he was speaking to and about. I return home and purchase a plot of my own, a stone's throw from Providence's favorite son, the un-chosen and anti-Semitic gothic writer H. P. Lovecraft. A Magen David remains unpurchased, a mezuzah left unattached to the door that is therefore figuratively unhinged, a faith, a belief that only goes without saying as a form of life that remains unobserved except where its symbols lie like totally unnecessary productions. "I" know who I am, after all. I mean this not as an objective certainty, not as an article of faith, not as an actual expression of self, only using "self" as a form of expression.

CRUEL WEST

Macbeth, of course, was not bar mitzvahed, not that it would have changed anything. I nevertheless invited myself to his party, knowing that I would unlikely find anything at the Scottish-themed table I would be willing to eat. But somewhere between the two cancers of my aged youth, I sat in Duncan's bedroom waiting for the king to be murdered by Macbeth.[2] I knew the murderer would come. He always does. The question is, how do I know? It has something to do, I think, we need to curate my fears in the context of Macbeth's "Present fears/ Are less than horrible imaginings" (1.3, 150–51). No amount of face-painting before going into battle, of streaming blood with such fearless abandon can offset the imponderable fear of Macbeth's self-making inevitability, that rank witchcraft ascribed to other(worldly) forces. Biological usurpers of the cutaway womb and fairy-tale trees that walk are impossible only as the negative unimaginable, the latter being a matter of self-limitation as aforementioned inevitability is as well. Inevitability is what death *calls* "aforementioned." Death by self-limitation. We don't go into battle. The battle comes to us, the inability to think beyond closing in on us, shrinking borders, our destiny being manifest, our manifest destiny

---

[2]In Punchdrunk Theatre's choose-your-own-adventure reimagining of Shakespeare by Hitchcock, *Sleep No More* (2011).

being self-defeating without being self-effacing—the sword, the knife, the walking trees entering Macbeth as if self-absorbed. I am waiting in Duncan's bedroom for the murderer to arrive, now beginning to realize that the murderer *has already* arrived in this carcinogenic tale, among all of the blood and ashes.

In *Written on the Body* (1992), a title the warrior king Macbeth might understand, Jeanette Winterson writes of (her) cancer:

> The inside of your body is innocent, nothing has taught it fear. Your artery canals trust their cargo, they don't check the shipments to the blood. You are full to overflowing but the keeper is asleep and there's murder going on inside. Who comes here? Let me hold up my lantern. It's only the blood; red blood cells carrying oxygen to the heart, thrombocytes making sure of proper clotting. The white cells, B and T types, just a few of them are always whistling as they go.[3]

"It's only the blood." But isn't that the gist of it? Bloody Duncan, Lady Macbeth's bloody hands, bloody Banquo's Ghost. In chemotherapy, they test your blood prior to each session to make sure that your white blood cell count has not been unduly compromised by previous treatment so they can continue non-strategically killing you on the inside in the hope of killing your potential murderer in the process. You are comprised of acceptable losses—hearing, hair, feeling in your extremities, immunity to other diseases, and a recognizable self. You become the victim of your body's own replicant cell bloodlust, worked up like that weird sister, performance novelist Kathy Acker's self-puncturing fiction in which the identities of self and system, of self *as* system constantly shift. Kathy Acker was, of course, Jewish (née Lehmann) *and* heavily tattooed and also died of cancer.

"This is the very painting of your fear" (3.4.60), Lady Macbeth tells her husband upon glimpsing the recently slaughtered Banquo at his "Today I am a king" dinner celebration. Macbeth sees in his ex-friend's ghost the cruel irony that he has killed Duncan so Banquo's sons can be future kings. He now must become a killer not just of men but of their children, a proto-Oppenheimer, his face marked with Japanese characters that depict vertical lines of succession. The final image in the 2015 film *Macbeth* (whose director Justin Kurzel called it a Western) is of a small

---

[3] Jeanette Winterson, *Written on the Body* (London: Jonathan Cape, 1992), 115–16.

boy running with bloody sword into a deep reddish-orange-suffused nuclear sky counterfeiting the dawn of a new day. All have become viscera that give only improper readings of how origins produce endings— invaders of the lost womb and trees that walk. The being of Macbeth can only be taken by what cannot be. The question is whether impossible being is just that which cannot yet be imagined, pictured in the mind— death by self-limitation. Or is impossible being just what we call the desire to self-disengage from the things that can kill you.

The parsing of Wittgenstein's last words, "Tell them I've had a wonderful life," most often confronts the seemingly confounding paradox of the "wonderful life" and the actual life he lived. What should really be looked at though is the "I" elided with a verb so that it does not stand on its own, which Wittgenstein might well have intended? Wittgenstein did not subscribe to a Cartesian self that reasons its way into being through thought so much as he believed in the "I" as an applicable function of language. Wittgenstein was partial to putting "I" in quotation marks and rendering it non-transparent in sentences like, "The word 'I' does not mean the same as 'L.W.', even if I am 'L.W.', for it does not stand for the person speaking." So, Wittgenstein would look at the initialized Western six-shooters I played with as a child in faux-Western get-up and say (substituting his own initials for mine), "I am not L.W., even if I am 'L.W.'" (*BB*, §67). This apophatic self-abnegation allowed Wittgenstein to sit close to the screen to watch the Western movies he and I regularly attended, although not together in space or time: "I" for escape, "L.W." to appreciate fully the "wonderful life" of the screen minus the necessity or even the possibility (save as "L.W.") of self-absorption. "I" saw identifiable characters auditioning to be me. "L.W." saw identity-behaviors, which "I" did not know it at the time, were what I was seeing too, seeing and learning to define myself through: tropes of friendship (loyalty and betrayal), of self-sacrifice, of generational animosity, and of the ethos of polarity. I learned the ropes, so to speak via these and other behavior-tropes, spinning them as one would a lariat on the old "frontier," which, as it happens was no more grounded in "the land" than I was, "Frontierland" being the name of Disney's California theme park created in the 1960s to model Western movie tropes in real life. "Freedomland" in the East Bronx being another. I visited both. (Tell them "I" had a wonderful time.)

Parks, themed or otherwise, post maps with arrows indicating, "You are here," the "you" in these cases being read as "I." "'You'/'I' are *physically* here." But what the indicator is really saying, per Wittgenstein, is "Here is here," since neither "You" nor can "I" stand-in for "a description of the body," and it is the body that the maps are referencing (eliding its physicality and citationality), not "Your *mind* is here," for example. The arrow, though, is pointing at something, at the expectation that there is a body put in place by the sign that is "sight[ed], say, along the barrel of a gun," says "L.W." alluding, no doubt to the cruel west.[4] Why "cruel"? Because the idea of "the West" borrows our personal anxiety over one's place in the world and returns it to us as an attractive mythology of self-creation, biographically removed from the self. Wittgenstein's notion of the language game, whereby we take a step back from life and recognize its constructedness (like language) did not seem cruel to "L.W." who pronounced his life to have been "wonderful." One thinks here as well of Chekhov, whose surgically lyrical work Meyerhold thought should be staged cruelly, and whose dying request (at age 44 from chronic tuberculosis) was for a glass of champagne.

Wittgenstein's concept of the language game left something unspoken insofar as he did not finally define what he meant by "game." Nor could he say, "what is common to all these activities [games] and what makes them into language or parts of language" (*PI*, §65). In his *Blue Book*, a rehearsal for the more complete *Philosophical Investigations*, Wittgenstein went so far as to say that, "language games are the forms of language with which a child begins to make use of words" (*BB*, §17). One wonders what happens when, as we often do, seat children before movie screens at an early age. For the child, image and action are absorbed as part of the one general language he is getting to know. He is seeing family resemblance prior to knowing that there are even rules governing this. "All it means is that these words are different instruments in our language," as Wittgenstein said of "L.W." and "I" (*BB*, §67). The child's syncretic seeing of, say, an image composed entirely of words is somewhat akin (has a family resemblance) to Wittgenstein's famous example of the "duck-rabbit," in which one has to re-learn that seeing one element or the other in/as a picture rather than both simultaneously (or one through the other) is not a necessity. Languages are like Tolstoy's unhappy families, each different in its own way, yet with a resemblance that enables them to be called "families." I was hailed in central Mexico

---

[4]Wittgenstein, *The Blue Book*, §§71, 72, and 74.

by a native unknown to me with the word "Ashkenazi," and I took this to be a sign of notoriety, like an outlaw known far and wide by the nick-name ("The Ashkenazi Kid") that will sooner rather than later kill him like it did Gregory Peck as "Jimmy Ringo" in Henry King's Western *The Gunfighter* (1950). All I really ever wanted to be was a *movie* cowboy who just performs the agonies of the self without regard for the limits of biography.

Long Island was not the place to invent yourself, the way Hollywood used to be.[5] I know this second hand as the person "I" once was, dreaming of California, where a place like Levittown with its "boxes made of ticky-tacky that all looked the same" could not exist except on a Hollywood backlot.[6] My babysitter lived in one of these match-box houses with her husband and three boys, all of whose first names began with the letter "K" ("Kirk," "Kenny," etc.) which I thought was odd, though not comic. She taught me the joy of the cine-democratic drive-in movie theater, "movie theatre" being a grand name for a large parking lot with a big screen parked in front of it and individual speak-ers hung on car windows. These personal speakers manifested the mental circuitry that in turn made the screened image feasible.[7] That babysitter, Audrey was her name, told me the story of a film she saw at the drive-in. It was a Western called *The Last Wagon* (dir. Delmer Daves) starring Richard Widmark as a good guy who gets tied to a wagon wheel leaving him vulnerable to attack. It was the most riveting tale I had ever heard and has remained for me a romantic lodestar of the West, as invented by Hollywood with the help of Audrey. The film came out in 1956, the annus mirabilis in movies that was for me like what "the magic hour" is to those who make movies—the perfection that comes right after sunrise or before sunset when the light is at its reddest, softest, and most unreal.

Among the pivotal movie Westerns released in 1956 were: John Ford's *The Searchers*, the first Western I recall seeing that represented the four seasons of the year, along with John Wayne as an Indian-hater, which I assumed made him an anti-Semite as well. Strangely, I hung onto the character's first name and gave it to my son, whom I told was

---

[5] Lenny Bruce, *How to Talk Dirty and Influence People: An Autobiography* (New York: Da Capo, 2016; orig. pub. 1965), 7.

[6] "Little Boxes," music and lyrics by Malvina Reynolds, 1962, was made famous by folk singer Pete Seeger.

[7] Paraphrase of McElroy, *Lookout Cartridge*, 7.

named after a great film, not a bad man. Budd Boetticher's (the not-so-poor-man's John Ford) *Seven Men from Now* starring his favorite leading man Randolph Scott who always looked very lean, clean, and like he knew he was acting in a Western. Scott got to play opposite two of the great Western villains, Lee Marvin in this one and Richard Boone (whose autograph I ate in a previous book) in the following year's *The Tall T*. Boone was later given the privilege of being one of only three men invited by *The Shootist*'s (dir. Don Siegel, 1976) eponymous gunfighter John B. Books to kill him in a fair fight before cancer did. As his character's surname "Books" suggested, this was a metadramatic role for Wayne, who was dying from a cancer of *his own*, no doubt picked up on the set of director Dick Powell's 1956 film *The Conqueror* shot in Utah near an active nuclear testing site in Nevada. Delmer Daves's *Jubal* arrived in 1956 with screen-easy Canadian actor Glenn Ford (also *The Fastest Gun Alive* that same year) and, from my perspective of character development, the redundant duo Ernest Borgnine-Rod Steiger. "I" couldn't be both or either one. George Stevens's 1956 film was *Giant* but "I" was more partial to *Shane* (1953), which famously ended with a young boy chasing after the eponymous blonde knight-errant on horseback, wanting something from him that he could not have—to marry his already married mother, but something which "I" read as friendship. *Davy Crockett and the River Pirates*, the first in a series by Disney brought me a coonskin cap that "I" used to cover up the horns on the head of "The Ashkenazi Kid."

It is said of the Jewish protagonist of Howard Jacobson's *The Finkler Question*, "He was a man who saw things coming" (a good tagline for a movie Western), but it is also said that "people who see things coming have faulty chronology."[8] So it was that in the 1950s John Ford film *Wagon Master* character actress Jane Darwell is seen unexpectedly blowing a *shofar* (a ram's horn associated with Rosh Hashonah, the Jewish New Year). Mormon Elder Wiggs asks cowboy Travis Blue to lead his people as wagon master to "a valley that's been reserved for us by the Lord. Been reserved for his people." They are, in a sense, the chosen people, as has been said of the Jews and by the Jews of themselves. When young cowboy Sandy asks Wiggs, "Are you people Mormons?" the Elder reflexively responds in terms generally reserved for the perception

[8]Jacobson, *The Finkler Question*, 3.

of prejudice, and in particular, anti-Semitism: "That's right, son. That's why I keep my hat on all the time. So my horns won't show." Dressed in a black suit with matching broad-brimmed black hat, Elder Wiggs and his party are surrogate Orthodox Jews—surrogate as Jews per se are invisible in the Old West(erns), unwelcome along with "show folks" and "horse-traders." When the people comprising the wagon train come across a stalled group of drunk (medicine) show charlatans, they disparage them as they had been disparaged in the last town in the time-honored tradition of intra-immigrant class prejudice and persecution. "I" felt right at home in what had been my father's cruel west.

A STRANGE ACT OF PROVIDENCE

Toward the end of the post-Western *The Last Picture Show* (dir. Peter Bogdanovich, 1971) set in the early 1950s, the local Royal theater in dusty-forlorn Anarene, Texas screens as its final offering Howard Hawks's coming-of-age Texas Western *Red River* (1948). How many of the already-failed lives in this half-life west Texas town dreamed they were Matt Garth (Montgomery Clift) physically overcoming larger-than-life father figure Tom Dunson (John Wayne) and taking over leadership of the 1000-mile post-Civil War cattle drive from Texas to Missouri? How many sons watching the film with or without their fathers felt the same way? The Royal's plaster cracks and threadbareness told the town what it already knew, that it was dying, if not already dead. Of the two movie theaters located in the unfashionable Long Island hamlet where I lived after moving from Queens, I only remember the town's first-born namesake that was rundown like the Royal and died from public embarrassment and neglect. "The Bellmore" asserted its ugliness, its age-inappropriateness like married and middle-aged Ruth Popper did with young Sonny Crawford in Anarene, which is a ghost town in real life. These two would not be caught dead together at the Royal, where everyone knew everyone else's business, but they would have found safe haven at the Bellmore, where there were neither ushers nor other patrons to shine a light on their indiscretions. They might have enjoyed the Bellmore's mature appreciation of the movie-going experience's origin story as the projected light of an over-articulated darkness. You didn't go to the Bellmore out of want, only out of need (to see a film that was only playing there), which is how "I" ended up in the sordid darkness, watching a color 1956 (of course) film version of television's *The Lone Ranger*

(1949–1957) on the big, ripped screen, hoping that the Ranger's silver bullets would kill any mice, rats, or bugs that might be tempted to crawl up my leg while I watched the show.

The Lone Ranger features an origin story par excellence. When the Butch Cavendish Gang ambushes an undermanned group of Texas Rangers in a box canyon, all of the lawmen appear to be dead. John Reid, the Lone Ranger who survives the ambush keeps his face hidden from the camera so as not to be recognized by us, since we are the only ones left who can identify (with) him. Surprisingly then, when the Indian Tonto enters the canyon, he identifies the Lone Ranger as a onetime trusty scout or childhood acquaintance (the story varies on this point) who saved his life when they were both young. The Ranger has a wet cloth covering half of his face. Tonto nurses the Ranger back to health, covering his face with bandanas. We learn from the Ranger that the leader of the doomed squad of Rangers, Captain Reid, was his brother, which leads the Lone Ranger to tell Tonto, "from this moment on, I'm going to devote my life to establishing law and order in this new frontier, to make the west a decent place to live…No one is going to know I'm alive. I'm supposed to be dead and I'm going to stay that way. I'll hide my identity somehow. I'll wear a disguise of some sort…From now on I'll wear a mask." The now "Lone Ranger" bases his new identity on not being identifiable as one of an ilk. Similarly ilk-less Tonto (in one version of the story, a mistake he made cost many of his people to lose their lives), quickly becomes the Ranger's best and only friend, making him his first mask out of his brother, Captain Reid's vest. The Texas Rangers' motto, "One Riot, One Ranger," became for me "One Lone Ranger, One Friend," which appealed to me as it lowered the odds of what I needed from friendship in order to survive growing up.

Although the Lone Ranger speaks with what appears to be strong moral authority, Tonto is *his* rabbi. It is Tonto who recalls hearing "a white parson" refer to "an act of providence," an idea to which the Ranger relates and instantly coopts: "Yes, that is true," he muses, "*A strange act of providence has protected my secret.*" With its talk of providence, *The Lone Ranger* is itself a parable supported by the Ranger's homiletic adages and instructional dialogue and especially by Tonto's naming of the animals and other things of this world. This contrasts dramatically with the awkward, embarrassing faux-"Injun-speak" Tonto is given, an immigrant's English that is, however, sometimes used to lexical advantage. When Tonto sees only a small wooden house instead of an expected "secret silver mine" and asks, "Where mine?" his absenting of the article "the" stakes his claim for an "I" the white man disallows him. By saying what is not evident (the secret "mine"), Tonto asks for what only he can understand—Native American self-possession.

Tonto is a functional "I." He gives the Ranger his silver bullets, because they're more accurate than the standard issue. Tonto calls the Lone Ranger "Kemosabe," which we assumed means "friend" but which was derived from a boys' summer camp of the same name (Camp Kee-Mo-Sah-Bee) in northern Michigan owned by the father-in-law of a man who worked on an early radio version of the story.[9] And with this, the Wild West draws that much nearer to suburban New York Jewry and becomes more of a boychick's own tale. It is just as I thought, not as I imagined: I may be lone but the world will never see me as The Lone Ranger. I accept that I am not "I." I am "me," Tonto, or at least I thought of myself in this subaltern position relative to the other boys who attended my all-Jewish summer camp. (And *I* went to camp with two brothers surnamed *Kafka*.)

I imagine that somewhere in the darkness of *The Lone Ranger*'s ripped-screening I sat through literally on the edge of my tattered seat at the back of the Bellmore Theater was another local misfit, whose biography had not yet carved some alternative to friendship from the anxiety of exclusion—the then Leonard Alfred Schneider, the future (previously introduced) Lenny Bruce who grew up in the same town as me. A true landsman in the life fiction-making sense, Lenny claims to have attended Hollywood High, whose superintendent (he says) was Spencer Tracy, whose principal was Vincent Price, "Lana Turner sat at the next desk, Roland Young was the English teacher and Joan Crawford taught general science." In his comic sketch "Thank you, Mask Man" (1971), Lenny took the Lone Ranger another way, reveling in exposing his "decency" and humility (like Shane, he rode off to forestall being thanked by those he had saved) for what they were—social masks.[10] Lenny teased out the Ranger's wants and more deeply his needs, sloughing off the mantle of morally stand-up guy and easing him into the kind of sixties hipster jargon and experimental morality characteristic of the stand-up comic

[9]James Van Hise, *Who Was That Masked Man? The Story of the Lone Ranger* (Las Vegas: Pioneer Books, 1990), 16–18.

[10]Although the Lone Ranger is commonly referred to as "masked man," Lenny calls him "mask man."

himself. The answer to the question that ended each episode of *The Lone Ranger*—"who *was* that mask*e*d man?"—is: he's a vintage 1950s repressed id and ego who wants and needs oral and physical approbation wherever and with whomever or even whatever he can find it. And the community he serves, for whom he has been created as a social mask must pay through the nose, the mouth, and every other orifice for all he has endured for them. His appetite is enormous. He eats his fifties' audience alive or as alive as a fifties' audience could pretend to be.

The town elders determine that the silver bullets Lenny's "*Mask* Man" leaves in his wake are Dr. Ehrlich's magic ones, the cure for syphilis (elsewhere re-configured as Lee Marvin-as-gunslinger Tim Strawn's syphilitic silver nose prosthesis in the 1965 comedy Western *Cat Ballou*). "He's saying in his own way that the whole world has syphilis and that's why he rides off with his mouth closed," opines the Mayor who has become miffed with "the schmuck" for leaving without accepting his "presents." "He don't want no part of nobody" [of "no body"]. The Ranger (Lenny never calls him this), who has become addicted to receiving "thank you's," loses his savior status when the "actual" Messiah returns, ending the "continuation of segregation, violence, and disease" that "men like yourself [men like Jonas Salk and Lenny Bruce] thrive on…Now that the Messiah's returned, you're in the shithouse." (This thought may be balanced with the Jewish concept of a God who can only be seen from the back, with "back"—in Hebrew, *achorai*—being conceived in a temporal rather than a spatial sense. "God says to Moses, You can see My afterward."[11]) One of the thank you notes the Mask Man reads is signed, "Leo Guroff, Freeport, Long Island." Freeport was the hated suburban hometown of angst-ridden, non-heteronormative Jewish singer-songwriter Lou Reed, who could well have played Lenny's ambisexual antihero and whose evocatively entitled album *The Blue Mask* (1982) deals, among other things, with gun violence as part of the American way of life. This "what-have-you-done-for-us-lately" attitude wrapped up in some newfound rejection of the way of the gun once it is no longer needed is a typical Western trope. But Lenny has something different in mind, something that speaks to colonization of racial memory via the Mask Man's link to "segregation, violence, and disease," his desire to

---

[11] Lawrence Kushner and David Mamet, *Five Cities of Refuge: Weekly Reflections on Genesis, Exodus, Leviticus, Numbers, and Deuteronomy* (New York: Schocken Books, 2003), 73.

perform "unnatural acts" with both Tonto and his horse, demonstrating the hetero-psycho-non-normativity of himself *and* his ilk.[12] Mask Man rides away without accepting the gratitude of a majoritarian people who are comfortable with him only so long as he doesn't demonstrate for them not who is behind the mask but what the mask means.[13]

Given the message and the messenger and the Yiddish shtick that pervades his routine, "men like yourself" (i.e., Mask Man) are Jews, the irony being that with the exception of parodies like *The Frisco Kid* (dir. Robert Aldrich, 1979), which features a rabbi played by Gene Wilder as an unlikely Western hero, there *are* no Jewish cowboys. As a Jewish character remarks in Mordecai Richler's *St. Urbain's Horseman* (after Russian Jewish writer Isaac Babel), "When a Jew gets on a horse he stops being a Jew."[14] I used to think the same thing about Nazis until I saw SS-Hauptsturmführer (Captain) and Commandant of the Kraków-Płaszów concentration camp Amon Goeth on horseback in *Schindler's List* (dir. Steven Spielberg, 1993). Since it is Lenny doing *all* of the character voices with the Mayor's being the most identifiably Jewish and even the apostles who announce the Messiah's coming speaking in Jewish vernacular, there is evidence here of something virulent. I vividly recall my reaction to seeing Arthur Hiller's 1975 film version of Robert Shaw's 1968 play *The Man in the Glass Booth*, in which a young Jewish man testifies at trial that the Adolf Eichmann-manqué defendant is in fact a wealthy Jewish industrialist and Nazi concentration camp survivor seeking to expiate his survivor guilt. The defendant cannot be a Nazi, the young man asserts, because "No gentile could ever be as anti-Semitic as Mr. Goldman." Sander L. Gilman says that (much disputed and hyperbolized) Jewish self-hatred "has been dismissed as merely the reflection of the incomprehensibility of the Holocaust," which in turn unearths the myth of a Jewish secret language. "The Jewish writer in the act of

---

[12] Mamet, *The Wicked Son*, 11.

[13] When the town turns against Mask Man, we see a white German Shepherd growling at him viciously, foreshadowing Samuel Fuller's controversial 1982 film *White Dog* concerning the unsuccessful attempt to recondition a similar dog that has been taught to attack Black people.

[14] Gene Wilder more famously played a cowboy of unspoken but evident Jewishness alongside Cleavon Little's African-American sheriff "Black Bart" in Mel Brooks's *Blazing Saddles* (1974). Both Westerns were *comedies*. Babel, quoted in Mordecai Richler, *St. Urbain's Horseman* (Toronto: McClelland and Stewart, 1971), 35.

writing disproves the damaged nature of the Jews' discourse...[while also serving as] the writer's proof of the intactness of the writer's Jewish identity."[15] The public face is a mask that performs concealment of rather than actually concealing Jewish identity. The mask is the not-so-secret secret language and as such is only as mythic as it needs to be.

The transcript of Lenny's stand-up version of *Thank You, Mask Man* makes the title character's true identity clear:

> *Dominic:* Look at these kids here, they made cookies and wrote a song called "Thank You, Mask Man." There's your hero! The man too good to accept a "Thank You" from little children, little children in the crey-paper costumes. Right now, buddy, you're going to explain or I'm going to whup the hell outta you, you hear?
>
> *Mask Man:* I'll explain if you get your god-damn hands offa me, you barbarian! You see, the reason I never wait for "Denk you" izzat I put two boys true college.
>
> *Sheriff:* What's that?
>
> *Mask Man:* Dot's right! I put two boys true college and I don' even get a "Denk you"!
>
> *Sheriff:* A "Denk you"?! Oi veys mir! The Mask Man's a Jew!
>
> *Mask Man:* Of course, schmuck! Dot's why I never talk on the radio show—all you ever heard me say on the radio show was "Hi Ho Silver!"—dot's all! You see .... Some goyim are coming? Zugnish! Don't zay a void! ....[16]

Mask Man's reference to his not talking on the radio show that bears his name (*The Lone Ranger*) speaks not only to the character's and the sketch's performativity but to the lack of an unmediated origin and identity. Lenny's characters refer to the heroically white horseman as "*Mask* Man" rather than "*Masked* Man" for reasons that feign innocence: the innocent voice of the child regarding an emperor who may or may not have on any clothes and of the defenseless citizen who cannot or will not defend himself (a longstanding indictment of the Jews, leading to the advent of the "never again" "muscle Jews" and the Israeli military state). More than this, "Mask Man" extrapolates to a formal surname, "Maskman" and, as with Superman and other superheroes, to the character's possibly hidden Jewishness. On the popular television sitcom

---

[15] Gilman, *Jewish Self-Hatred*, 360–61 and 361–62.

[16] http://www.notbored.org/mask-man.html.

Friends, Phoebe asks Chandler one of her typically out-of-the-blue questions and this dialogue ensues:

> *Phoebe*: Hey! Why isn't it "Spiderman?" Ya know, like Goldman, or Silverman?
> *Chandler*: Because it's not his last name.
> *Phoebe*: It isn't?
> *Chandler*: No, it's not like Phil Spiderman. He's a spider-*man*. You know, like Goldman is a last name, but there's no "Gold-*Man*."
> *Phoebe*: Oh-h, okay. There should *be* a Gold-*Man*![17]

While many family names are assembled from former professions or places of origin, Jewish names have generally been altered at Ellis Island, if not later in the process of assimilating to an already inhospitable society. Mask Man may represent alias as a particular form of subterfuge linked to this assimilation process, in a way that the more extrinsic Masked Man does not. Still, both Masked Man and Mask Man represent someone a person has become, with the element of choice deriving from a situation of duress. Lenny has made what was for him a logical association that renders the cruel west more timely and timeless than the wild frontier. Tonto is manifestly who he is and his plight as a Native American is written into all versions of the Lone Ranger story that I know. This manifestness serves to further mask the Lone Ranger's true identity while deepening the condition of maskedness. The Lone Ranger is quite possibly also the Lone Jew or else the lone character in Lenny's scenario who won't admit to being a Jew, who has chosen to mask his Jewishness beneath some cockamamie story about being left for dead and continuing life as a disguised dead man. He is ambiguous to everyone but Tonto and one retired Ranger as to why he must conceal his identity, but even they don't know that his reason hides another. (It's a good thing "I" have already claimed the "Tonto" role, although I suspect "I" did so to prove that "I" am transitioning from being

[17] "It may not be true in all cases, but it's a pretty good rule of thumb. If the word 'man' appears at the end of someone's name you can draw one of two conclusions: (a) they're Jewish, as in Goldman, Feldman, or Lipman; or (b) they're a superhero, as in Superman, Batman, or Spider-Man." Zeddy Lawrence, "Web Master," *Totally Jewish—Lifestyle Channel* (July 8, 2004). http://www.totallyJewish.com/lifestyle/features/?disp-_feature=jHO skA (site discontinued); *Friends*, "The One with the Tiny T-shirt," Episode 3.19 (March 27, 1997) wr. Alan Chase, dir. Terry Hughes. http://www.friends-tv.org/zz319.html.

The Lone Ranger, who as a cowboy Jew is "all hat and no cattle.") The Lone Ranger's real mask is not black but the overall whiteness of his attire, bearing, and his overly articulated speech—resembling someone learning to speak in a newly acquired tongue. In *The Frisco Kid, yeshiva bocher* Avram, who travels west from Poland and then across the USA to become Rabbi of a San Francisco congregation is aided by good-hearted bank robber Tommy who becomes his best and only friend as well as a yarmulke-wearing best man at Avram's wedding. Along the way, Tommy asks Avram how to say various things "in Jewish," as if he is trying to fill a void or else to coax out his own hidden identity (Harrison Ford, the actor playing Tommy, is Jewish on his mother's side.). The Indian Chief played by Italian-American actor Val Bisoglio asks Avram in what language the Torah is written. Not unlike the historical African-American cowboys who for many years were written out of Westerns, Jews have only been written in subscript. For many, like Billy Crystal in *City Slickers*, they only learned to sit a horse and still be Jews by starting out as comics who did stand up.

Why does it occur to somebody (and to whom) that Jews are comical as cowboys? Because they are quintessential urbanites and specifically (even for Jews) New Yorkers? Because they value brains over brawn and yet cannot master mind over body, riddled with neuroses as they are, obsessing over death manifest in a hypochondriacal life? Because they themselves default to humor (see hypochondria)? Because they are still regarded less as cattle ropers than as cultural interlopers? In *City Slickers* (dir. Ron Underwood, 1991), Mitch (Billy Crystal), whom his wife calls "Mr. Death," is one of three friends on a cattle-drive vacation trying to battle their way through male mid-life crisis. Mitch and Phil are Jewish. Ed is Italian, but as Lenny Bruce said, "All Italians are Jewish."[18] Mitch wears a New York Mets baseball cap instead of a cowboy hat, referring to the thought-to-be unlikelihood of a Jewish boy growing up to be entitled to don either hat professionally. By wearing a New York Mets baseball cap (the Mets are Long Island's team; the Yankees are New York City's, i.e., Manhattan's team) while becoming a two-week-long fantasy cowboy, Mitch uses earning power to buy his way into an assimilationist experience. It's a calculated move. As a New York Jew whose diaspora, like mine, consisted of moving out of the five boroughs (going East to

---

[18]Lenny Bruce, "Jewish and Goyish," in John Cohen, ed., *The Essential Lenny Bruce* (New York: Ballantine Books, 1967), 13.

Long Island), going West is, beneath the saccharine surface of this movie fantasy, largely unachieved.[19] When Mitch chases what looks to be the Lone Ranger's white spirit horse "Silver" in *City Slickers II: The Legend of Curly's Gold* (dir. Paul Weiland, 1994), a herd of culturally unassimilated wild horses ends up chasing *him* to the very border of death into which we all assimilate and his Jewish hypochondria nominally aspires (a.k.a. "Mr. Death").

Lenny Bruce's Mask Man refuses to shake hands (to receive "thank you's") for fear of being contaminated by the disease of assimilation. He refuses to take credit for wearing the social mask of majoritarianism. What Lenny has done is to make Mask Man the only member of the minority Jewish community that acts like a majoritarian culture who is honest and at the same time critical of his personal assimilationism, his taking up the mantle of *the masked American hero of the West*. How can I be of the West he asks himself like Billy Crystal's Mitch, when I am from the East, specifically New York City and vicinity, and even more specifically, a Jew? If the secret of life is indeed sticking to one thing as leathery trail boss Curly (played by *Shane*'s villain, Jack Palance attests) and if that one thing as Curly's twin brother says in the film's sequel is "honesty," can you be true to yourself *and* be assimilated?[20] If as David E. Kaufman suggests, "the comedic equivalent of assimilation is masking, impersonation—the humor com[ing] from our apprehension of the mask and the simultaneous knowledge of the true identity behind it," then "Lenny Bruce" is his own character, and he is asking the question, "Who was that mask(ed) man?" of himself.[21] He can't tell anyone his real name, *because he has already changed it.*

The Return of Frank James (dir. Fritz Lang, 1940) is a film about the afterlife of myth. Frank, who is thought to be dead after the murder of his brother Jesse by Bob and Charlie Ford, discovers the assassins melodramatically reenacting on stage the deed that made them infamous.

[19] All three writers of the *City Slickers* movies are New York Jews. Lowell Ganz was born in Manhattan and grew up in Queens. Marc "Babaloo" Mandel grew up in the Bronx. Billy Crystal, who starred in both films, moved from Manhattan to the Bronx in his very early years and was raised in Long Beach, Long Island.

[20] *City Slickers 2: The Legend of Curly's Gold* (dir. Paul Weiland, 1994).

[21] David E. Kaufamn, *Jewhooing the Sixties: American Celebrity and Jewish Identity* (Lebanon, NH: Brandeis University Press and University Press of New England, 2012), 106.

The tale has been recast with the Fords playing the heroes' roles and the James boys the villains'. This is more than Frank, who is sitting in the Lincoln box watching the play, can bear and he stands up like Hamlet's father's ghost before the frightened eyes of Bob Ford who exits the play post-haste, followed by his brother, running for their lives. Bob Ford runs to Creede, Colorado, where there also happens to be a repertory theater in which he might be able to reinvent himself as an actor in his own life's drama. In an unexpected turn of events, Bob Ford later shows up larger than life looking for all the world like one of the rhetorical actors his impersonator John Carradine so often played in movie Westerns, to witness Frank's sentencing for a murder he did not commit in the course of the robbery of the railroad company's express office to gain funds for his pursuit of Jesse's killer (Bob Ford). The manner in which Ford plants himself just inside the entrance to the courtroom without taking a seat rhetorically announces that the Western's structural strategy plays the straight line of cause and effect (the self-reliant westerner solving his own problems any way he can) versus the circularity of fate. Frank chose to return and give himself up in this post-Civil War drama in order to clear his innocent Black farmhand—a freed slave—of a murder charge brought against him as Frank's surrogate. Bob Ford fires on Frank (after he has been acquitted at trial) when the latter turns his back, which is precisely how he murdered Jesse. This time around a wounded Ford misses and dies in the return fire. Frank James lives on and in an ironic replay of the Fords' emploi (not depicted in this film), worked among other jobs as a ticket-taker at the Fresno movie theater in Los Angeles. "GET YOUR TICKET TORN BY FRANK JAMES" the ad read, and "people came for that rather than the film."[22] Had he been "Bob Ford," Frank would have appeared in a mock-heroic story of his own life rather than having to wait for Fritz Lang's *The Return of Frank James* to appear a full 25 years after his death. As Frank had witnessed Ford's play from the Lincoln box and Ford had hoped to witness Frank's demise from inside a Kansas City courtroom, Frank might have appeared in ghostly fashion (as the film tells us, the James boys were wont to do) to watch his own life's drama enacted by Henry Fonda, who was, in name only, just one tick away from a Ford, also named Henry (the anti-Semitic industrialist) and from the theater in which Lincoln

---

[22] Michael Ondaatje, *The Collected Works of Billy the Kid* (New York: Vintage, 1970), 24.

was shot. Was Tonto in director Gore Verbinski's 2013 version of *The Lone Ranger* part of the Wild West show owned by the investment group that employed Frank James? Was the fictional "Lone Ranger" actually a Black man, US Deputy Marshal Bass Reeves, as some have claimed and does this conform with Lenny Bruce's vision of the west more than, say (John) Ford's?[23] Does any of this hybridic fact and fiction give a Jewish boy hope of riding a horse with the confidence of an outlaw or a lawman or an Indian, as "I, myself"?

Who am "I"? The lady with the camp number forearm tattoo had me pegged as a "Bobby Gold"-like Jew (from Mamet's *Homicide*, 2001), years before "I" had a name for it. "You caught the case, you *got* the case," Bobby's lieutenant tells him. (The form of life is everything that *is* "the case.") "Bobby, you *live* with this candy store," Gold's lieutenant tells him. "The candy store case." An elderly Jewish lady, a camp survivor, is killed behind her candy store counter for the mythic treasure that Jews are believed to hide in the basements of the small shops dotting my ancestral landscape from Belarus (where my paternal grandmother was a small shopkeeper) to the Bronx (or *Homicide*'s Baltimore) where the new poor stole from the old poor. The "fortune" is said to be hidden in the basement where Lenny Bruce joked his family discovered Uncle Morty's suicide note admitting (once and for all) that he (standing in for all Jews) killed Christ. The he/we-ness that underlies this joke bears within it the me/they-ness of the assimilated or even alienated Jew complicit in his/our persecution. One catches in this as well an ironic reflection of the hurtful accusation that Jews are always making things up, specifically their fantasy that someone is trying to hurt them. (Perhaps the source of my own "cruel west" trope where it seems like everything and everyone is trying to kill you.) "There's so much anti-Semitism in the last four thousand years, we must be doing something to bring it about," says Bobby Gold, to which the dead lady's granddaughter asks rhetorically, "You hate yourself that much? You belong nowhere." And there we have it, the utter placeless-ness, the living in the deep recesses

[23] In 1861, John T. Ford converted the former Baptist Church into the theater that bears his name. The original theater burned in 1862 and was rebuilt. It was there on April 14, 1865 that Abraham Lincoln was assassinated in the presidential box. Bob Ford was shot to death in Creede, Colorado. Unlike Lincoln at Ford's, he was not at the theater. http://www.indiewire.com/2013/07/was-the-man-behind-the-lone-rangers-mask-a-black-man-in-theaters-tomorrow-73-166997/.

of time where locatable space will not suffice. The living in racialized myths, theirs and ours, the constant need to escape into or out of
affiliation. "The attraction of flight," Mamet suggests, "as Jonah from
Ninevah, as Abraham from the imminence of God's pronouncements
is the burden of the Jews. It is not that we, uniquely, have been given
the burden but that we, uniquely, have been *ordered to resist*."[24] Above
all, argues Mamet, to resist identifying with or passively submitting to
our oppressors while attacking other Jews who are our only real line of
defense. When a man in police custody for murdering *his own family*
tears the restraining strap off of Bobby's holster while going for the latter's gun, the cop takes this transgression, this unlocking of something
held close to his body, this Jewish body in peril, *personally*.

Did the movie stars of my youth encourage me to change identities by showing me what it looked like for an adult to indulge childhood fantasies? Issur Danielovitch (a.k.a. "Kirk Douglas") got to play
a Norseman, along with Bernard Schwartz (a.k.a. "Tony Curtis") in
Richard Fleischer's *The Vikings* (1958). Like Philip Roth's *The Anatomy
Lesson* (1983), *The Vikings* is about pain (the loss of functioning body
parts) as the price paid for struggling with one's personal and racial identity, a point not lost on Lenny Bruce, who drew attention to the casting of Douglas and Curtis as Viking warriors and secret blood brothers.
"What a son!" Viking king Ragnar constantly says to and about his only
legitimate heir, Einar (Douglas). In a strange parallelism, Eric (Curtis)
is the issue of the Viking lord Ragnar's rape of the English Queen Enid,
sent away as a boy to save him from the new English tyrant King Aella
who would kill that throne's rightful heir if he got the chance. (This par-
allels the Old Testament story of baby Moses being placed in a basket
and sent down the Nile by his mother to save him from the Pharoah's
order to kill all Hebrew sons.) Raised as a Viking slave, Eric runs afoul of
his unrevealed half-brother Einar when his hawk tears out Einar's eye. In
return, Eric escapes torture and certain death when the Norse god Odin
moves wind and water to save him so that he may fulfill his royal destiny
as the future English king. He is aided in this by Aella's English noble
enemy Egbert, the preponderance of names beginning with the letter
"E" bespeaking a genealogical circle awaiting closure as in some secret
language that only appears to be broken to those who cannot read it.

[24] David Mamet, *The Wicked Son: Anti-Semitism, Self-Hatred, and the Jews* (New York:
Schocken Books, 2006), 5–6.

(Richard Foreman's Hebrew-letter-designed stage production of *The Vikings* awaits such reimagining.) My father was proud of his son, even though I never learned to speak the Yiddish language nor mastered the Jewish orthodoxy into which he was born. My son is another "E", Jews using only *the initial* of the departed from which to create a new name.

A.K.A.

Swede Levov, the content of whose "substratum" writer Nathan Zuckerman regards under the Macbethian soubriquet "unimaginable," was another Jewish masked man. At the time of their reunion, both Swede and Zuckerman have been through prostate cancer but only the writer appears to have been impaired by it as he misreads his subject's athletic body's inability to deeply experience its own incapacity and irrationality. (The "fact" that Swede, not Zuckerman, "actually" dies from cancer in the plot, in the double plot of fiction burying a character, as it were, standing up—speaks again to how appearances, including literary appearance, deceive.) Misreading enables the writer's obsession with the other person as his subject, a character that is made up to resemble an apparent self, a self of appearance alone. In recounting the neighborhood where Swede and Zuckerman grew up, the writer contemplates how the details he remembers relate to surfaces like the one he ascribes to the athlete who exhibits no interior life (someone not having an inner life is as unimaginable as the inner life that someone has). The writer's thoughts go to death and burial: "The *detail*, the immensity of the detail, the force of the detail, the weight of the detail—the rich endlessness of detail surrounding you in your young life like the six feet of dirt that'll be packed on your grave when you're dead." Not only death in the neighborhood, but death *as* the neighborhood, "the ultimate reunion story" of "the interior life that is unknown and unknowable," of the burial that prefigures death as life observed (seen and lived so as to be seen).

"Perhaps by definition," Zuckerman muses, "a neighborhood is the place to which a child spontaneously gives undivided attention: that's the unfiltered way meaning comes to children, just flowing off the surface of things."[25] Fear gripped my neighborhood with the rumor (which in a child's mind is always self-substantiating) that a murderous inmate

---

[25] Roth, *American Pastoral*, 42–43 and 80.

had escaped from a nearby insane asylum disguised as a mummy. Why a mummy? In those days before fear became my literary imaginary, "my best friend" and "I" regularly watched late-night horror movies on television that were so old and so bloodlessly black-and-white (no hacking, no severing) as to be almost palatable to a tender young mind. These monster movies, hosted by a self-and-genre-parodying local New York City disk jockey in ghoulish makeup named "Zacharley" (a.k.a. John Zacherle), featured Dracula, Frankenstein (Jewish?), Wolfman (Jewish?), and the Mummy—anxiety tropes preceding the age of self-recognition, children's monsters, not yet adult demons. The Mummy's return brought the *Caligari* theme of no-escape, no-asylum from the madness of self-imagining down from the slivered screen. The Mummy turned the corner from the street where "my best friend" lived and proceeded down mine. As he drew close, "my best friend" *as* the David who slew Goliath felled the Mummy with a punch to the nose. (We learn in Genesis 6:4 that "The *Nephilim*, these Goliaths [plural] who inhabit the Promised Land...were then on earth," the repressed, unconscious memory of which bubbles up inside the child who is living in a world of giants.[26]) The Mummy bled. The Mummy fell. The Mummy rolled around on the ground like he was on fire, shouting airlessly that he could not breathe. The Mummy grasped desperately at his wrappings and unspooled to reveal the neighborhood bully, an unsurprising "a.k.a." given that mummies don't bleed or breathe. Was the Mummy Jewish? "I" ask only because the Kantor-esque emballage might represent a preserved dialogic self-questioning, after the *gemarrah*, "the commentaries or disputations that are never straightened out" in relation to the teachings on the law written in *The Talmud* ("Study") and within it the *Mishnah* ("Repeating").[27] Spalding Gray recalls seeing the 1950s über-popular ventriloquist Paul Winchell and his dummy Jerry Mahoney (the Dean Martin and Jerry Lewis of the wooden doll set) on television

[26] Kushner and Mamet, *Five Cities of Refuge*, 112.

[27] "Talmud (literally, "study") is the generic term for the documents that comment and expand upon the *Mishnah* ("repeating"), the first work of rabbinic law, published around the year 200 CE by Rabbi Judah the Patriarch in the land of Israel. Published at the end of the second century CE, the Mishnah is an edited record of the complex body of material known as oral Torah that was transmitted in the aftermath of the destruction of the Second Temple in 70 CE." https://www.myjewishlearning.com/article/talmud-101/; https://www.myjewishlearning.com/article/mishnah/; Debra Shostak, *Philip Roth—Countertexts, Counterlives* (Columbia: University of South Carolina Press, 2004), 11.

talking about the horror of being confined inside an iron lung (something like a sarcophagus) as part of a medical cure. The image of Paul
Winchell's human voice emerging from the wooden confines of Jerry
Mahoney's wooden body merged with that of the same human voice
emerging from the metal confines of the iron lung. Folded into this
transference was my mummy story (life-threatening self-confinement)
with Spalding's own fearful childhood memory of "the Blaine brothers...
eight-foot-tall hairy men [who] had been seen loose roaming the Rhode
Island countryside," where "I" now live.[28]

The a.k.a. "David" who slew the Mummy was a "Jewish hammer," a
Judah Macabee, a muscle Jew from a Philip Roth novel, a David Mamet
film. When something "my best friend" saw on the giant screen scared
him as a child, he ran at the screen to attack it. I crawled under the seats,
because I was an "I", a figment of the screenal imagination, scaring itself.
It was years later, when "my best friend" said he could not remember
who I was that "I" was released to write this book. I discovered he was
not the hero of my youth, he was *the Mummy*, living a secret inner life
that ruined a childhood that needed to be forgotten. I recall performance artist Cynthia Hopkins's character Cameron Seymour, "a neurologist specializing in the memory function of the brain (and suffering
herself from psychogenic—emotionally driven—amnesia that blots out
much of her childhood)."[29] There was a gap of many years between the
moment when "my best friend" unwittingly pummeled the external representation of his own inner angst and his vanishing of the figure of the
Mummy from his formerly half-life's life story. A Jewish golem, a savior
but also a potential world destroyer.

REUNION

It took decades for Frank Sinatra to stage-manage a reunion between
the estranged comedy team of "best friends" Dean Martin and Jerry
Lewis, who at the conclusion of their penultimate film, the Western
Pardners (1956) literally shot down the rumor of their imminent split
by six-gun-shooting out the letters spelling out "The End." The film

[28] Spalding Gray, *Sex and Death to the Age of 14* (1979), recorded October 29, 1982,
The Performing Garage, New York City, supplemental material on *And Everything Is Going
Fine* (dir. Steven Soderbergh), Criterion Collection DVD, 2012.

[29] http://cynthiahopkins.com/shows/accidental-nostalgia/.

was released on the same day that Martin and Lewis gave their last live performance as a team at New York City's Copacabana nightclub. Don't believe something just because it is represented, their live appearance said, unless, of course, you are satisfied living inside the fiction of a film. Films are, after all, often only looped after the fact, a fact that Martin and Lewis exposed nightly at the Copa.

The unwrapping and unfolding of mummies and zombies and their haunted logic figure prominently in the Martin and Lewis vehicle *Scared Stiff* (dir. George Marshall, 1953). In the film, Dean as nightclub singer Larry Todd is introduced as "that clown prince of song," suggesting that he is a double threat. This first impression is quickly contravened when Jerry as waiter Myron Mertz interrupts Todd's act and they appear to be a song-and-comedy duo. The first bit they do is a love triangle in which Larry is the husband and Myron is his wife's lover, then Myron is the husband and Larry is the lover, and finally, Myron is the wife, and in each case, Larry gives Myron a beating. It turns out that Larry and Myron have been friends since childhood with Larry getting Myron a job wherever he is working. Even Myron's mirror reflection tells him that Larry is "his best friend," which says something about the "self"'s fictional creations. When Larry learns from showgirl Rosie with whom he has been carrying on that she sent Myron to deal with her gangster boyfriend Shorty on the amorous couple's behalf, Larry packs heat and, as "best friends" do, goes to save Myron. For his part, Myron later comes upon the police gathered around a corpse he thinks is Larry's (a man whom Larry in turn mistakenly thinks he killed). When the cops ask Myron whether he knows the dead man, he responds: "Do I know him? He's my best friend. I worked with him, I sang with him, I ate with him, and you want to know if I *know* him?" The police detective impatiently interrupts: "Do ya?!" and Myron taking a second look at the corpse says, "No, I don't know *him*." And that about says it, says what for Jerry-as-Myron is the unsayable, the thing he thinks he knows about someone who is ultimately unknowable, his strong and silent partner Dean Martin. That Jerry can only say the unsayable over the unthinkable, the unimaginable—i.e., Dean's dead body—is instructive and also premature in terms of both their lives and their careers. Later, in a bid to escape the gangsters on the pier, Myron/Jerry is coerced into playing a dummy to Larry/Dean's ventriloquist and much is made of Myron/Jerry's dummy-hood. Escaping from a steamer trunk into which he had to fold his body, Myron suffers from a back injury that foreshadows the condition that would eventually lead to Jerry Lewis's Percodan addiction and near-suicide. Perhaps it was Jerry who appeared as a nebulous form sitting on the edge of my hospital bed as a Percodan-induced hallucination following my latest cancer surgery. Maybe it was he who was keeping me at the edge of madness that led me to believe "I" would die if I could not escape from my hospital room/asylum.

Jerry's "best friend" no longer recalls him either. It all seems so fake to Dean, like one of the celebrity-specific dreams Jerry used to tell him about, in which he seemed to know everyone in Hollywood but always only out of context. (This makes "Jerry" my landsman, twice over, however, groundless our dreams are.) There's Carmen Miranda thanking Jerry for dropping his tray while she was performing. The disturbance, Miranda says, got her fired from that job which led her to a bigger, better job that led to her current celebrity. This clearly wish fulfillment causality sustains itself only within the confines of a dream. The chance meeting between Jerry and Miranda leads to he and best friend Dean joining her act on the ship that is taking them all to Cuba where they have a date with a haunted castle inherited by a young woman named Mary Carroll who is being threatened and with whom he, i.e., Larry has become smitten. Jerry's dream is haunted by the promise/premise of premature death, perhaps like Carmen Miranda's at age forty-six. How did he know? Mary tells Larry that she is planning to dream about him, and a brochure impersonating a map to conscious dream logic is unfolded:

Myron: (He reads.) "Cuba is truly the island of romance. A land of flashing-eyed señoritas seasoned with onions and a dash of garlic, all for fifty cents."

Mary: Come on. Let me see that. "A land of flashing-eyed señoritas, many of them continental stars spread out all over the sidewalks" (?)

Larry: There's a trick, there's a trick to this. See, you got to know how to fold these things. (He proceeds to show them how.) "Cuba is truly the island of romance. A land of flashing-eyed señoritas equipped with red, green, and amber lights to control the traffic." See?

Once at the haunted castle on Lost (a.k.a. Long) Island, which Mary now owns and where "my best friend" and "I" saw them on TV, attempts are made to scare off Larry and Myron with monster effects. Mary plays the ghost of her dead great-grandmother, the castle's

former owner, to counter the zombie/mummy narrative with the spec-
tral reunion of embodied *spiritual* remains. Railway tracks in an underground crypt remind Larry of "my hotel room in Steubenville," Dean's
real hometown, folding biography back upon itself. Myron accidentally
causes a wall panel to open, revealing the most frightening sight of all,
their friendly buddy-movie competition, Bob Hope and Bing Crosby,
i.e., their real heads superimposed on skeletons' "bodies." Here, the
armature of celebrity intervenes, as it often did in film comedies of this
era (Martin and Lewis made an earlier appearance in a Hope and Crosby
film) as a fear of self-impersonation. Scared out of the castle and their
own film by Hope and Crosby's comedy-team zombie-ism, Larry and
Myron as (for the purpose of this film) the fictional "Martin and Lewis"
tell the film audience, "Well, that's the end." But the end of what—the
sense of uncertain being? Jerry's fear of not really knowing Dean, not
knowing the real "Dean"? The team split and these recurring themes
appeared in Jerry's solo zombie-idiot films, made in the afterlife of his
"best friendship" with Dean.

"I" took this personally. I have the framed *Life* magazine cover
(August 13, 1951) in which the boys are caught in the act of jumping
with a sort of manic exuberance as if in direct response to the legend
accompanying the photo that shouts, MARTIN AND LEWIS: TOP
MONEY ACT IN SHOW BUSINESS. The comic duo share headline
space with WHAT TO Do DO ABOUT GERM WARFARE. When
"Martin and Lewis" professionally split, it was for me like the dreaded
nuclear fission threatening childhood's end that the boomer generation managed to survive only to enter the afterlife of what Susan Sontag
called "Apocalypse From Now On," a waiting for/writing of the dis-
aster.[30] Dean quickly got over what was for Jerry an earth-shattering
split and found himself another group that was largely devoid (save for
lone Jew and marginal member Joey Bishop and racialized Jewish con-
vert-as-mascot Sammy Davis, Jr.) of compulsively self-questioning tics.[31]
Dean, though, mostly wanted to be left alone to watch his Westerns
(in which he sometimes co-starred) on his hotel room TV. Dean's pins

[30] Sontag, *AIDS as Metaphor*, 176.

[31] "Davis doubled down on Lewis's metaphoric cancer—the Black, the Jew, the
Immigrant, the Native American (i.e., the Indian) the Urbanite, the Entertainer, the
Liberal as alien, other, cancer in the fascist lexicon of miscegenation." Sontag, *AIDS as
Metaphor*, 83. One thinks also of Coleman Silk in Philip Roth's *The Human Stain* (2001),
a black man whose counternarrative is to pass not only as white but as a Jew.

seemed unsuited to the Western, though. They were thin and tapered down to the top of the boot and did not appear to know how to run outdoors. They counted steps like playing cards. Running was something Dean needed to think about. Urgency was not his emploi. He moved as if not wanting to upset a certain balance of effort and effect. He'd rather sit back and deal, and it showed.[32]

I doubt Dean thought much about the Western he made with Jerry, *Pardners* (dir. Norman Taurog), in 1956, the year in which Cinemascope and Technicolor made sense of the transcendental long before I had any sense of what it was or that the transcendental might even be. It was the same year in fact that Martin and Lewis's *Hollywood or Bust* (dir. Frank Tashlin) came out, the movie that finally made their personal and professional friendship, well, go bust. Lewis's casting in *Pardners* as a rich and spoiled New York City Jewish child-man, struck a nerve, impinging on Martin's adult childhood cowboy dream and as such was a perfect vehicle for the duo's constitutional unease with one another. The movies are filled with partners who split up with the understanding that the Western in particular is a one-man journey that stops to pick up others as circumstances dictate but not as a matter of personal policy or preference.[33] Gangs are gangs for a reason. They are bodies of intentionality. Once that intention has been fulfilled or even while still in transit, hierarchical order (there are only nominal equal splits where money, not power, is concerned) is meant to break down. After the take has been divided, gang members go their separate ways, because their working is not sustainable as friendship, any more than friendship is a good premise for pulling a job.

[32] Martin's biographer Nick Tosches describes him at age 54 filming the unmemorable Western *Something Big* (dir. Andrew V. McLaglen, 1972) as he (Tosches) imagines him (Martin) saw himself, "wearing a toy gun and all dolled up like Giovanni Mack Brown" (a reference to B-movie Western star Johnny Mack Brown). Ironically, "Howard Hawks' instructions to Dean Martin who showed up in an almost comical cowboy outfit on the first day of shooting (his best, most famous Western, *Rio Bravo*, dir. Howard Hawks, 1959), were not to play a cowboy but just play a drunk." Before Martin signed on to play the drunkard "Dude," Hawks tried to get Martin's good friend Frank Sinatra, who always looked out of place in the painfully comic Westerns in which he starred. Nick Tosches, *Dino: Living High in the Dirty Business of Dreams* (New York: Dell, 1992), 1 and 17–18. http://www.imdb.com/title/tt0053221/trivia?ref_=tt_tr.

[33] See most recently, Quentin Tarentino's *The Hateful Eight* (2015) which uses this Western trope as its premise and its plot.

"Ride away" croons the soundtrack as John Wayne's Ethan Edwards in *The Searchers* turns his back *on family* and returns to the solitary inwardness of Western space.[34] Ford shot a number of his Westerns in Monument Valley owing to a familiarity with the site that paralleled the circularity of the anti-hero's apparent journey through a necessary community back to a majority of one. Friendship and family are liabilities when the West is waiting to attack you where you are most vulnerable. Better to be a spy in your own house, sleeping with one eye open and a pistol, a pin, a button, or a fuse at the ready. Do not let campfires or home fires fool you. You ought to be allergic to them (as I am) and act accordingly. Don't get too near the warmth. This, Dean understood but Jerry who modeled urban Jewish neurosis to a fault (there is in fact no other way) could not accept this, and Dean came to shrink from his figurative touch. Martin and Lewis film plots often had as their premise Jerry's misapprehension that he was being hired to behave or perform as Dean's partner, which Dean's character resisted because he was not. By film's end, a partnership had been formed but one feels that financial residuals and a residual loss of affection will soon attach, the latter as a predictor of interpersonal detachment. Fear of abandonment and fear of entrapment given the control factor of lawful partnership makes for anxious comic enactment and hysterical overacting of a theatrical kinship. Unlike what *Pardners's* theme song says, being partners is not the same as being "pals." "You and me, we're going to be partners, you and me we're going to be pals" acknowledges this fact by staking its claim semantically in futures, partnership as a dividend of work, for which friendship is not just unnecessary but counterintuitive. Knowing this allows Dean Martin to enter into this every odd man out for himself celebration as a nominally bonding duet, in which it is Jerry not Dean who sings harmony. Dean casually addressed people he *didn't* like or else gave no thought to as "pallie," as if belittling the notion of having or even needing a pal.[35]

"One's mind betrays one's body," as Sontag asserts. Following his split from Jerry, Dean's mind gave into its own noncompliance with all

---

[34] I discuss *The Searchers* in my book *Incapacity: Wittgenstein, Anxiety, and Performance Behavior* (Evanston: Northwestern University Press, 2014), 233–38.

[35] When Dean is trying to smooth talk Jerry out of something that is rightfully his in *Hollywood or Bust* (dir. Frank Tashlin, 1956), the film that un-partnered them, he addresses him as "old buddy, old pal."

but the most formal of social realities, the performance of kinship in the Rat Pack, which gnawed at him until he only performed sitting down with a drink in his hand, when he performed at all. Jerry's body metastasized its own (minus a partner as foil) physically spastic irrationalism—the woefulness of the spastic body fighting itself like a cancer. And to make matters worse, having to fight minus former boxer Dean, so that Jerry's shadow boxing now displayed in its full comic horror the truth that "the body is, all too woefully, just the body."[36] Objects that got the better of Jerry in the team's films now multiplied in number and intensified in difficulty so that he laid entire scenes to ruin in a spatial metaphor for overacting and over-emoting ("one's body betrays one's feeling"), turning pathos into bathos. As Jerry's body grew bloated on high doses of percodan to ease his aching back (the result of too, too many comic pratfalls), Dean wasted away to nothing, "Nothing" rather than "Cowboy" being the role he now appeared to have been born to play. Having cut out the cancer of overweening ambition, need, and desire from his body in the form of "Jerry Lewis," Dean became a ghost of his former self, the former healthy one who balanced his partner's neurotic, abnormal, incoherent "act."[37] Jerry's solo act now identified as a source of inchoate, not just childlike but primitive energy. In retrospect, Dean was for Jerry "the mechanism which 'restrains' growth," that growth being not just of a rampaging ego but of the body's counter-effective ambition for itself to be free of everything but itself. "The body's treachery is thought to have its own inner logic."[38] Like the man said, "It's a very big subject, betrayal."

OPERATION IMBECILE

Jerry Lewis is a dybbuk desperately struggling to exorcise (for which Jews have been said to have a particular talent) the *loshan hora*, the body's own evil speech. This evil is, however, only exacerbated by his spastic movements, which likewise only serve to advertise himself as the very taboo he cannot suppress. Jerry's anxiety or "nervousness" as

[36] Cancer has been metaphorically linked to the repression of energy, of feeling, emotions. "The tumor has energy, not the patient." Sontag, *Illness as Metaphor*, 18, 62, and 63.

[37] Although, it was Dean rather than Jerry who manifested cancer's early associations with "idleness" and "sloth." Sontag, *Illness as Metaphor*, 14.

[38] Ibid., 40.

he calls it holds a mirror to this condition and reflects itself. Jerry does not so much hate himself as he hates the person he sees in this mirror, whose distortions he regards as being real but unlovable. He does not lack for confidence so much as he is overly confident in the wrong thing, in the effect his distorting ugliness and negative assertiveness has on other people. He sees himself as being literally untouchable and so performs a sort of self-touching, a desperate embrace that explodes its own constraints. He cannot stop talking. Smilesburger (his surname a sort of Jewish joke on itself), a crippled old Jew in Roth's *Operation Shylock*, contends that *"inappropriateness is the Jewish style,"* by which he means particularly "the sin of Jewish speech," of which Jerry's rhythmically inflected Yiddish-American stands as exhibit A in the crime of self-presentation. Smilesburger quotes the eighteenth-century Vilna Gaon (Rabbi Elijah ben Solomon Zalman or Eliyahu of Vilna) as proclaiming that the Midrash says, "What should a person's job be in this world? To make himself a mute…Words generally only spoil things."[39]

Jerry tried to be quiet, he really did. Some of the most famous sequences in his post-Martin-and-Lewis film work from *The Errand Boy* (1961) to the nearly silent *The Bellboy* (1960) resort to what is, however, equally assertive pantomime. Lewis's Newark landsman, Philip Roth could not keep quiet either, violating as he did the unspoken Jewish law, "Thou shall not be a talebearer among your people."[40] Roth plays the role of the spoiler ("Words…spoil things") for many Jewish readers who regard him as telling trade secrets that in post-Shylockian terms say not

[39] "Gaon is the modern Hebrew for genius. In the Bible, gaon means glory or arrogance, depending on the context." The term was later used as an honorific for particularly distinguished rabbis. https://www.thejc.com/judaism/jewish-words/gaon-1.7355; http://www.jewishvirtuallibrary.org/rabbi-eliyahu-of-vilna-the-vilna-gaon.

[40] Aside from scattered references to Roth and Lewis's common birthplace, there is little in print that links them in either a factual or fictional way. Scott Bukatman mentions in an endnote that the "Jewish self-hatred" Lewis performs specifically in *The Nutty Professor* maintains "the parallel between Lewis and Philip Roth," but this parallel line is not sighted or cited beyond this and another brief mention in which Bukatman generally notes the similarity between Roth's self-flagellating (my term) novel *My Life As A Man* and (again) Lewis's *The Nutty Professor*. Scott Bukatman, "Paralysis in Motion: Jerry Lewis's Life as a Man," in Andrew Horton, ed., *Comedy/Cinema/Theory* (Berkeley and Los Angeles: University of California Press, 1991), 203, 204, n. 7, 8. There is one brief mention in an article discussing an independent film's screening states, "[Alex Ross] Perry's film [*The Color Wheel*], a feast of eruptive performance, harsh physical comedy, and ideal comic distance, has something to do with Jerry Lewis and is also inspired significantly by the work of Philip Roth." This same article compares the work of Frank Tashlin, perhaps the greatest

only that the Jew bleeds but bleeds himself into a puddle of guilt and helpless self-abnegation. The standard instruction given to the beginning writer, to "write what you know" loses its broad, overdetermined appeal among those who contend that what Roth is doing is writing even more of a counternarrative than he himself believes he is constructing. Still, even Smilesburger likens Roth to Dostoevsky who likewise took a Bakhtinian dialogical, an internal counternarrative approach to literary fiction.[41] The problem is that to be Jewish (which in this one way resembles and promotes obsessive-compulsive behavior) "is a[n internal] dispute, incarnate." Jews cannot stop speaking says the spokesman for the (mock) self-confessional Philip Roth, because inside each Jew *"are so many speakers."* Jew-hater Dostoevsky, though, who invents divided characters with doubles throughout his oeuvre, in an odd way sets the stage for the Newark blood brothers Roth and Lewis, a fact that *Operation Shylock* makes clear at least to me as it nears its end. The real Philip Roth, that is, the real writer Philip Roth speaking of himself as the subject of his work, in referring to "the instinct for impersonation by which I had so far enacted and energized my contradictions [his doubles and doubleness] solely within the realm of fiction" confesses:

> I really couldn't see what was behind what I was doing, and that too may have accounted for why I was doing it: I was enlivened by its *imbecilic* side [my *italics*]—maybe *nothing* was behind it. To do something *without* clarity, an inexplicable act, something unknowable even to oneself, to step outside responsibility and give way fully to a very great curiosity, to be appropriated unresistingly by the strangeness, by the dislocation of the unforeseen....

Compare this with Jerry Lewis's statement regarding the emotional infantilism that was his professional stock and trade and that only appears to make him different in his lack of control (a cover for his

---

director of Martin and Lewis's as well as of Lewis's solo films, to that of Alfred Hitchcock, whom Tashlin greatly admired. Richard Brody, "What to See This Weekend: BAM's Independent Lineup," *New York Magazine* (June 22, 2012). http://www.newyorker.com/culture/richard-brody/what-to-see-this-weekend-bams-independent-lineup.

[41] Russian theorist Mikhail Bakhtin clearly sets forth his idea of dialogism in his book *The Dialogic Imagination: Four Essays*, ed. Caryl Emerson and trans. Michael Holquist (Austin: University of Texas, 1982), as well as in *Problems on Dostoevsky's Poetics*, ed. and trans. Caryl Emerson (Minneapolis: University of Minnesota Press, 1984).

hyper-controlling nature) from Roth's apparent authorial control (in the guise of forfeiting control of his own narrative):

> I have never been able to develop a façade to hide behind [he could have been a Philip Roth character but not Philip Roth in his own character.] My emotions function on a separate wire. I can stand toe to toe with two oxes and never know I'm hurt until I'm picked up bleeding. But if a guy doesn't say good morning back, I can have a heart attack. I'm more than just a great movie star. I'm also a neurotic, temperamental *imbecile*.[42] [my *italics*]

Smilesburger (an anxiety dream's ham-fisted name for a comic super-villain) points out that "the talking Jews" went to Freud who told them to keep talking about everything, i.e., the talking cure, which ("I" say) effectively turns the means of the cure back to the apparent cause, talking aloud of one's psychological condition as a rehearsal for writing about it. "No word is forbidden. The more *loshon hora* the better."[43] Perhaps the greatest of all modern talking Jews and a textbook case for psychoanalysis was Lenny Bruce, a fact, as I have said, *was never talked about* in the town where we both grew up.[44] In 1959, Lenny told a story on national television in which he referenced a widely reported news story from 1957. Although the story was intended to illustrate America's social hypocrisy, there is, for me, something else going on.

> There was a child that was trapped in a well. And a doctor attended him and they got the kid out and, you know, the doctor sent a bill. Alright. Now, the nation screamed, you know. "What?! What *finks* those doctors are! How about that? Sending those poor people, you know, a bill... Okay, but how about the poor person [who received the bill]...maybe he's a TV repairman...he wants to be paid *now*, daddy, two-dollar home repair...

---

[42] Roth, *Operation Shylock*, 358; Shawn Levy, *King of Comedy: The Life and Art of Jerry Lewis* (New York: St. Martin's Press, 1996), ix.

[43] Roth, *Operation Shylock*, 332, 333, 334, and 335.

[44] In a non-historical footnote (which I'm aware this footnote inexactly doubles), "The *New York Review* assigned Philip Roth to cover one of Lenny Bruce's [public obscenity] trials. But then Bruce got sick, the trial was postponed" and Roth went to the Yaddo's writer's retreat, presumably to work on his fiction. Howard Junker, "Will This Finally Be Philip Roth's Year?," *New York Magazine* (January 13, 1969), 46. Appropriately, if you read this article online and follow the long line of ciphers in the website page address to the very end, you arrive at Philip%20Roth%20and%20Jerry%20Lewis&f=false.

from the doctor, anyone...." So the doctor naturally should get paid. So, I satirized it...I said, so they sent the doctor bill and it brought so much heat on the AMA...that all the doctors got together, and the doctor kept saying, "I want my money." So, they got the kid out of the well, and the report came from Patchogue, [Long Island,] New York, that the child is out of the well. The doctor bill will not have to be paid. Of course, the child will have to be returned to the well.[45]

So, this is how I feel about psychiatry. Only you keep paying *and* you keep getting returned to the well without ever achieving wellness. Only an imbecile, like the fake "Philip Roth" in *Operation Shylock*, adopts the identity of his obsession and names it his cure.

Odd Friend Out

Boychick in "the Unlocatable Room" of Harold Pinter's play, *Old Times* (1971), fraught with time's immanence minus a temporal fix, full of him-selves—the x, y, and z axes called "Kate," "Anna," and "Deeley." The play's manifest insistence on spatial and gestural specificity—a crossed leg, a semi-absent focus, a sofa's half-shell embrace of a body making a physical impression—pokes his immanence repeatedly in the figu-ral camera "I." The self is here always camera-ready and in that sense reproduced and inauthentic, but only if we map the space as we would a room and not as something else that is not *someplace* else. Perhaps it's a picture, shedding planes like skin cells in my father's silkscreen shop, caught between "the painter's analytic" and my own character('s) "abstraction."[46] Hearing loss like mine, augmented perhaps, by chemo-therapy, effects scenic im/balance and so I find myself even more given to in-between readings of spaces as texts than before, although as/like a character in Pinter's play I don't really know what or when "before" is/was. In dispute in this play is "the anthrochron of friendship" (an image-coinage McElroy borrows from timekeeping), which catches me

[45] *Playboy* magazine founder Hugh Hefner, with his ever-present pipe-in-mouth and creepily avuncular manner plays the role of undiscerning psychiatrist/audience for Lenny's improvisational session-player monologue. "Lenny Bruce's Playhouse Penthouse 1959." https://www.youtube.com/watch?v=dh09K-4R69I.

[46] McElroy, *Lookout Cartridge*, 142, 144, 145, and 147.

in its reflected light.[47] My *Old Times* overhears McElroy's apparent mondegreen of paraphrase as "paraphase," with the latter not merely resay-
ing (saying differently as "paraphrase" itself does) but resetting meaning.
In a sentence that could have been spoken in the play, a McElroy character says: "For thus these spaces could have been around us throughout this night of time that seemed urgent one way when I came in your
unlocked door but now spreads like an inestimably charged field ever,
yet, within the coordinates of this room, to a mode like time, but solute—a paraphase."[48] The characters' (mostly Deeley and Anna's) contestation of words, people, and events as though they were song-lyric
memories ("Seems Like Old Times") speak to this. The fact that Deeley
cannot or will not get Kate to admit to the fact that Anna is her "best
friend" speaks to me in the role of an anxious Deeley and of Kate as his
inexpressible desire. The play can likewise be cast with "*my* best friend"
in Kate's role and Deeley asking his question on behalf of a friend (me)
as one sometimes does when first talking in transparent disguise to a
psychiatrist or to a reader. But perhaps "I" am miscast as Deeley or as
Deeley alone and am rather Kate's mind obsessively interrogating itself
(Goldberg and his interrogative subject Stanley provided the template
for this in Pinter's 1957 play, *The Birthday Party*, no less than a critique
of Judeo-Christian civilization):

> *Deeley*: Did you think of her as your friend?
> *Kate*: She was my only friend.
> *Deely*: Your best and only.
> *Kate*: My one and only.
> *Pause.*
> If you have only one of something you can't say it's the best of anything.
> *Deeley*: Because you have nothing to compare it with?
> *Kate*: Mmmmmm.
> *Pause.*
> *Deeley*: (Smiling) She was incomparable.
> *Kate*: Oh, I'm sure she wasn't.
> *Pause.*
> *Deeley*: I didn't know you had so few friends.

---

[47] McElroy, *Ancient History*, 203.
[48] Ibid., 236–37.

Kate: I had none. None at all. Except her.
Deeley: Why her?
Kate: I don't know.
Pause.

And yet there is evidence that "I" could be Anna inviting herself to rekindle a friendship with Kate, who tells Deeley, "I hardly remember her. I've almost totally forgotten her." And yet it is Deeley who asks Kate in the role of "*my* best friend" the pertinent and prescient question: "Why isn't she married? I mean, why isn't she bringing her husband?" This is the reason why "Anna" did not remember *me* in the first place.

To make some impression (i.e., to appear), Deeley tells Anna about a film he made in Sicily that he wrote and directed, adding for good measure, "my name is Orson Welles."[49] The real Welles's six-year sojourn in Italy was punctuated by his accepting acting jobs like Cesare Borgia in *Prince of* Foxes (dir. Henry King, 1949, released the same year as Carol Reed's *Odd Man Out*, Pinter's rough template for *Old Times*) to help finance completion of his own film *Othello* (1951). In the latter, of course, a man and a woman contend for the affections of the eponymous *male* with predictably tragic results that do not necessarily speak to the gender fluidity this recasting makes permissible. At almost the same time, Welles played Harry Lime in Carol Reed's *The Third Man* (1949) and a Mongol warrior in *The Black Rose* (1950) likewise for the money, also "borrowing" wardrobe from each film to use in his own. By appropriating the name "Orson Welles," Deeley is paraphrasing himself, possibly as negative, in a figuratively immersive developing solution, as a multiplicity of selves as roles acted to make the actor whole, creatively and mostly, financially, Deeley tells Kate that when he first met Anna, "She was pretending to be you at the time...She thought she was you...Maybe she was you. Maybe it was you, having coffee with me." Pulling back his camera "I" from "she was you" to "it was you...with me" opens up the scene to make it viewable to someone else, someone *other than* him—other than his "best friend," other than "I" in the cruelty of the moment, silent and still. The three of them, the two of them, the one of them in a tableau, sitting and lying on furniture, which is not necessarily just to say lying down.

Marlon Brando's self-made Western *One-Eyed Jacks* (1961) opens with his outlaw character Rio eating a banana while waiting for his

[49] Pinter, *Old Times*, 8, 9, 10, and 28.

partner Dad Longworth to empty a bank safe. Rio tosses one banana peel each onto the two-sided scale set before him, proleptically recalling Nietzsche's saying, "Sometimes in our relationship to another person, the right balance of friendship is restored when we put a few grains of injustice on our own side of the scale."[50] Being pursued by the Mexican Federales following a bank heist and trapped with just one tired horse between them, Dad and Rio (whom he calls "Kid" to his "Dad" deepening the film's abandonment and betrayal theme), decide that one of them will ride off in search of two fresh mounts while the other will stay and attempt to hold off their pursuers. After Rio fixes it so that Dad gets to go for help, Dad cheats Rio by riding off with the two horses and the bank's gold, leaving Rio to be captured. Rio is sent to prison in Sonora but escapes five years later and locates Dad, who is now a sheriff and family man (as his name predicted) having run as far as the land could take him, to Monterey by the Sea.

Rio assures Dad he bears him no grudge. The one-time prisoner, now free of all delusion, declaims like Nietzsche's free spirit in *Beyond Good and Evil* (1886), "Enemies, there is no enemy!" as if either he or Dad believed it.[51] Dad views this rhetorical avowal for what it is, the Kid's repayment of a debt or deficit in friendship—the withholding of truth in the appearance of trust. Dad applies his bullwhip, aggressively, even hyperbolically to the Kid's bare back, not only assaulting but insulting his flesh, mortifying it as a trope of embarrassed friendship, a tainted subject that is to be sent packing. "You're a one-eyed jack around here, Dad. I've seen the other side of your face," Rio tells him through the bars of the jail cell where he waits to be hung for a bank robbery he did not commit. When Rio asks whether he is going to get a trial, Dad answers, "You'll get a fair trial, and then I'm gonna hang you, personally." Dad breaks Rio's right hand with a gun butt for good measure turning the Kid into a memento mori of Billy the Kid, who Method actor (after Brando) Paul Newman played earlier in Arthur Penn's Western psychodrama *The Left-Handed Gun* (1958). In that film, Billy the Kid breaks his promise to his one-time friend-now-sheriff Pat Garrett by shooting and killing a man at Garrett's wedding celebration to avenge

[50] Friedrich Nietzsche, *Human All Too Human: A Book for Free Spirits*, trans. Marion Faber and Stephen Lehmann (Lincoln: University of Nebraska Press, 1996), §305 and 177.

[51] Friedrich Nietzsche, "Beyond Good and Evil," in Walter Kaufmann, ed. and trans., *Basic Writings of Nietzsche* (New York: Modern Library, 2000), §376 and 194.

a long-standing grievance. This precipitates Garrett's decision to pursue and eventually kill Bill. In *One-Eyed Jacks*, Rio's murder of a man at Dad's wedding (do all kids, even in their dreams, secretly hate seeing their dads getting married to someone other than their mothers?) is meant to precipitate the showdown that Dad's original betrayal set in motion five years before. Actor Slim Pickens plays the sadistic sheriff's deputy Lon Dedrick who terrorizes Rio with a double-barreled shotgun in hand, a role he essentially reprises in Sam Peckinpah's *Pat Garrett and Billy the Kid* (1973). Peckinpah was hired to do rewrites on *One-Eyed Jacks*. Katy Jurado also appeared in both Brando's and Peckinpah's films. The severing of friendship in these intersecting actor scenarios enacts an interesting compulsion to repeat.

And this, minus the inevitable shoot-out and Dad's subsequent death, returns us to the scale upon which is balanced friendship and the "few grains of injustice" that tips it toward our "best friend's" narrative, in which the Kid, here not named Oedipus files his adult version of a childhood complaint. He has historically conceived this imbalance as being chemical, a mental disturbance precipitated and perpetuated by his sense of having been treated unjustly not solely by friends but by relationship in general. This potent traumatic cocktail of being watched over and yet overlooked is characteristic of many grown-up children who have beaten the plowshares of youth into the weapons of neurotic adult self-determination, the rhetoric of writing the self as a concealing yet visible one-eyed jack. Perhaps it is this failure to forge relationships in my formative years that has enabled me to make up my own rules and relationships between seemingly random, unallied ideas and things, to extract and erase causality from cause, and so to make trauma repeat as pattern and form. In this way too have I adapted Nietzsche's example of the man whose talent for friendship is expressed in his "find[ing] an exactly appropriate friend for each phase of his development" ("David," "David," "David"). I have reinvented this "talent" as the phased process of writing to different topics, partnering with the proper subject to help me develop my idea of relationship in mental mise-en-scènes that (perhaps) obviates the need for "real" friendship. The self-lacerating nature of this writing in its various forms of relationship, however, suggests otherwise, writing being acknowledged as the thing that keeps you from seeking out friends except as the cause and causality of writing on the self-chosen subject. Jerry Lewis's self-authoring of Dean Martin as "big brother"/"best friend" to his childhood abandonment neurosis shouts like mad Nietzsche in the wake of so much fraternal cruelty, "Enemies, there is no enemy!" where the friends had been, shouts this like the part Jerry by his own will and finally under his own direction played, that of the infantilized idiot, Nietzsche's "living fool" who I claim here, contra Nietzsche, to be an *un*free spirit.[52] Self-delusion is never really reality's benefactor when it is made visible as hyperbolic performance. One is not, after all, *compulsively* free.[53] And Nietzsche, as we know, could not, would not sit a horse.

---

[52] Ibid., §376 and 194.

[53] Bob Dylan's title song to Peckinpah's *Pat Garrett and Billy the Kid* contains the refrain, "Billy, they don't like you to be so free." Dylan (a.k.a. Zimmerman) appeared in the film as a character called "Alias." Soundtrack album to the film (Columbia, 1973).

CHAPTER 7

Dog Anabasis

In his essay, "The Name of a Dog, or Natural Rights," Emmanuel Levinas relates an anecdote concerning his internment in a German prisoner of war camp:

> And then, about halfway through our long captivity, for a few short weeks, before the sentinels chased him away, a wandering dog entered our lives. One day he came to meet this rabble as we returned under guard from work. He survived in some wild patch in the region of the camp. But we called him Bobby, an exotic name, as one does with a cherished dog. He would appear at morning assembly and was waiting for us as we returned, jumping up and down and barking in delight. For him, there was no doubt that we were men.

Hitler famously said, "The Jews are undoubtedly a race, but they are not human."[1] The Jews have a long history of wrestling with matters of racial difference (of being white but also not-white), which has at times been folded into the ameliorating concept of ethnicity.[2] In Quentin Tarantino's *Inglourious Basterds* (2009), Nazi Colonel Hans Landa

---

[1] Emmanuel Levinas, "The Name of a Dog, or Natural Rights," in *Difficult Freedom: Essays on Judaism*, trans. Sean Hand (Baltimore: The Johns Hopkins University Press/The Athone Press, 1990), 153; Hitler is quoted in the epigraph to Art Spiegelman, *Maus, Part I "My Father Bleeds History"* (New York: Pantheon, 1986), 10.

[2] See, for example, Eric L. Goldstein, *The Price of Whiteness: Jews, Race, and American Identity* (Princeton: Princeton University Press, 2006), 165–66.

© The Author(s) 2019

S. Golub, *A Philosophical Autofiction*, Performance Philosophy,
https://doi.org/10.1007/978-3-030-05612-4_7

echoes Hitler and Goebbels's comparison of Jews to rats but says that unlike his masters he does not "consider the comparison an insult," owing to the Jews'/rats' capacity for hiding, for self-concealment. This is a talent conditioned by duress that results, Landa says, in abandonment of dignity. Levinas and his fellow Jewish inmates' naming the stray dog "Bobby" humanizes the dog they felt re-humanized them. The wandering dog returns like the spirit of the wandering Jew and as such is not an "it" but a familiar, a landsman. Meanwhile back in the secret annex, Anne Frank and company are watching *Rin Tin Tin Saves the Day*, a precursor of the popular television show of my youth (*The Adventures of Rin Tin Tin*, 1954–1959).[3] It didn't seem to me that any of the people being saved by the heroic German Shepherd were, like me, a Jew. But I was raised in my religion to be wary of saviors in any case, as was Anne Frank.

It was while belatedly reading Bruce Jay Friedman's 1962 novel *Stern* that I recognized and was able to admit to what I had long been rehearsing, a Jewishness whose affective faith was defined in the form of physical and nervous complaint. "My Favorite Complaints" is the Jewish riposte to Rodgers and Hammerstein's "My Favorite Things," the latter sung by a novice nun to the innocent Aryan children in her care at the onset of the German occupation of Austria and of my childhood preoccupations. The lyric "When the dog bites/When the bee stings" is augmented by me with "When the ulcer, the tumor, and the death terrors fill the void left by an uncertain faith." The dog biting is, however, left intact. The Von Trapp family lives in leafy mountain's majesty. Stern mentally lives where "I" do, growing some "black and mottled trees [he] call[s] his Cancer Garden," a metaphor rooted more deeply than at first expected. Another Rodgers (née Abrahams) and Hammerstein (a "third," although his father was born Jewish) Christian heroine, the English governess Anna in *The King and I*, instructs her charges, "Whenever I feel afraid/I hold myself erect/And whistle a happy tune/So no one will suspect I'm afraid" in counterpoint to a fearful comorbidity that is my birthright and cultural commonplace of sympathetic, generational Jewish angst, fear, and pain. Stern's Jewish college roommate twisted popular

---

[3] The screening of a scene from *Rin Tin Tin Saves the Day* appears in the remake of *The Diary of Anne Frank* (dir. Jon Jones, 2009). This particular title refers to one of the serials shown during World War II that may or may not have been released under this name.

song lyrics "to get Jews into them."[4] Jews named "Ulcerstein" and "Tumorberg," "I" presume.

"When the dog bites." Stern's walking home route from the train station put him in direct contact with "the giant gray dogs *[that] took his wrist in their mouths*" [my italics]. My solo walking route to and from synagogue on the Jewish High Holy Days of Rosh Hashanah and Yom Kippur to expiate my family's suburban survivors' guilt (my parents drove themselves to shul later in the day) was marked by a paralyzing fear of and ardent watchfulness for the dogs who were variants of my neighborhood German Shepherd Sabre who once took *my* wrist in *his* mouth, as "I" recall, despite not leaving a mark, except, that is, on my psyche: the indeterminate memory of a Spalding pink rubber ball leaving my hand, a playmate's shouted warning, the attack dog charging at me. At the start of his first performed monologue, *Sex and Death to the Age of 14* (1979) at The Performing Garage in New York City, Spalding Gray tells the story of being bitten by his dog "Jill." He says that she took a chunk out of his arm, "it felt like a bite out of an apple" although he acknowledges it couldn't have been that bad because it left no mark.[5] In this early monologue, Spalding was not yet confident that his memory would translate directly into performance without some paper trail, some walking route to follow. I have become a student not so much of dogs as of my fear of dogs, a lifelong lookout for the great unleashed, where they are and when. I have become in this regard as dogged as the mailman the dog so readily and reflexively attacks, taking personally as it does the letter carrier's vainglorious claim of superior doggedness. ("Neither snow nor rain nor heat nor gloom of night stays these couriers from the swift completion of their appointed rounds.") "I" am as much like Stern as "I" am his daughter who when asked to say what the neighborhood anti-Semite (the so-called kike man) did to her says she doesn't remember, that maybe he didn't do anything at all. "But he saw me." It is *the scene* of watching yourself being watched, of self-picturing fear that denotes the pain of experience as being "actual." "I" was always making scenes, so "I" know, in the thea*t*er of Sab*r*e, the manifestly unyielding there/not there.

[4] Richard Rodgers and Oscar Hammerstein III's, "My Favorite Things" from *The Sound of Music* (1959) and "I Whistle a Happy Tune" from *The King and I* (1951); Bruce Jay Friedman, *Stern* (New York: Grove Press, 1962), 63.

[5] Gray, *Sex and Death to the Age of 14*.

Like so many postwar diasporic Jews, I grew up overwhelmed by the legacy of being overkilled in the Holocaust, the Shoah, and parental memory of it; also, by a feeling of belatedness, of being born too late to offer even token resistance. So, "I" became a dog soldier in the fight against the Nazis I grew up watching in the movies. In these films, as in recorded events, we are trapped or else imprisoned, gassed, flooded, burned out, and shot-dropped into mass graves. We escape into forests and fields, only to find that even outside there is no way out. We are outmanned, outgunned. (Leading to the appeal of *The Lone Ranger* and other Westerns, at least for this Jewish boy.) We are betrayed by our friends and neighbors, by the man or woman who sells us our food. We are on lists and subject to absurd and humiliating rules and requirements that single us out as a race. We are made to wear our Jewishness on our sleeves and on our actual coats. We are dragged from our houses and apartments, robbed of our possessions, our professions, our family, our dignity, our history, our voice. "I" never get to shoot, blow up, or otherwise kill Hitler, Heydrich, or Himmler. Someone or something always comes between me and the targets and they escape into the next movie. Sometimes the gun jams, sometimes there are betrayals or a simple change of plans, a car, bus, tram, even a pedestrian cuts off my route, or there's an armed escort, or another movie recorded over the one in which "I" take the shot. "This one's for my father!" "I" shout, while remembering my father cheering on the televised movie "kills" in the upstairs bedroom of my childhood home. But I am shooting at ghosts. The report from my weapon is a generation late. How can I account for this gap and how does this gap elide with my lapse from Jewishness? "There is less neurosis in observing then there is in lapsing," Shylock tells Strulovitch in Howard Jacobson's novel *Shylock Is My Name*. "You have as many things to remember not to do [as the observant Jew performs]. As many festivals to miss, as many mitzvahs to forget, as many obligations to turn aside from."[6] How can I be tested in the afterlife of history's making? How do I exhale memory? Why would I forget those set-jawed faces barking orders at me like so many vicious dogs? I am conditioned to resist, and yet the means and modes of my resistance, along with the timing of the assaults, surprise me, take over my mind, as if my father is still speaking *his* mind through *me*. "I" chase Mengele across

[6]Jacobson, *Shylock Is My Name*, 90.

fictive hemispheres with my co-writer (one of the David's), ripping off one after another of the Nazi doctor's disguises and displacing his name onto common objects to disperse the phantasmic power of the original's charismatic authority over me. Ira Levin read my mind when he turned Mengele's beloved German Shepherds on him in *The Boys from Brazil*, like my neighbor's Doberman Pinscher turned on him after many years of loyal service, as if it had seen the same movie(s) I did.[7]

Donna Haraway has commented on the popularity of dog origin stories, with humans likewise being invested in "evaluating the decadence or progressiveness of breeds, judging whether dog behavior is the stuff of genes or rearing." At the heart of some of this interest is the question of "who and what counts as an actor" and perhaps how they become or became one. Do dogs (only) play dog parts and are these parts preordained not solely by biology but also by "the neurosis of caninophiliac narcissism" that makes them meet our demands for kinship (friendship, unconditional love) but also mastery? I am a practicing caninophiliac narcissist but with a difference. I look to discover the seeds not only of kinship between myself and one particular breed of dog but rather of dissociation, fear, even hostility. Of course, even though the dog may not like me, he must still *be* somewhat like me for this negative argument to work according to my anthropomorphic desire. We ask of those that do not directly reinforce us with their verbal language (my deaf grandfather, our Hebrew God), what (or who else) could they be thinking (of)? With Haraway's call for dog-human or human-dog coevolutionary origin stories in mind, I note after her, that "we [dog and man] both inherit their consequences in our flesh."[8] Each of us has external markings and is also internally marked. Had my mother not been so afraid of dogs (and cats, even before Art Spiegelman turned them into Nazis in the graphic novel *Maus*, 1980–1991), she would have marked for me my first encounter with a dog, no matter how afraid I was initially, as not needing to have a fearful consequence. Instead, it became traumatic.

---

[7] My vivid recollection of this scene is from the film version of *The Boys from Brazil* (dir. Franklin J. Schaffner, 1978; adapted by Heywood Gould from Levin's 1976 novel). This story does for Hitler what David and I did with Mengele. But whereas Levin widely distributes his DNA among Hitler's "boys," we release Mengele's DNA into both the animate and inanimate world.

[8] Donna Haraway, *The Companion Species Manifesto: Dogs, People, and Significant Otherness* (Chicago: Prickly Paradigm Press, 2003), 2, 26, 27, and 33.

Might the same thing have happened to Sabre with *his* mother or with a previous owner? I knew another German Shepherd that somewhere in his past must have been beaten with something leather resulting in its hiding whenever his current master produced his leather satchel to take on a trip. Maybe Sabre attacked me not just because he was raised to protect his owner (a small blonde girl in a stroller on a driveway) but also because his experience demanded of him that he translates his fear into aggression. Was Sabre's mother as anxious as mine? Did Sabre, raised to be sensitive, even helpful to disability as his breed sometimes is, attack in me whatever weakness or imperfection he felt but could not express in himself? As a father impatient with a child who shares my psychological disorder, this is something I might understand. And this understanding is in part what makes me something of a stranger to companionship with those who may be of the same ilk. I learned this involuntarily from *my* father, who became an American at an early age and was impatient with his unassimilated family who did not. Historically, German Shepherds track, search for the missing, not merely those who are lost but for those who choose to stay hidden, who fear being found, of trusting in another, who are terrorized by the mere fact of knowing (or assuming) that this particular breed of dog is on the job. The thought of being followed and found out dogged my relatives to their deaths and continues to live in me in the form of obsessively unwelcomed thoughts. They are my mental otherness's hyper-vigilant weaponized companion.

Of me it has been said (passing as Jacobson's fictional Strulovitch), "Being a Jew was everything to him, except when it wasn't. Which is a debilitating characteristic of the Jewish mind, unless it is a strength." I am David Mamet's "wicked son" at the Passover Seder, situated apart from the ceremony, asking rhetorically, "What does this ritual mean to [*me*]?"[9] I am Mamet's Bobby Gold barking at a paralyzed young policeman at the scene of a Jewish woman's murder in *Homicide* to shoot the dog that is nominally protecting her. "Jews guarded by dogs? Historically, very, very wrong," Philip Roth says.[10] I resist the idea that Jews indulge in paranoid fantasies of being followed and persecuted, the ghost of which Mamet invokes in order to attack as being anti-Semitic.

[9] Jacobson, *Shylock Is My Name*, 225; Mamet, *The Wicked Son*, x and 5–6.
[10] Roth, *Sabbath's Theater*, 363.

Neurosis is not a fable, although it is not unrelated to the tales told to us by our parents and grandparents, the media, and the stories we tell ourselves in our own name and in the many pen names we assume.

Like the old woman in *Homicide*, the old man at the heart of *Remember* (dir. Atom Egoyan, 2015) is wearing a Star of David. Of *David*, the Jewish king. His shield. His protection. We see it hanging from around the neck of Zev Guttman while he is lying in a bath and looking up at the steam from a shower head he will not use. A Jewish survivor of Auschwitz, he cannot separate showers from the screaming voices that haunt his memory. In a sort of ritualized cleansing or perhaps an act of appropriation, Zev later showers perfunctorily with his clothes on in the house owned by the neo-Nazi he just killed after first killing the man's German Shepherd who was ordered to attack him. The dead man's State Trooper's star worn upon his uniform shirt served as a perverse testament to the memory of his German-born father's enthusiastic participation in the chaos of *Kristallnacht*, in which he hammer-smashed the windows of Jewish shopkeepers. Zev was looking for the man's father whom he believed murdered his family at Auschwitz along with the family of fellow octogenarian Max Rosenbaum who sent him on this mission. Zev Guttman has dementia. Each time he awakens from sleep he calls out for his recently deceased wife Ruth and forgets where he is and where he is going. (His dementia likewise calling out for my similarly addled aunt Ruth who believed someone was stealing the dresses she hung in her shower, perhaps because *she never used it*.) Zev has to write reminders on his skin that unconsciously mimic prison camp numbers tattooed on his forearm. Barking dogs, steaming, streaming showerheads, and railway platform loudspeakers remind Zev of the camp and seemingly provide him with the muscle memory necessary to shoot quickly and accurately when he has to—the German Shepherd; the dog's owner whose dead father Zev erroneously thought was his original target; the thought-to-be-final option for the original target; and finally, himself, upon remembering that *he*, "*Zev*" ("Wolf" in Hebrew) and the man he has been sent to hunt were *both* murderous SS guards whose tattooed camp numbers stolen from executed Jewish prisoners allowed them to pass through the gates of Auschwitz during the Allied liberation. (The small scar visible under Zev's left arm in his bath scene being where his SS member blood type would have been tattooed, allowing for another kind of identification that was overlooked after the war.[11]) In his short story "Reunion," Nathan Englander shows how this theme of appropriation can be spun by Jewish humor in another way. Two Holocaust survivors living in the same US retirement community are shown to have camp arm tattoos separated by a mere three numbers. This amazes the men's children more than it does the two old men. "So I say to my dad, 'He's right ahead of you... 'Look, a five,' I say. 'And yours' is an eight.' And the other guy looks at my father and says, 'All that means is, he cut ahead of me in line. There, same as here. This guy's a cutter. I just didn't want to say. Blow it out your ear,' the other guy says. And that's it. Then they get back to putting on socks." Being of the children's generation I acknowledge that I may be sustaining an obsession that more properly belongs to my predecessors, who have chosen not to be as obsessed as I am, not as obsessed with "I" am.

The sound of dogs barking punctuates the death, suffering, and humiliation in the Warsaw (Jewish) ghetto depicted in *The Pianist* (dir. Roman Polanski, 2002). All the dogs are on the non-Jewish Polish side of the wall that cordons off the captive population. The starving Jews, it seems, have no dogs. If they did, they would boil them and eat them like the Indians being slaughtered by the cavalry in *Little Big Man* did. The morning after Dustin Hoffman's white man Jack Crabb awakened in the Cheyenne Indian camp in *Little Big Man*, he was accosted by a mongrel dog the size of a dachshund, or that's what the shadow of genocide that wafts across Arthur Penn's 1970 Viet Nam-era film made me think. That and the apparent monstrosity of Jack being served this same dog boiled as the next day's breakfast. The latter was tainted by thoughts of genocide as well. Jack does not differentiate between Jesus and Moses, at the start, reflecting an in-between-ness encoded in the film's Jewish fish-out-of-water subtext. Much is also made of Jack's short stature, as if to say that he is somehow not up to the task, whatever that task might be. I was shortsighted back then, like (Hoffman as) Jack, not wanting to discuss genocide and other matters of Jewish identity that were force-fed me by my father across the dinner table and in books with titles like *Forged in Fury* (wr. Michael Elkins, 1971) that he placed inside my desk drawer for me to discover. I read the Jewish-American-lite novels of Leon Uris (*Exodus*, [1958]; *Mila 18* [1962]), heroic narratives whose politics, even having just finished college, I was expected to embrace still

[11] Englander, "Reunion," in *What We Talk About When We Talk About Anne Frank*, 12. *Remember.* http://www.imdb.com/title/tt3704050/trivia?ref_=tt_trv_trv.

without yet fully understanding what they meant. As with the small dog that was not actually a German breed, I learned early on to see what was there but also what wasn't there as equally disturbing.

Do the dogs fear that I might eat them and so attack me first, the idea of "dog eat dog" being the behavioral code of the animal world and of humans who (are made to) behave like animals? Does the dog attack me because it thinks I won't fight back, that I don't know how to fight back, that I would not fight to save my life (Mamet's)? This is what was said about my ancestors. "Well, off they go to the melting pot," a Nazi officer observes as the Warsaw Ghetto Jews are loaded like cattle on to the train bound for the camps. The melting pot, what we call America, the term that came to signify productive assimilation, used as a sign off for those who would only assimilate to death because the body politic would not absorb them. The pianist hides beneath the platform upon which he once played. Hiding beneath the platform of one's own performance to forestall death. Neurosis is the generational abstraction of this paradox, still no real defense against anything. In *The Painted Bird* (1965), had Jerzy Kosinski imagined a stray dog journey for himself like Wladyslaw ("Wladek") Szpilman's, the eponymous pianist? Had adult neurosis imposed itself on the past creating fictional childhood trauma? Can you take food from the mouths of those who have really suffered? Can you play someone else's ghostly music, hands miming at some distance above the keyboard, as your own?

Jewish characters in both *To Be or Not to Be* (dir. Ernst Lubitsch, 1942) and *The Pianist* recite Shylock's famous, "Hath not a Jew eyes" speech, a plea for and to common humanity. But whereas *The Pianist* is intentionally orthodox, *To Be or Not to Be* makes the speech into one part actor self-realization and two parts delay-and-distract tactic so that Jews may escape under German noses, masked as harmless comedians— comedy again appealing to a hardwired universality. I used to pass an English professor on the campus where I also taught who always hailed me with the merchants' recurrent greeting from Shakespeare's *Merchant of Venice*, "What news on the Rialto?" but whether this was meant as a call to a fellow professor, a theater practitioner, or as a fellow Jew, I do not know. I think, maybe, it was some kind of test, not a calling to but a calling out, a way of saying I am imbued with what you only pretend to know or else *should* know. As both a presumably text deficient theater professor and a Jew, I read his greeting as a possibly unwitting or at least deniable indictment and not, as it might have been, his effort to prove himself to be at least textually worthy of *my* theatrical expertise.

Guilt, shame, and the precariousness of life, the last of which arrives 67 pages into Paul Auster's 2013 memoir *Report from the Interior* in the form of a neighbor's cancer (a single case whose gravity immediately vaulted over that of the contemporaneous polio epidemic) and his own realization that he was himself a Jew.[12] I knew of cancer earlier in my own narrative owing to "my best friend"'s mother's fatal bout and my paternal grandfather's ongoing pain whose source I would much later find out only betrayed its hiddenness physically. I grew up not in the "watered-down brand of Judaism" practiced by Auster's Reform congregation but in Conservative Judaism, which valued the language and look of authenticity ("conserving" rather than "reforming")—old men davening (bowing from and halfway down to the waist) in their black hats and tallises (prayer shawls), while chanting obscurely. Conservatism argues with but submits to many Orthodox Jewish teachings. It discomforts with ambivalence. Reformism accommodates by drifting into communalism. It does not so much comfort with faith, as it makes you (and a much wider range of people) comfortable. The local Reform synagogue resembled a recreation center, complete with a swimming pool (we were told) on the roof. Our synagogue, my synagogue knew only discomfort. The air conditioners always ceased functioning for the high holy day religious services in the same way that the elevator in a New York City apartment building is inevitably out of order on the days you move in and out, causing personal stress while avoiding system overload.

My father remembers as a young boy marching behind Russian soldiers, singing their songs without regard for lyric content, recalling from rote, as they did their anti-Semitic ways following the defeat of the Nazis in World War II. They were creatures of habit and conditioning like the black German Shepherd that attacks a Jewish woman in the inspiring Belarusian muscle Jews-in-the-forest film *Defiance* (dir. Edward Zwick, 2008), as if it has been waiting for her for generations. The dog wants the food in her bag, but her body will do if the former does not suffice. There is a fearful continuity at work in its most savage form, and another no less palpable continuity in the weight of historical authoritarianism. I am still living figuratively and yet concretely in my father's

---

[12] Paul Auster, *Report from the Interior* (New York: Henry Holt, 2013).

house, wrapped up like old King Saul, whose "long unsought role in life...itself comes to resemble if not a disguise then an unwanted garment that has grown into his flesh, mastering him, impossible to remove as the tormenting shirt of Greek myth."[13] "What do you want me to continue?" I ask like Jacobson's on-again, off-again "Jewishly" protagonist Strulovitch's estranged daughter Jessica of him. "The thing you were born to be," he responds. She: "Jewish?" He: "Continuous." Taken as a piece, the question and answer reads less like dialogue than a religious recitation, something like a secular Jewish catechism.

I want to say that this no longer torments me as it did Saul to the end, when David replaced him as king of the Jews. But "I" would not be writing this book, if it did not. My Jewishness was not originally my theme, but it insinuated itself into my thinking once my memory gained momentum. My going back means fighting back against the passivity of non-encumbrance by memory, and it has arrived when so much else has been forgotten. These fears that had been allowed to grow and fester without resistance to foster unwanted growths—cancers, neuroses, obsessions, compulsions, fear—have been my crude, symbolic offerings for deliverance in kind, like the golden tumors the literal-minded Philistines offered the Hebrew God to deliver them from the Bubonic plague.[14] I have now beaten symbol into metaphor, like swords into plowshares (Isaiah 2:4) in order to take back history and make it my own fiction. So much of what I now recall or think I do that left an impression, began a pattern, transpired at a very young age, roughly up to age nine or ten. My father was roughly nine when he left Belorussia and yet remembered almost nothing about it, or perhaps had been schooled in not speaking of it like his brother and especially his two sisters clearly were by their parents in a vain attempt to bury family trauma. What did my father learn in his first several years of school in the Russian language he was made to learn, the Hebrew read in temple and the Yiddish spoken at home? What was it like not to have been given a middle name at birth and different first and last names thereafter? When he remembered things about the past, did his parents tell him, "It's only your imagination" not so much to allay his fears as their own? Strulovitch, who finds kinship with Shakespeare's "infuriated and tempestuous"

[13] Robert Pinsky, *The Life of David* (New York: Schocken Books, 2005), 44.
[14] Ibid., 50; Jacobson, *Shylock Is My Name*, 185.

mental muscle Jew Shylock (whom he meets at a cemetery where both men are visiting their wives' graves), believes he understands "why [the Jewish imagination] sets no limits on chronology or topography, why it cannot even trust the past to the past, and why his mother probably did see Hitler," as she claimed, buying aftershave in the local department store. *Defiance*'s fighting Bielski brothers and the many they saved from the Nazis and near-death experience of hiding in the forests of Belorussia told their story to their grandchildren when they asked. But not my family. They wished to belong to (but were nominally excluded from) the "family association" of "*Shapiro, Shakespeare, Shylock*," all Jews, Strulovitch imagined, each name with "a *shush* in it."[15]

SABRE

Sunshine (dir. István Szabó, 1999) is a story about how guilt becomes a neurosis that struggles to work itself out over *generations*. The Hungarian Jewish protagonists' family name of Sonnenschein means "Sunshine." The overdubbed voice (of actor Ralph Fiennes) belongs to the great-grandson of the man who creates the family's origin story with his money-making recipe for "Sunshine tonic." "Sunshine" or "Sonnenschein," a name that is changed over generations of assimilation that colludes with the Austrian Empire, Hungarian and Soviet communism and the attendant morals, inter(personal) histories, titles, faiths, and traditions that must be concealed. The great-grandmother puts a curse on the family after her son Ignatz (Ralph Fiennes) and her "sister" Valerie (actually a first cousin taken in by his family) marry and have children. Ignatz's father Emmanuel had warned him that only God wants. We can only wish. When ambitious Ignatz (a judge, a dispenser of justice, a Jew's highest calling) seeking a promotion that requires him not to seem Jewish informs his father that he wishes to change the family name to the more Hungarian-sounding "Sors" (meaning "prophecy," "destiny"), Emmanuel remarks: "Well, names are not given to us by God." But when Ignatz says he wants to assimilate, his brother Gustave (who will later become the family's first communist) tells him society will never let him do this, a sentiment that their father essentially reinforces in cautioning him not to climb too high, to know who you are.

---

[15] Jacobson, *Shylock Is My Name*, 3, 5, and 8.

Hitler's rise to power and Hungary's collusion with fascism bear this out in their sanctions against and quotas enforced on the nation's Jews according to their specific definition of the factors that, they say, make a Jew a Jew.

The iterations of Jewish self-denial, the cleaving to the illusion that origin stories can be forgotten or else finessed by dress, manner, position, celebrity, name-change are finally destroyed at Auschwitz where Ivan, the great-grandson narrating the tale, watches while *his* father Adam, the gold medal fencer for the Hungarian national team at Hitler's 1934 Berlin Olympics, is literally frozen to death by Nazi guards for refusing to admit that he is Jewish. For his part, Ivan, who converted to Roman Catholicism to advance his fencing career before the war, does not admit during Adam's torture and death to being his father's son. No German Shepherds are shown in the Auschwitz scenes, but Adam's weapon of choice throughout his fencing career was the *saber*. Future SS-Obergruppenführer and architect of Hitler's "Final Solution" Reinhard Heydrich competed with a saber in fencing tournaments as a young Kriegsmarine officer, the saber being "the most brutal of weapons…Unlike the foil, which touches only with the point, the saber [variant spelling] cuts and thrusts with its sharp edge, and its blows, like lashes from a whip, are infinitely more violent." In recounting this, Laurent Binet speculates on who might have been Heydrich's opponent. "I imagine a left-hander," he writes, "quick, clever, dark-haired. Perhaps not Jewish—that would be bit much—but maybe a quarter Jewish. A fencer who's not easily impressed, who shies away from direct combat, who provokes his opponents with feints and parries." Someone like Adam Sors, née Sonnenschein. It was rumored that Heydrich was himself Jewish, that "his grandmother remarried a Jew," that his father's real last name was Süss.[16] Sors and Süss, Süss and Sors: thrust and parry, parry and thrust. Both men shadow fencing with the *shush*.

Following his liberation from the camp and the end of the war, in his capacity as a high-ranking policeman in the new communist government, Ivan Sors carries out the interrogation of his mentor Knorr. Knorr, a non-religious Jew, who survived Auschwitz but will not survive the new order, tells Ivan: "Even you will never be free of Auschwitz. Auschwitz was our baptism. But there is something you must know, though. Surviving Auschwitz doesn't make a man better or greater. It's just burnt

---

[16]Laurent Binet, *HHhH*, trans. Sam Taylor (New York: Picador, 2012), 20, 26, 27, 38, and 39.

into your brain! It can never be erased! That's the problem...We're children of an unfortunate race...Who's the traitor, you or me?" The talk here is not of politics but of morality and of breaking faith with yourself. With the deaths of Stalin and Knorr (great-grandfather Emmanuel's death was proximate to the Emperor's), Ivan seeks to make amends for his and his forbears' assimilation, self-denial and even self-protective anti-Semitism. Ivan, played by the voice-over's Ralph Fiennes, becomes a prominent voice for revolution and is incarcerated for three years. He discovers upon his release that his grandfather's pocket watch, gifted him by his father, has been lost (probably stolen). "I thought great-grandfather came and took it back from me," Ivan tells his grandmother, who at a loss asks her, "If there's no God and there never was a God, then why do we miss him so much?" What is it that we miss that matters? Not the Sunshine family recipe that only acts as a real tonic when it is allowed to slip away and the original Sunshine family name is reclaimed. And with this the family curse is lifted, the incestuous taint of intramarriage having morphed into the concrete metaphor of uroboric assimilation finally dispelled by Ivan's awareness that you may survive guilt, but you will not escape it. Guilt is itself a survival mechanism that is also a neurotic one. In this sense, the assimilationist surname Sors proved to be what it said it was, a prophecy, but a self-fulfilling one minus any personal fulfillment. For the first time, Ivan understands the framed quotation he found after the war on his father's desk: "We are afraid to see clearly and of being seen clearly...this is precisely what happened to us."

Ignatz tells his son, "Study has always been our religious duty as Jews. Our exclusion from society has given us an ability to adapt to others and to sense connections between things which seem diverse." Ivan applies to change his name officially from Sors back to Sonnenschein. "For the first time in my life," he says as himself, the narrator, "I walked down the street without feeling like I was in hiding. I knew the only way to find a meaning in my life, my only chance in life would be to account for it." I had some cousins on my father's side named "Sunshine" who I remember coming once to visit us at our house when I was young, although when I tell my mother this she has no recollection of it. My mother is now very old, but she did not remember them even years ago, despite my sister recalling that they were cousins *on my mother's side*. When my mother saw the film *Sunshine* years before I did, she did not make the connection between the Sonnenschein family and our own, *her* own Sunshines. I remember the first name of one of my missing Sunshine cousins (I don't know what their original surname was) as being Spencer. My sister, though, remembers that his name was Larry from Lawrence, my father's American name.

PILGRIM'S REGRESS

"It was," writes Kurt Vonnegut, in *Slaughterhouse-Five* (1969), "a flying saucer from Tralfamadore, navigating in both space and time, therefore seeming to Billy Pilgrim to have come from nowhere all at once. Somewhere a big dog barked."

"I" am something of a time-traveler, a dog soldier in someone's army sniffing for clues, barking up and down a stunted, branchless family tree, wagging my history behind me like a tale. "In case Billy dies, which he didn't, half of the [dog] tag would mark his body and half would mark his grave."[17] Billy Pilgrim is first seen wandering a blasted German war-scape like a stray, unidentified, treated by others of his species like a cur (no one's "Bobby," as in Levinas's memory). Never knowing who he is in the sense of knowing his place or what constitutes his pilgrim's progress. Dog anabasis. Not so difficult to identify with, especially given our slim purchase on personal identity compared to the hold it has upon us. Decades later, I'm staring at the mosque domes and minarets of Istanbul, thinking "I" might be on Vonnegut's planet Tralfamadore, raising an oversize teacup in a photograph not to my lips but to my nose, like a veil that covers all but my eyes, to hide or disguise myself. Now, standing stooped, highlighting the cracked spines of the books in my small corner of Borges's library in the Tower of Babel mere steps away from my desk chair, and sneezing away the degraded pages that age along with me. I don't know whether what I am missing is no longer necessary or just no longer accessible to me.

Terrence Malick's contemplative travelogues of this alien Earth (*The Tree of Life*, *To the Wonder*, *Knight of Cups*) are made for the hearing impaired such as I. Subtitles tell you when phones are ringing and birds and crickets are chirping (one assumes, differently), dogs are barking (*"Dog barking."*) and the wind is blowing. But perhaps I am, as always, analogizing to the human. Perhaps these talking pictures are made for dogs, for Tarkovsky's dog in *Stalker* (1979), for Godard's dog in *Goodbye*

---

[17] Kurt Vonnegut, *Slaughterhouse-Five* (New York: Dial Press, 2009; orig. pub. 1969), 95 and 116.

to Language (2014). Unheard sounds speaking of unexpressed, perhaps inexpressible feelings. (Window curtains ripple like fences dappled by light. These are *heard* as well.) The grass, made of bugs invisible to the naked eye, biting at your ankles as they do in the plains states, leaving marks where you walk and run and fear to sit. The skin is raised where it has been ruptured, irrupted, interrupted. The field of experience bites you. There is no passing through it without interruption. The dog is sleeping in the field, awakening to your approach. Biting you is just what it does. This is likewise part of your experience, even if all you have to show for it is the anticipatory fear of being bitten. Marina, who appears to be undone by experience in *To the Wonder* (2012) and forever dances away from the camera, is followed closely by a dog at film's end, leaving us not knowing whether or not it is her(s'). (*Birds chirping.*) "One day I'll put a raft of these interruptions together as if they were one life and the *rest* were interruption," a Joseph McElroy narrator reflects.[18] When that happens, all films will be made for dogs, or dogs for films.

The introductory overdubbed narration (spoken by actor Ben Kingsley) in Malick's *Knight of Cups* (2015) speaks of a pilgrim's progress (quoted from John Bunyan) and of a king forgetting who he is when he drinks from a cup. The protagonist Rick says, also in overdub: "All those years living the life of someone I didn't even know." We next see children at play and dogs playing among them. The subtitles tell you what is inaudible, what you're *not supposed* to hear. And it's clear from the mindless, drunkenly forgetful antics of Rick or Rick's image minus a self-image, that he cannot hear any of this either, not his own inner voice which is posthumous in relation to the life he has been living. The image of children playing with dogs playing with children tells you this. (All I need is one dog to serve as a tuning fork to signal the earthquake, the catastrophe.) A dog runs amid the ruptured water pipes and mains, as if signing its name to chaos: Chaos is when/where dogs run unleashed in mostly urban settings. (Tarkovsky could not set a film in Los Angeles because the rumbling disturbances of objects in space by earthquakes would overwhelm the spiritual, paranormal trembling of his objects in space that speak of other spaces and other objects of knowledge.) Dogs

---

[18] *To the Wonder* is set mainly in Bartlesville, Oklahoma, site of my brother-in-law's first marriage. The film tells of man played by Ben Affleck with his Batman's dark-valley-of-doubt and self-unforgiveness, who cannot decide which of two women to marry or stay married to. McElroy, *Ancient History*, 225.

dive for objects underwater. Balls and other toys, mimicking human figures. Underwater, dogs are, like these human figures, "(INAUDIBLE)" and so somehow equal. They paddle in place like running in their sleep when they dream. Humans now are bouncing these balls off the wall, awakening me to memory, as if I've broken the water's surface. A dog is rolling like a ball, side over side. "I think you were afraid of going astray," Rick's ex-wife Nancy tells him, and I hear "a stray," wondering why any seemingly random, stray dog keeps pressing up against (my) words, my worlds, wanting to speak and be heard. Not kept underwater but breaking the surface of language, forming a new language that Godard, Malick, Tarkovsky tell us needs some other name, a name that does not partake of language, a wordless, letter-less name, or something Kabbalistic wherein the letters have hidden meanings without naming the secret. "Dog," an inversion of letters that spoofs what meaning is. A nod to Wittgenstein on the limit-meaning of words, something the dog is made to understand, as far as understanding goes when you are made a certain way, in just one way that embodies and expresses limit. And yet even with this, dogs do not forget who *you* are. Their memory is not blocked or altered by what you or they think you have become.

I've heard that Malick has his actors "torpedo" or walk into each other's scenes unannounced to elicit honest reactions. This creates lifelike performances. The actors are not given scripts, sometimes only lists of character ideas and other lists of books to read. His male leads are silent and reactive, but still predatory. His female characters are archetypal. So, one wonders how real these interactions can potentially be. Malick's people do not so much inhabit space as they spatialize their lives. Cities and mountains grow up around them so that they can stage themselves acting. Cross-temporality is no problem since no one ever seems to be living entirely in that one time we call "the present." Malick's reality makes everyone an actor and every actor more of an actor than he or she has ever been before, although there is no "before" in Malick's world save for glimpses of what might be an invented past. Characters are torpedoed by the actor's question, "Who am I?"—the identity question never being far from conscious thought. These people try to crowd out thought with experiences of which they manically partake. They live lives of permanent distraction, so that experiences don't really add up. The people themselves leave no trace of having been, like they're mere images on a screen, coming attractions of the movie-going experience they already affect. They keep speaking of wanting to be free without

ever letting us know the ways they are bound. All we see are the trap-
pings of their lives as if they were life's equal. But nothing equals "life."
So, all of the lifelike acting is just a bill of goods being sold to those of
us who think we can live our lives through film and as though these lives
were films.

Male characters in Malick's contemplative films want credit for struggling with their fathers and their impact on their all-interruptive lives in
which no choice makes them feel wholly adult. They are stunted children, which they tacitly believe makes them creative and opens their
lives to options of which they cannot, nevertheless, partake. They speak
in overdubbed voices, distant from themselves in what McElroy calls
"Outer Paraspace," moving from self to self as easily as Malick's plot
moves from song to song (*Song to Song*, 2017).[19] Then again, Malick
shoots thousands of feet of film, leaving many characters and the stories they brought with them on the cutting room floor. Did I mention
the dog? He shows up somewhere in the middle of all of this just to
remind us that these overheard lives are dog-eared, pitched to its hearing
and level of incomprehension. Knowing this takes the pressure off knowing. Ground-level shots of bow-legged boots walking through puddles
are just that. Moodiness is just a certain blending of sensations that dulls
clarity. Pretense just looks like something strangely human.

In *Everything Is Illuminated* (dir. Liev Schreiber, 2005), "Jonathan
Safran Foer," who is (also) the author of the novel on which the film is
based (2002), is a cynophobe. On arriving in the Ukraine, he is forced to
share the backseat of a cab with a dog, and a bit of a crazy dog at that.
The dog's name is Sammy Davis Jr. It's a black and white female "seeing
eye" dog for the grandfather who thinks he's blind. Jonathan informs
the driver and his grandson Alex that Sammy Davis Jr., the grandfather's
favorite entertainer, is a Jew (who also happens to have one glass eye).
The grandfather and Alex refer to Jonathan as "the Jew," like Sinatra
did "his Sammy." The family business is to drive around "rich American
Jews" who are searching for their roots. The sign atop their car has a
sign featuring the Star of David. The grandfather lives with the secret
of his own Jewishness and so naming his dog after a convert to Judaism
is probably no accident. If the German Shepherd who almost took my
hand off were not named Sabre, but something more Jewish friendly

---

[19] McElroy, *Ancient History*, 251.

("Lenny," perhaps, but not "Leni"), a name that atoned for German-ness would "I" remember the incident differently? Who names their dog "Sabre" without expecting it to cut something off? Lenny Bruce tells of encountering "Brutus the Doberman" who came "bounding seemingly out of nowhere," as they always do. "Dogs seem to take a particular delight in scaring nine-year-old boys," Lenny wrote, speaking for all of us grown-up cynophobes. "...I think it's really a game for them...For *them*. I didn't understand the rules of the game when I was nine years old. I was a prepubic spoilsport." Is biting for a dog what might other-wise be a language game for us humans, or is it their means of interrupt-ing such human behaviors?[20]

In his short story, "Investigations of a Dog" (1922), Kafka's narra-tor says: "Recently I have taken more and more to casting up my life looking for the decisive, the fundamental error that I must surely have made; and I cannot find it. And yet I must have made it, for if I had not made it yet were unable by the diligent labor of a long life to achieve my desire, that would prove my desire is impossible and complete hope-lessness must follow." The speaker is a dog that values its community of species, yet feels somewhat apart from it, that investigates its uniqueness while admitting to sharing a dog nature and form of life that is common to all, that asks questions that interrupt on impulse without revealing meaning, conceding that it is common to all dogs to ask questions "con-fusedly, all together...as if in doing that they were trying to obliterate every trace of the genuine questions." In the face of real-life experience and endless self-questioning, the dog who acknowledges the limitations of his knowledge asks, "All this ceaseless labor—to what end?" Kafka's "dog" is certainly Jewish in its devotion to questioning as its own pursuit and its problematical relationship to assimilation as a principle. The dog examines insights gained "when we are beyond ourselves" and recalls the childhood origin of questioning in an encounter with a group of seven musical dogs who physicalized a score of actions that articulated what might otherwise be called the sound of silence. All this talk of dogs, who walk on their hind legs, know doubt and fear, similarity and difference, credits ancestry with guilt and community with laws and institutions, even if meant metaphorically, slows my response time to the inevitability of

---

[20] Bruce, *How to Talk Dirty and Influence People*, 63 and 69.

the dog attack while seducing me in the ways of the dog anabasis.[21] Can fear withstand rational consideration? Isn't this the point on which prejudice pivots? Beyond this, by wearing a dog costume do I draw closer to the terrible gifts that intuition and the search for totality in the face of self-abnegating critical analysis bring? Does recognition of myself as a dog increase impatience with what I see in its behavior rather than empathy? Am I here no longer speaking of dogs but of my child in relation to me? Kafka wrote this story, as he did his others, while still living with his parents.

On one of his periodic walks, Rousseau says he was knocked unconscious by "a Great Dane rushing full tilt toward me, followed by a carriage." In this state, Rousseau writes, "I had no distinct notion of myself as a person nor had I the least idea of what had just happened to me. I did not know who I was, nor where I was; I felt neither pain, fear, nor anxiety."[22] Unlike Rousseau's, my own walks do not engage with solitariness so much as with relationship with a partner not of my own choosing. It is a situation that Dean Martin's "Steve Wiley," the character he played who was forced to share a new car lottery prize with Jerry Lewis's "Malcolm Smith" and the latter's pet Great Dane "Mr. Bascomb" in *Hollywood or Bust* would understand. Martin was by that time (1956) performing his own perturbation. "My best friend"'s dog was running under cars in 1956, whenever it got out of the house, so that the car seemed to be running on the dog's legs. By 1961, "my best friend" and I had de-partnered, which for some reason known only in but not to my hyperbolic and hypochondriacal mind sent me into life as a solo act listening for footfalls behind me, for the big dog gaining on me from the rear projection, never real but always present-to-mind. My lifelong fear was always coming into being as expectancy always is. Whereas Rousseau spoke of walking around "in a kind of ecstasy, abandoning all my senses and my heart to the enjoyment of all, yet sighing a little that I was alone in enjoying it," my own walks became strictly narrative, hyper-observational yet sense-free, dumb to what enveloped

[21] Franz Kafka, "Investigations of a Dog," trans. Willa and Edwin Muir, in *The Complete Stories*, ed. Nahum N. Glatzer (New York: Schocken Books, 1983), 278, 281, 282, 291, 292, 292, 293, 297, 299, and 309.

[22] Jean-Jacques Rousseau, *Reveries of the Solitary Walker*, trans. Peter France (New York: Penguin, 2004), 38 and 39.

me other than my own fear and my counternarrative of attempted control.[23] My body ticks like Malcolm's does when he feels lucky, but for me it is not so much luck as the body's own intuition of what the mind is telling it irrationally that replaces luck or chance. The rear projection, a technical strategy designed to underscore the unreality of representation, aligns "Steve" and "Malcolm"'s stationary cross-country road trip with Martin and Lewis's flattened friendship in *Hollywood or Bust*. I cannot be harmed by the two-dimensional, I think, although, anxiety and attendant obsessive-compulsive behaviors both flatten and deepen dimension at the same time. The big dog, the Great Dane, the *melancholy Dane*, now rides up in front with me, between me and my partner, my friend, friendship, his paw on the death driveshaft, his formal name (here "Mr. Bascomb") suggesting that he has a right to be (t)here, that my lot, my lottery is only mine to share with him, my fellow traveler who is not, after all, my friend.

When Steve sends Malcolm for a run with Mr. Bascomb "way over the hill" so that he can abscond with the car, the dog is back instantaneously without Malcolm but standing in the way of Steve's escape. There is no escaping the big dog (Churchill's "black dog," melancholy, arch villain Melancholia) who in a sense is already in the driver's seat. "Mister Bascomb can't drive," Malcolm admonishes Steve. "He doesn't have a license." That is, he has not been properly screened. Although in a film in which DEAN MARTIN AND JERRY LEWIS appear on a marquee at Las Vegas's Sands Hotel unnoticed by "Steve" and "Malcolm," it is difficult to ascertain what proper screening is, save as rear as in *mere* projection. That is what "I" am doing, projecting my hyperbolic counternarrative of fearful control, of observing the unobservable, as if as Boswell says of Johnson in his treatment of the latter's life, he will be completely seen "as he really was." "Bascomb" or "Boswell" "liv[ing] o'er each scene" [in meticulous detail] with him [matching my "Samuel Johnson in his obsessive-compulsive detail-making"], as he actually advanced through the several stages of his life," traveling without transport, without escape or release from the ritualized structure of the peregrination. Do "I," not like Johnson but like *Boswell's* Johnson, want "to be seen in this work more completely than any man who has ever yet lived"? Is it even possible to split subject and biographer in two when

---

[23] Rousseau quoted in Peter France, "Introduction" in *Reveries*, 16.

Johnson himself opined "that every man's life may be best written by himself"?[24]

My walks of late which were meant to reinforce compulsive ritualized patterning have slowly been transforming into perambulations via permutations to the accepted paths. (*"Ideas come as you walk,"* Nietzsche said. *"Walking dissipates thoughts, Shankara taught."*[25]) The inside versus the outside or the outside contra inside of the signpost, the hydrant, the telephone pole metal-tethered to the pavement in their around and between choices, the return along the same as opposed to the opposing side of the street, the sidewalk past the open gate rather than the small shoulder separating street from parked car or curb, the explicit "BEWARE OF DOG" warnings and the implicit warning represented by old man McGready's Service Station since 1939, where live animals are kept behind the garage are no longer sidestepped except where my OCD mind is jaywalking across the straight and narrow. It sure beats walking down the center of streets as I did growing up. The playing field is dramatic and so never level. It is all an uphill climb, an anabasis, a long march through hostile territory, derived from just such an ancient Greek expedition that may have been apocryphal and became a template for too many Westerns to count. Cue the scalping parties, rival gangs, and unleashed dogs lying in wait for the lie "I" tell myself about uncontrollable fear.

Standing, or perhaps less aggressively sitting between strip mall storefronts for *The Kingdom of God* and *Die Hard Games* is the altogether unprepossessing *Angels of Mercy Karate Academy*, which I pass on my walks when I have it in myself to pass by the sign that reads FUNERAL HOME. (Given what its neighbors advertise, I wonder if it is an exclusively Christian home.) I might be less reticent to do so if the sign read FUNERAL *ACADEMY*, because it would indicate only what we already know, that we are in training for death, and not what we know but choose not to acknowledge (especially as being Jewish I do not necessarily believe it) that in death we are all going home (or becoming permanently homeless). The counternarrative note is struck by an advertisement I pass on my way back from the FUNERAL ACADEMY (as I have renamed the building for comfort's sake) that reads BERETTA

[24] James Boswell, *The Life of Samuel Johnson* (New York: Penguin, 2008), 19 and 21.

[25] Adi Shankara, Eighth-century Indian philosopher. E.M. Cioran, *The Trouble with Being Born*, trans. Richard Howard (New York: Arcade Publishing, 2013), 28.

REALTY. BERETTA, as in Beretta, as in gun. If this kind of thing were not Nabokov's intellectual property, most notably Humbert Humbert's real gun with the unreal name of "Chum" (a.k.a. "Friend") in *Lolita* his American travelogue of cultural-behavioral signs (published in 1955 while I was still watching movie Westerns), I might regard this gold-lettered sighting as YELLOW GUN's (one of my anxiety's aliases) self-citation of a surreal writer's tic.

Today I counter-walked my usual route, doubling back to view places I had chosen at most to pass by before. I walked past what used to be the offices of a now gun-to-mouth suicided local lawyer and not just past but into the vast, unmarked gray parking lot of what is again the FUNERAL HOME in front of which was parked an immaculate white car resembling something out of Cocteau's surreal cine-Liebestod *Orphée* (1950). More precisely, I walked the *perimeter* of the gray, non-reflective drowning-pool into which one had to descend. Further on, doubling back I caught sight of my fear in the distance in the form of two parallel metal bars hanging from the rear of a delivery truck marked "Eclipse" and advertising "Nightscaping" that to me resembled a dog's two stifle-jointed hind legs. *Yellow Gun is here.* I am not a Nietzschean nor am I well-read in Eastern religions, but I do know that I have taken to walking not once but twice around the funereal parking lot in death's shadow and will likely hazard a third-time round.

CHRISTMAS IN COLONUS

William Gurevitch saw Santa Claus in a vision, had this vision tattooed on his forearm and took as his name "Willy G. Christmas" (one letter shy of "Jesus H. Christ") to initialize his rebirth in Auster's novel *Timbuktu* (1999), which is narrated by Willy's dog "Mr. Bones." The fact that Willy retained both his first name and the first initial of his former (actual) surname as the middle initial in his new moniker suggests that he had not altogether let go of his past in the effort of making himself into a new man. ("You are still who you were, even if you are no longer the same person," Auster said elsewhere of himself about losing his father at age twelve.) Or perhaps, citing Wittgenstein, it was Willy's way of saying that he is still who he never was. A grandson of Jewish concentration camp survivors, Willy's mother saw the Santa Claus tattoo on her son's arm and "shrieked at him…called him a Nazi." And "rather than beating a dead horse" and activating in himself a Nietzschean madness by trying to explain again why he had so corrupted his Jewish flesh with permanent ink, Willy left his mother's house and became homeless. His mother saw a tattoo that counteracted her own parents' as betokening not just madness but betrayal.[26]

Willy G. Christmas, late of Poe-land (he fancies himself a writer and is stuck in the gothic author's old haunt of Baltimore) with an ancestral home in Poland, is dying on the road to Timbuktu, beyond Colonus, the sweet hereafter of the harshly body-and-soul-tattooing "here-before," from which he will be reborn. In Timbuktu, deceased Willy tells his now abandoned dog Mr. Bones, "dogs...speak man's language and converse with him as an equal" (as Levinas would con*cur*). Maybe Timbuktu looks like the world Godard (Dradog spelled front-words) depicts by mixing two- and three-dimensional photographic imagery in his dog's eye-view film, *Goodbye to Language* (2014).[27] Like the dog seen traversing stagnant pools of water in the inter-dimensional and possibly intra-dimensional Zone in Tarkovsky's *Stalker*, the dog has wandered beyond separateness, conditioned by language, which gives life its tragic dimension. The dog is like the cowboy whose partnerships interrupt his solitary wandering, whose separateness is harsh, who lives to be loyal and so to be betrayed. "And Darwin, citing Buffon [first in a line of "B"-initialed dogs that includes (Mr.) Bascomb and (Mr.) Bones], maintains that the dog is the only living creature that loves you more than it loves itself." It is only the animal's gaze, said Rilke, that teaches us about what it is to see outside the self, the true face-to-face-ness of which Levinas dreamed his dream of relationship, the basis of friendship, the disarmer of men of war.[28] Man must forsake home and em*bark* on an anabasis that leads to that place that dogs know as clearly as the sound that only they can hear. Mr. Bones, who lived in fear of his master's demise, the sort of catastrophic fear known to obsessives, dreams of Willy after Willy's death. But it's more than a dream. It is a dream-within-a-dream and then within-a-dream again, a working through of Godardian dimensions in the skins of other non-talking dogs, the hides of horse, cow, and pig, and the corpus of a fly. Bones is testing his "old dog self" in terms of a life that is no longer capable of authenticating

---

[26] Paul Auster, *Timbuktu* (New York: Picador/Henry Holt and Company, 1999), 22 and 23; Auster, *Report from the Interior*, 5.

[27] Auster, *Timbuktu*, 49.

[28] Quoted in *Goodbye to Language*.

as "waking" or "dreaming" a life, which at the same time, no longer brooks the deadly miscommunication and misunderstanding of language (*le mo[r]t*).[29]

On a bookshelf in my study is a postcard with a photo on the front of a grassy knoll. In the foreground is a mailbox with the number 1517 painted on it by an unknown hand. In the background is a convertible sedan (not coincidentally) from 1955 to 1956 without a front license plate or a driver, leaning precariously on the angled ground. Does the car "live" here (as the mailbox might suggest) or has it been abandoned? Perhaps the car lives here *and* has been abandoned. Between the car and the mailbox stands a street sign marking the intersection of what would normally be a cross street and a through street. But the cross street is actually the grassy knoll which may account for why the sign naming the cross street is unseen. The sign for the through street is, however, clearly visible. It reads: DREAM.[30] Is the sign even there? Are we looking at an un-delineated image-collage? And does DREAM indicate the assertion or end of a binary? Does a dream contain as many dreams within it as there are lines inside a line? Is Timbuktu the space, in the way that memory is a virtual space where dreams and lines come to rest without number, a space in which, as Mr. Bones was wont to say, "It's not the end of the world"? Is the signpost there to mark dimension rather than context, the possibility of three dimensions where we are only seeing in two? "What's difficult," an overdubbed voice says in Godard's film (citing Céline), "is to fit flatness into depth" (or, as Godard later paraphrases, "to turn depth into flatness"). Godard accomplishes this forking of dimensions, among other ways, with a chair placed before a car, the chair not the car abandoned to be otherwise seen. Is this what the missing sign tells us in the DREAM photograph—that we are missing a dimension? Speaking of how 3-D is uninteresting to him, Godard remarked. "We can't see anything beside what we could already see." By "beside," he surely meant "in addition to" but I will allow myself to think also "proximate," sharing the space inside the frame. "Sometimes painting [and its analogue, film] is a frame," Godard adds, "but sometimes you can see what's beyond the frame. You couldn't really see it but you

---

[29] Auster, *Timbuktu*, 77–78.

[30] Eugene Smith, "Pennsylvania 1955–1956," black and white photo postcard. Nouvelles Images S.A. éditeurs and E. Smith. Magnum Photos 1995/45700 Lombreuil-France off-set. Printed in France/PH 1186.

could feel it." Words, however, he says, "are lost with the animals, or the poor, or the mentally impaired, or the homeless."[31] Lost with Willy, with Mr. Bones, with all the dog-men who cannot or no longer search for "the right words" in forests where stray dogs roam and in frames, also in books, who abandon words in the perhaps futile attempts to escape themselves. "Timbuktu" is not a made-up word but it is a word that has become synonymous with a foreignness commensurate with the ends of the earth (actually an inhabited city in Mali, West Africa). It is the forked answer to the imminently/immanently mortal Mr. Bones's "it's not the end of the world," because it is not and yet it is, etymologically speaking. The car in the picture frame, along with the word DREAM was abandoned from where I sit viewing and writing these words, left road-less and speechless at the point where the journey must be continued on foot, which is to say on two feet or maybe four. It is the riddle the Sphinx posed to Oedipus retold to and by a now much older man. Does the dog, who walks on four legs at all times of the riddle's figurative day, know what friendlessness means? We sense he knows loyalty, but does he understand betrayal, the people and language that fail him, that turn on him as might a dog on its master? But even here the dog who turns does not know this as betrayal.

On the scenic horizon, we see the recurring figure of the Tramp, unseen benefactor of the blind flower girl in Chaplin's *City Lights* (1931), as always, going it alone. Does his depersonalized designation "The Tramp" suggest that his identity status is unchangeable? For some unknown reason, he has been stunted, traumatized into remaining in a childlike state of being able to pass through the world without getting an oversized toe-hold in it. We do not ask whether his life can sustain a narrative, since narrative is his life. Context is him fitting into whatever vacancy presents itself to him—a role, a dance, a scene that is even for a moment missing a character, a suit of clothing. *City Lights* features a musical chairs sequence at a nightclub in which the Tramp is either pulling away some-one else's chair or having his own chair pulled away in turn, with none of the chairs properly belonging to him as he is only a guest of a rich man who befriends him when he's drunk and then roughly discards him when he's sober. The Tramp is a fantasy friend of the rich man whose wife has left him. The Tramp himself is friendless, albeit willing to fit into the

---

[31] Interview with Jean-Luc Godard, included in DVD disc of *Goodbye to Language*.

role, the suit, the dance, the embrace of the friend for as long as someone wants it to be so. He is a savant whose idiocy is fitting in but not really. He sidles up. He lives for being other. It is, like the money he earns by stepping into the ring as a last-minute substitute boxer, easy and not easy. The on again-off again friendship that the Tramp shares with the rich man is not something to be counted on, nor is there any degree of self-evaluation in the counting. Unlike the push-pull friendship of famous comic teams, the Tramp's solo friendship act is always performed with strangers and is always one-sided. The Tramp receives friendship and returns affection as might a stray without any basis for understanding what a real friend is except as a source of immediate creature comfort, a place to catch your breath but not to stay. It is no wonder that so many dogs are named "Tramp." They can never truly outlive ownership and to own their own freedom is to go homeless, away from a home. I think, maybe, in my former life, I was a stray dog who even in its next life as a man cannot outlive the anxieties inculcated in the last. I experience the phantom dog bite as a reality I have devised to forestall further contact with what lies beneath the skin once it has been broken.

REDUCTIO AD HITLERUM

Watching *Amores Perros* (*Love's a Bitch*) (dir. Alejandro González Iñárritu, 2000), a film of endless dog-on-dog violence is like plunging your face into a bucket of contaminated blood. It's a horror show that I have sought out to confront an age-old fear. It's a reduction of humanity on the backs of dogs. Dog-on-dog genocide, inhuman reduction. Where is the humanity? Why can't they be better than us? What have we taught them to do? How can a dog-man act this way? Black Rottweiler Cofi's big money fight is against a German Shepherd, whose owner shoots Cofi in mid-contest. You can't trust the breed *or* its owners. I have to fight against my hard-earned prejudice. The horror is inbred. It never was in the movies as I thought, or else the movies read my mind. The fact that this particular movie wraps around, circles back to my dog-nemesis is certainly no accident (accident being at the heart of this film). At least it is nothing that I can conceive as being an accident. *Reductio ad Hitlerum*—all fear derives from one source.[32] A dog lover, Hitler helped

---

[32] German-American Jewish political philosopher Leo Strauss coined the term *reductio ad Hitlerum* in 1951.

popularize German Shepherds as pets and was the breed's most famous owner. Hitler and his mass of German Shepherds whittled down the Jewish population in central Europe to nothing, to no mas(s). Hitler killed his beloved German Shepherd Blondi with the poison he then used on himself and Eva Braun in their bunker as the Russian army was closing in on Berlin. Had this not happened, Hitler and his legion of killer German Shepherds would have killed all the Jews, making what you are reading here ghost-writing sent from a place of impossible origin.

A little dog chases a ball down a hole in an apartment floor and disappears in *Amores Perros*. The dog belongs to Valeria, a model who seriously injures and later loses her leg in an accident caused by Octavio fleeing from the man who shot his dog Cofi, the latter bleeding out in the backseat of his car. Four-legged, two-legged, and now one-legged creatures suggest some savage retelling of Oedipus's origin story related to his solving of the Sphinx's riddle. But this is just by way of preparation. A homeless man with long gray hair nicknamed El Chivo ("the Goat") is wandering the street where he picks up stray dogs, including the mortally wounded Cofi, whom he rescues from Octavio and Valeria's car crash, which interrupts him like fate as he is closing in on his murder-for-hire target, an Abel whose death has been paid for by his brother Cain. El Chivo has himself lost a daughter to the figurative death of (self-)imprisonment and estrangement.

Avi Shafran recalls the Yom Kippur ritual of the two goats, one ascribed to G-d, the other "to Azazel—the name of a steep cliff in a barren desert. As the Torah prescribes, the first goat was solemnly sacrificed in the Temple, attention given to every detail of the offering; the second was taken to the cliff of its name and thrown off, dying unceremoniously before it even reached the bottom." From this oft-told tale, Shafran gleans the following lesson:

> There are two ways to view human life, as mutually exclusive as they are fundamental. Our existence is either a result of intention, or of accident. And the corollary follows directly: Either our lives are meaningful, or they are not. If the roots of our existence ultimately lie in pure randomness, there can be no more meaning to good and bad actions than to good or bad movies; no more import to right and wrong than to right and left. We remain but evolved animals, our Mother Theresas and Adolf Hitlers alike. To be sure, we might conceive a rationale for establishing societal norms, but a social contract is but a practical tool, not a moral imperative;

it is, in the end, artificial. Only if there is a Creator in the larger picture can there be true import to human life, placing it on a plane apart from mosquitoes... the sending off of the Azazel-goat could be seen as an acknowledgement of the idea that sin's roots lie in the madness born of our self-doubt. And those who witnessed its dispatchment might well have been spurred by the thought to turn instead to consider the other goat, the one sacrificed in dedication to G-d. So stirred on the holiest day of the Jewish year, they might then have been able to effectively commit themselves to re-embrace the grand meaning that is a human life [as the Torah states].[33]

Susana, with whom Octavio planned to run away but who betrayed him to her savage, criminal husband (Octavo's brother Ramiro) at the latter's funeral tells the still dogged Octavio who was trapped in her romantic ambivalence: "My grandmother used to say, 'To make God laugh, tell Him your plans.'" I realize now that *Amores Perros* is an after-the-fact template of a plan I have myself been spinning. El Chivo is an Old Testament God, after which my despotic mind is fashioned, arbitrarily deciding what thoughts, images, memories, and ideas live, die, or recur without giving sufficient reason as to when and why they do. *Amores Peros* is to me ultimately not about the violence that makes us inhumane but the ambivalence that makes us human, the denial of any independent life-plan we nevertheless pursue. The God-Goat abandons Cain and Abel in a figurative desert of their own incomprehension, as Dog (Cofi) is his witness. "A man has to believe in something" was the final line of my last book. Until now I have believed in fear, or perhaps given what Jacobson calls my (Jewish) God's "over-particularity" in terms of being represented, in a dog named "Fear."[34] And "Fear" always comes when I call.

Performance artist Laurie Anderson's *Heart of a Dog* (2015) includes video footage of her blind dog Lolabelle playing piano for audiences, *who laugh at her.* I hadn't taken into account the idea that people might laugh at a dog's earnestness. Suddenly, I am not fearful of the dog, I feel empathy for the dog I am. Anderson dedicates *Heart of a Dog* to her husband Lou Reed, "my Lou" as we Jews say of our own, a "magnificent spirit" who died from liver cancer. Lou, adrift in his Long Island home,

---

[33] http://www.chabad.org/holidays/JewishNewYear/template_cdo/aid/4590/jewish/Dispatching-the-Goat.html.

[34] Jacobson, *Shylock Is My Name*, 239.

as much as I was as a boy growing up. Lou discovered necking with girls in the movie theater which I also attended (the Eden-like "Grove") but I was alone, a stray. Under the dedication in her movie, Laurie shows Lou, the perennial outlier, lying on his side holding Lolabelle near his face. During my chemotherapy, they brought in a comfort dog that immediately climbed onto my lap and fell asleep. And the fear went right out of me for a time.

CHAPTER 8

I'm Not Like Everybody Else

In Raúl Ruiz's *Mysteries of Lisbon* (2010), there is a window inside a room through which a Magritte-like assemblage of physically unlike multiples stare from some other inside-outside space and possibly time. Ruiz's monk gifts to the son he gave away at birth (for having killed his mother when father and son were different people with other names), a baroque cabinet containing her ashes and with them, her skull. This completes the mind's anamorphic redesign of the parent–child relationship as a troubling of history and external reality.[1] When another parentless child being raised by Father Dinis, the first monk's son, ventures into the latter's private room, the adult Dinis, although angered at his young charge's violation of his interior space, shows him historical relics of his past (the various physical disguises he has worn, the rolled-up scrolls of plans he made), culminating in the unveiling to the boy of the mother's skull only recently given to Dinis by his estranged father. Dinis then locks the child inside the dark room to contemplate how he will confess his violation of another's memory that is, however, something of a shared memory of parental abandonment and biographical split.

We have already seen that boy, a bastard given only the first name João, having his picture drawn. "I was fourteen," his narrative voice tells

[1] The framing of a somehow remembered, hoped for but ambiguous escape from a painful interiority recalls man-child Hedwig's (one of a single mind's multiple personalities in M. Night Shyamalan's 2016 film *Split*) revealing to a captive girl that her hoped-for window of egress is only a child's painted picture of a window on the wall of a window-less room in the labyrinthine prison beneath the Philadelphia Zoo.

© The Author(s) 2019
S. Golub, *A Philosophical Autofiction*, Performance Philosophy,
https://doi.org/10.1007/978-3-030-05612-4_8

us on the movie soundtrack, "and I didn't know who I was at all." He is
knocked out with a wooden ball used to knock down game pins and has
feverish dreams about which he wonders whether they are real. He recovers
in a room that has a small toy theater in it whose stage figures he imagines
are moving and continue to move as the narrative is taken from him for
nine years during which time João grows up. He reenters childhood now
through another door—other people's guilt, the price of what the past
has cost them, in murders, adulteries, prematurely ruined reputations,
ruined lives set in motion by *his* birth. The adult João carries around
with him the portrait of himself as a boy we saw being drawn, together
with the small baroque toy theater and the wooden ball that hit him in
the head, introducing him to an undreamed unconsciousness. These
things remind him of a destiny that is written in childhood but only partially understood even many years later. "They all had surnames," he
remembers. "Four, five, even more. I was just 'João'." He speaks these
lines aloud while lying ill in what appears to us to be the guise of no one
in particular. These names, these multiples gnaw away at an identity that
as João's life manifests is indeterminate. Genealogies twist around one
another like vines. Trap doors open in people's pasts that deposit them
elsewhere in time with new names. "I thought I had dreamt it all," João
says, entranced by the same cholera fever that killed the mother he hardly
knew in Portugal, the birthplace to which he had returned. Memory
felled by a fever dream of a multitudinous reality that has come to rest.
Narrative's split consciousness says it is the "everybody" that you are not
like in all the names you give your thoughts and the one name you give
yourself.

The film noir *Crossfire* (dir. Edward Dmytryk, 1947) begins with a
Jewish man being beaten to death by an anti-Semitic soldier, although
all that we see at first are their interior shadows (the thoughtlessness of
light) abandoned in the wake of a lamp being knocked to the ground
in the struggle. The room is seen from floor level, as if the camera were
hidden under a coffee table or swept under the rug. From this perspective, the space and light inside the room appear to be anamorphic and
the room itself, figurative, a ghost room. What we are then seeing in a
word is "bias." Ray Davies wrote a song for a 1960s BBC series called
Where Was Spring? entitled "When I turn off the Living Room Light,"
which opens with the line, "Who cares if you're Jewish?" the reason-
ing behind this question being that everyone "looks" the same in the

dark, where being Jewish does not leave a mark.[2] This cold comfort is on the order of salutary neglect, as it suggests at best that bias requires the absence of manifest difference to be calmed enough to nod off from racist vigilance. Suddenly *not* being like everybody else was not such a good thing. So, what will it be—I'm not like everybody else, or I am? This is only a Jewish question to the extent my answer is I am a Jew. And I am a Jew no more obsessed with cancer than cancer is obsessed with me.

In Philip Roth's 2001 novel *The Dying Animal* (and the 2008 film *Elegy* adapted from it), sixty-two-year-old writer-college professor Dave Kepesh, a self-described "devout hypochondriac," "in the theatrical company of 'Mr. Reality'," instills in his students a certain unpreparedness to deal with something like cancer except as a real-life fiction that belongs in someone else's body.[3] His young student and one-time lover Consuela Castillo, who as they say is both "to die for" and "too young to die," literally wears the "perfection" Kepesh attaches to her on her chest in the form of a double "C" carcinoma, an expression of the writer's own phobic narcissism. Having endured his own Kafkaesque metamorphosis into a giant female mammary in Roth's earlier novella *The Breast* (1972) (akin to Gogol's Major Kovalyov's transformation into a giant nose), Kepesh sees Consuela's breast cancer as being a cruel joke on his fictional self.[4] At the beginning of their origin story, Kepesh had shown Consuela a framed letter Kafka had written to his beloved Milena, as if the professor were trying to interest his student in the role in which she was already pre-cast. In time, Kepesh will consult his oncologist son Kenny, who resents his father's divorcing his mother and abandoning him, on Consuela's behalf. Kepesh requires an *ontologist* for himself, but, of course, they don't exist except in cases where "oncologist" is misread or misheard. In Roth's novel, Kenny is not a doctor but rather "runs a little company that restores damaged works of art," a profession that might have served (the object of) his father's obsessive desire better than any doctor could. Kepesh's artistic appreciation of Consuela's body cruelly hinted at the surprise ending in which this "big, ersatz something special" that "flattered her vanity" would be reversed in the form of cancer's

[2]Johnny Rogan, *Ray Davies: A Complicated Life* (London: Vintage, 2016), 373.

[3]Philip Roth's novel *The Breast* (New York: Vintage/Random House, 1994), 4, 38, 59, and 88.

[4]Nikolai Gogol, "The Nose" (1836).

irreversible damage and unflattering physical humiliation.[5] "I'm stuck inside myself," Consuela says, which must be what this means.

I attended Union College in Schenectady, New York whose Web site boasts that it "was the first college in the country to be built according to a master plan" [by eighteenth-century French architect and landscape painter Joseph-Jacques Ramée].[6] The students of what was then an all-male college (or at least *this* student) could never figure out why at the center of his plan Ramée chose to position a sixteen-sided building that resembled a Rothian giant female breast, why the male president for which it was so built was surnamed "Nott" <sic> (a tumor or k/not?), and why they ringed the building's aureole with a Talmudic one-off citation that reads, "The day is short, the work is great, the reward is much, the Master is urgent." This sounded to me like the riddle Sherlock Holmes must translate into a map to solve the "Musgrave Ritual." Holmes does this by tracing the shadow cast by a large elm tree onto a unique architectural façade (both suggesting campus life) to discover the correspondence between ancestral legacy (Union was founded in 1795) and living death (tradition and its codes).[7]

It was inside the giant "Nott" that we staged our first amateur performances "under the laws of Minerva," as the college logo read. I came to bucolic Union under the delusion that I was entering a movie shot to my mind's specifications and not to the way things were. When they later shot a movie there called *The Way We Were* on campus it was a romantic confection of "misty, watered colored memories" I did not have.[8] Women did not matriculate at Union until the year following my graduation. The surname of a Union classmate of mine, Caden Cotard (another

[5] Roth, *The Dying Animal*, 44 and 77.

[6] www.union.edu.

[7] Ibid., In Sir Arthur Conan Doyle, "The Musgrave Ritual," originally published in *Strand Magazine* in 1893, the location after generations of the concealed royal crown of Charles I results in the accidental entombment of the longtime Musgrave family butler Brunton who is attempting to steal it. I discuss this story in my book *Infinity Stage* (Ann Arbor: University of Michigan Press, 1999).

[8] They shot the college scenes for the historical romance *The Way We Were* (dir. Sydney Pollack, 1973) at Union, three years after I graduated. The movie showed what college was supposed to look like. Of course, in the movie Union was co-ed, which gave the star romance between Jewish Barbra Streisand's and Gentile Robert Redford's opposites-attract characters a place and a chance to begin. I am quoting part of the lyric to the film's theme song written by Alan and Marilyn Bergman (music by Marvin Hamlisch).

double "C") refers to a delusional state of mind in which the sufferer thinks he is dead. This is probably not so much what bonded us as defining where we were bound. Caden also saw his time spent in Schenectady as being some sort of movie dream. He thinks he starred in a film called *Synechdoche, New York* (dir. Charlie Kaufman, 2008), the film's title being a play upon Schenectady, of course, and a nod to the architecturally unique Nott, part of theatrical death's master plan as memento mori.

Toward the start of his theater-of-life-within-the film, Caden, who is married to a female miniaturist named "Adele Lack," depresses the red flag on his mailbox (one of many red flags in his theatrical narrative) after removing a circular for "Attending Your Illness" that features a cover photo of a gray-haired man apparently wearing a CPAP mask used to correct sleep apnea. Caden probably doesn't recognize me from this photo. It has been decades since we last saw each other and he wouldn't know about my condition despite me knowing about his. "Caden"—in Arabic the name means "friend," but neither one of us knew this at the time. Over the course of the film, an ER doc recommends that Caden see an ophthalmologist, which Caden mishears as a urologist, which I hear as my old "friend"'s attempt to track the path and site of my cancer—my new old friend that has been with me now for the worse not better part of twenty years. My cancer has metastasized into Caden's film, which likely says something about the capaciousness of his and my hypochondria. The structure of Caden's narrative—a theatrical presentation as large as the film that contains it (a nod to Borges's map the size of the territory it designates)—may speak to Caden's haphephobia, the need for more personal space than other people require, an ever enlarging and tessellating series and overlay of spaces that belong to him.[9] Taking his cue from Ramée and his college-scape, Caden has become his life's master planner after the delusional Union.

"You're actors playing actors," Caden tells his "doctors" in the scenes he later writes for them (including a death scene in which he is featured). As Caden's reality metastasizes during the run of his staging of *Death of a Salesman* featuring all young actors, his father dies riddled with a cancer he didn't know he had until it was too late. Even though he had been told that death "comes faster than you think," Caden rehearses his play for seventeen years (an idea of the years between my two cancers), unaware of the time until an actor points it out. Caden hires a non-actor

[9] http://voices.yahoo.com/haphephobia-fear-being-touched-2370796.html.

named Sammy Barnathan to play him in the theatrical remounting of his life as/in synechdoche/Schenectady, but Sammy, who we first see observing Caden taking the "Attending Your Illness" circular from his mailbox, began following him *three years earlier* in preparation. Whereas Kepesh literally played a fictional part (a breast), Caden imparts his fictional part to a real-life appendage (Sammy). Caden watches an upbeat commercial for chemotherapy on a paint-splattered portable TV in his wife's art studio following her departure. As he watches "Ad"'s (as he familiarly calls "Adele") screen ad, he puts himself in the picture, metastasizing the death his mind counterbalances by metastasizing his life on the outside, as scenes requiring their own inventive frames. Caden's theater box office person Hazel is reading Kafka and later Proust as guides to shopping for a house in which to die. Caden fails to understand or read into his psychiatrist's book her first name, which is the Proustian "Madeleine." In fairness, the book's claim to explain an "unapproachable phenomenology" is more abstruse than Caden's onto-logical-phenomenological Ür-theater can intellectually fathom, although not contain. (Caden on theater: "It's the beginning of thought. It's the truth not yet spoken. It's what a man feels like after he's been clocked in the jaw.")

Adele leaves Caden and sublets an apartment in New York under the name of "CAPGRAS," like the delusional syndrome of people substitution, imposture, and pathological playacting that someone is who he is not, namely someone else. Although as another former student of Dave Kepesh tells him about dating new people, "they're the same old people in masks. There's nothing new about them at all. They're just *people*." So, Capgras may have less today upon which to rest its delusional claim or else its shareholders may be more far-reaching.[10] The name on the apartment next door is BARTH, surname of the author John Barth who worked his postmodern magic on Scheherazade's serial narrative impersonations of the *1001 Nights*. Caden reaches Adele's apartment by pushing the elevator button marked "31," alongside the button marked "ALARM," as if mirror-reading unluckily absent but inverted "13" as what is, in fact, an "unapproachable phenomenology," which his young daughter's cancer perhaps has helped him to see. Cue the "TEAR SUBSTITUTE" that Caden uses to affect emotion. He owes as much to those who as with Kepesh are dying *for* him but only as actors he has cast (off).

---

[10] Roth, *The Dying Animal*, 107.

In Philip Roth's confused chronology of my college experience (*Indignation*, 2008), the war being fought is in Korea, not Vietnam and the student takeover of the administration building and the closing down of the college happens one year after my graduation. Conversely, the college is already co-ed in the 1950s, whereas it is *that event* that occurred the year after I left Union. The college *was* "the Mother of fraternities" and a "Technicolor college movie musical" dream as Roth described, although it is said that he modeled this after a college of a different name.[11] I prefer to think of it as being the same college but at a different time (i.e., *The Way We Were*). Like Roth's Marcus Messner in *Indignation*, I dated a blonde *shiksa* but while his called him blind for what he didn't see, mine laughed when I temporarily blinded myself in one eye with a direct shot from the plastic top of a cheap bottle of *André* (champagne) whose name may have given Roth the idea for *Escargot*, the pricey French restaurant where Marcus takes bipolar-glamorous Olivia Hutton on their first and only real date. Both Marcus and I were taken to the hospital, me for my eye, he for a ruptured appendix which almost killed *my son*, responding to the constant fear that Marcus's father had for *his* son, who is run through by an enemy bayonet in Korea and dies at age *nineteen* after being expelled for falsifying his college Chapel attendance, which was required at Union in my time there as well. Two years later my name is entered in the draft lottery that is surreally hosted on TV by my local New York City nightly newsman. My number does not come up, but I watched others die right there next to me on the living room sofa, while still others perished in the library when their call numbers were posted. And yet I remember my death as if I had gone to Vietnam or Korea, as if it were Marcus's, which, oddly enough, he also remembers as if it were happening in a book, a movie, a work of fiction to someone else. I read *Indignation* not as fiction but as the memoir of an old friend I never knew. This odd displacement of time and identity comes through Roth's writing of Marcus, who does not believe in God, despite having been raised in the Jewish religion that does not promote heaven and hell. All that remains is memory beyond time in which life's former "what if" theme becomes "even as."

---

[11] Roth attended Bucknell University in Lewisburg, Pennsylvania, as did the David with whom I co-wrote a novel. Philip Roth, *Indignation* (New York: Vintage, 2009), 18. https://www.union.edu/offices/fraternity-sorority/.

BROKEN

"We are all broken."-- Spoken to me on my way out of physical therapy by someone on his way in—a prophet, an angel, perhaps in human form, or else an empty vessel.

Chance the Gardner's (in Hal Ashby's *Being There*, 1979 from real-life impostor Jerzy Kosinski's novel) affectless silent and echoic observation allows others to use him to fill in the gaps in their own metaphors, like the cool medium of television which literally speaks to him as if he were a character inside an enlarged fictional frame. Chance has no origin story, has never been to a hospital but dislikes them, as he does doctors. Is this a response to some unspoken experience, like the kind my aunt Ruth endured as a child back in the old country where all record of her origin story was lost? Chance might have "actually" dated Ruthie but he wouldn't pick up the phone to call and she wouldn't pick up the phone to answer. If he did and she did, and I'm not sure they didn't, he would have attended one of my grandparents's Passover Seders with even less understanding than we kids had and with more terror at the cacophony of chanting and singing in Hebrew and side conversations in Yiddish and American English. First, he would have to contend with my father, Ruthie's younger (or as the family remade him, older) brother, playing upon his childhood doubts and his adult fears. As a large and chubby schoolboy, Peter Sellers, a.k.a. Chauncey Gardiner, a.k.a. everyone other than "Peter Sellers," a person he did not seem to know or could even seem to locate, used to recite a literary passage he had learned by rote. It was from *Gulliver's Travels* and spoke of "The Most Mighty Emperor, Delight and Terror of the Universe, Monarch of All Monarchs, Taller than the Sons of Men," of whom Sellers would add, "You know, that Emperor was no more than six inches tall."[12] The point here being, of course, that as a boy Sellers appeared to be Brobdingnagian but felt himself to be Lilliputian, shy, uncertain, alien, Jewish at a Catholic boys' school. My father, who like Sellers, never went to college, used to recite the beginning of the very Catholic Coleridge's "Rime of the Ancient Mariner," which he learned by rote, with the same de-contextualized frequency: "It is an ancient Mariner,/And he stoppeth one of three./ 'By thy long grey beard and glittering eye,/ Now wherefore stopp'st

---

[12] Roger Lewis, *The Life and Death of Peter Sellers* (New York: Applause, 1997), 26, fn.

thou me?'" My father never got any farther than this, as if beyond this there be dragons of some undiscovered, mysterious world to come (or maybe just the interpretive world of higher education in which poems are broken down by stanzas and *all* the stanzas are studied). Curiously, where the poem goes next is to a feast, a gathering, specifically a wedding. It's a cautionary tale of mistakes made, which would surely have discomfited the pale and trembling guest at the Passover feast sitting across from Ruthie, wearing the face and costume of "Chance." Given his penchant for discomfiting me in public, I have no doubt that my father would have done the same to poor Chance (whose reality he could not abide). At another feast served up at a restaurant to a long table of women single or without their husbands, my small family was present, eating at the next table. While I strained *not* to hear what these women were saying, my father approached the woman at the head of the table and the table conversation and asked her if she and her friends might speak louder of sex and such things as his son (me) was struggling to hear what they were saying so as to augment his education in these matters. "No I didn't, no I wasn't," the Emperor of Lilliput struggles to say, while the Brobdingnagian head woman smiles and nods conspiratorially in his direction. "You're on your own, Chauncey," my own smile and nod tell the quaking ghost of embarrassments past across the table he would now just as soon climb under. If he did, he would see one of my other aunts pinching my leg and the squirming that breached the surface of my smile.

As the self-consuming verses of the morbid holiday song "Had Gadya" mounted one another—a cat-ate-a-kid (goat)/a dog-bit-the cat/a stick-beat-the dog/a fire-burned-the-stick/water-doused-the-fire/the ox-drank-the-water/a slaughterer-slaughtered-the-ox/the Angel of Death-killed-the slaughterer/the Holy One-slew-the Angel of Death, Chance's terror and chance *as* a terror came into focus. Occupying a chair with his emptiness, who else would he be but Eliahu (i.e., Elijah), for whom we set out a plate and a glass of wine, which he somehow was meant to reach through the double-locked and staked to the ground door that Ruthie guarded with mythic vigilance. Eliahu, the ninth century B.C. prophet denounced Jezebel, which might account for his interest in my virgin (one presumes) aunt. Jezebel was thrown out a window and her corpse eaten by dogs. I was not checking on her but on our double-parked car through the window among the window-sill vegetation, while Chance or Chauncey or Eliahu watched me, *observed* me in my non-observant rote ritualizing while studiously *not* hearing this last bit about a dog's eating even (especially) death.

The prophet Chance's manifest literalness and passivity scare the life out of me, much as he sucks the lives out of others with such minimal prompts as "Yes, I know," and "I understand." People feed him with *their* metaphors until he grows huge, reaching millions of people through television. There is something atavistic as well as predatory about him as he, a so-called messenger or prophet, sits, silently observing us around the sacrificial platter. Leon Wieseltier observes that "One of the primary methods for the transmission of tradition is the premature termination of childhood."[13] M. Night Shyamalan, with his terrorized, traumatized, preternaturally insightful children who "see dead people" (in *The Sixth Sense*) must have a small Jewish boy living inside him as one of his personalities, maybe even the dominant one. I hear that he has a future project in mind that has the working title *Seder*. One item that has leaked about the story premise is that the Beast (the most violent, animalistic of numerous personalities—including an obsessive-compulsive one—devised and released by a single mind in "Night"'s 2016 film *Split*) is reanimated, like a golem, from the elements on the sacrificial platter at the Passover Seder: the matzot (unleavened bread) symbolizing escape from slavery (the bread had no time to rise); the piece of roast meat on a bone (*zeroa*, or shankbone) representing the lamb sacrificed on the eve of the Jewish exodus from Egypt; a hard-boiled egg (*beitzah*), representing G-d's desire to redeem us; bitter herbs (*maror* and *chazeret*) standing in for the bitterness of slavery, our bitter tears; a fruit, nut, and wine relish (*charoset*) to constitute the brick and mortar used by Jewish slaves to build the Pyramids; parsley, or "*karpas* in Hebrew, referring to the backbreaking work of the Jews as slaves, as the Hebrew letters of *karpas* can be arranged to spell the word *perech* plus the letter *samech*. *Perech* means backbreaking work, and *samech* is numerically equivalent to 60, referring to 60 myriads, equaling 600,000, which was the number of Jewish males over 20 years of age who were enslaved in Egypt."[14] 600,000 is, of course, a subset of 6,000,000, the number of Jews killed by the Nazi genocide in World War II.

[13] Wieseltier, *Kaddish*, 47.

[14] http://www.chabad.org/holidays/passover/pesach_cdo/aid/1998/jewish/The-Seder-Plate.htm.

"Earliest childhood," Lawrence Kushner writes, "is living in the unity; adulthood is surviving the brokenness."[15] Brokenness, like a child's nightmarish fable in which a giant (Goliath's return) grinds his bones to make his bread, in this case unleavened. Broken like the world, like the Hebrew Name of G-d, "made from the root letters of the Hebrew word 'to be.'"[16] Corresponding defects all the way down. A mystical, trickle-down theory of natural chaos. Bone-broken Elijah Price, a.k.a. "Mr. Glass" in Shyamalan's *Unbreakable* (2000) is a body broken inside itself, rend(er)ing its owner friendless in and to himself, looking for something to do with all of this ever-present, ever-pressing loss, a weight detrimental to being. Glass he is, so "Glass" he becomes. It's his nemesis name, nemesis for him being his own psychosis. This could have gone either way—toward a redressive constellation of harmonious parts or into a cultivated disharmony in the form of opposition to likeness, to isomorphism. Unlike the prophet Elijah whose name, like his brokenness, he bears, his delusional message merely reinscribes an isolation that brooks not even misunderstanding. It takes one to *know* one, and in this City of Brotherly Love (Philadelphia, where Shyamalan spent his childhood and sets many of his films), the sociopathic Glass has no one in whom to confide his darkest imaginings or to fend off their manifesting a brokenness in others. You don't have to hold a grudge for having entered life broken. You need not make art out of destruction or philosophy from or into myth. But this is clearly how this Glassworks. He manages a gallery that displays comic book art, awaiting the appearance of a superhero whose bones never break, so that he (Glass) can, by becoming his Nemesis, the archvillain in his own composition, find his place in the world. His brokenness is not "a mistake." He was born (this way) for a reason, which is only realizable via his self-making as a fiction, as the fictional "Mr. Glass" (a formerly derisive childhood nickname).

On May 12, 2015, at 9:23 p.m. EDT, a Northeast Corridor Amtrak passenger train carrying 238 passengers derailed in the Port Richmond neighborhood of Philadelphia, injuring 200, 11 critically and killing eight on impact. The train's engineer lost control of the train as it rounded a curve at twice the recommended speed limit. The National Transportation Board ruled that the driver lost "situational awareness"

---

[15] Kushner and Mamet, *Five Cities of Refuge*, 140.

[16] "*Yod, hey, vav*, and bey." Ibid., 4 and 5.

owing to distraction.[17] Specifically, he had been listening to radio chatter about another accident, a *different* accident, the one in 2000 depicted in the film *Unbreakable* from which a man named David Dunn emerged unscathed. Nor has he ever been sick. And yet how does the objective viewer who is not so invested in Dunn being recognizably different in this way reconcile this difference with the chicken pox scar clearly visible on the right side of the actor's face who plays him? Are we willing to overlook this potentially fatal flaw because the two myth-makers for whom this writing is an inside job—Dunn's son Joseph and fatherless Elijah Price—both need David Dunn to be a superhero so that they can reconcile themselves to death and disfigurement, mortality and abandonment—to potential realities that their minds will not abide. The fictional train crash *was real* in the sense of precognitive, making Glass's agency in making the accident happen real in some sense too. Or at least not definitively fictional. Glass the Prophet was born with his bones broken enabling him somehow to break time's arrow in half. He might have prophesied as a Martin Amis character did: "The future always comes true." That character was referring to the Holocaust, the Shoah, in which the Beast is risen.[18]

On a ship at sea in *Three Crowns of the Sailor* (dir. Raúl Ruiz, 1983), the eponymous narrator meets the Impersonator who tells him of having lost his best friend because the latter stole his fiancée. The Sailor realizes that the voice in which the Impersonator tells this story "belonged to someone I thought dead." (Ruiz double-tracks the Impersonator's voice on the film's soundtrack.) "You know who I'm talking about," the Sailor tells the murderous student who is his audience. "You've surely guessed what I was thinking about: We're all dead here. This is the other life." Earlier, we were told that when the student is bored, he refers to himself as "I." We are experiencing reality in the split between "you" and "I," and between "you-*as*-I." The "other life" of which the Sailor speaks is, he cautions the student, not necessarily the hereafter. Moore's paradox illustrates the problem as not being "you" and "I" or even "you-*as*-I." Confusion arises when the "I" is both implicit and explicit as

[17] http://www.nydailynews.com/news/national/amtrak-engineer-deadly-phil-ly-derailment-made-human-error-article-1.2639665; http://www.npr.org/sections/thetwo-way/2017/05/12/528206181/amtrak-engineer-charged-in-deadly-2015-phila-delphia-train-crash; https://en.wikipedia.org/wiki/2015_Philadelphia_train_derailment.

[18] Amis, *Time's Arrow*, 155.

in "It is raining outside, but I don't believe it." It might even express itself as in Moore's Paradox as understood by the fools of Chelm, one of whom declares, "I believe that water is sour cream" (so as to solve a sour cream shortage), "aches are mother's milk," and "darkness became freedom."[19] When the Impersonator throws himself overboard and then shows up alive the very next day, he tells the Sailor that it wasn't him who drowned. It was the other one. That "the other" is implicit in each of us in every "I" is obvious enough. But what does it mean to say that the "I" is explicit, that it is meaningful, if it is the other that is inside of us, the other that we kill off like the magician Angier does in Christopher Nolan's *The Prestige* (2006), and for what—to gain the upper hand, to fix the game of life as if it were a competition. A competition with whom—ourselves? Which one of "us" wins? The Impersonator? Is it the surviving passenger-as-superhero, whose identity is split, or the engineer who synthesizes his realities without getting a story in the film that is the real unbreakable protagonist? You cannot get him to testify against himself.

Magen Davids

At the Passover table, where I press on the rubber ball my grandfather gave me to relieve the tension, I preimagine I am Spalding Gray, my ubiquitous glass of grape juice channeling Treplev's miniature drowning pool in *The Seagull*'s final act. Spalding grew up in Rhode Island. It's called "The Ocean State," because it's surrounded by water. Water. Spalding's Kryptonite. The title of the performance he has in mind to give tonight is *Swimming to Cambodia* (dir. Jonathan Demme, 1987); ironic given that he is an admitted hydrophobe. "Displacement of anxiety," he calls what he does while facing a pool of water that is not a river or the sea. Like Archimedes displacing water from his tub, Spalding's mind shrieks "Eureka!" to seal in his "perfect moment" that aligns so perilously with death. The water is not after all for swimming, nor is it for drinking. It is tainted with a cancer-causing carcinogen that according to a legend Spalding retails is used in Cambodian beer. And yet, he is drinking. It beats getting bitten by one of the possibly rabid dogs of Cambodia. The overhead camera shot of the water in the glass recalls the glowing glass of poisonous milk in Hitchcock's *Suspicion* (1941).

---

[19] Englander, "The Tumblers," in *For the Relief of Unbearable Urges*, 27 and 28.

The glass of water is small but also metonymic, meaning that it is a good deal larger than it drinks, as big as your mental context for it allows. Spalding with his professorial hair loss on top, not shaved like David Dunn's former athlete with his life loss, is likewise soldiering on. This ordinary looking and sounding man in a broadly checked flannel shirt that passes for a superhero costume or else is an homage to a childhood pajama top. Spalding. Sp-a-a-a-a-l-l-l-ding. The ball thrown against the door locks ricocheting here and there but still within a narrow passage. The turning of the doorknob in series of three each way as Spalding did "for luck" that differed from OCD only because it was targeted toward an immediate goal—in his case, a movie role. If I perform my ritual with performance in mind I can perhaps normalize my compulsion by making it (seem to be) functional. "I am doing this because I am 'I'." This "because" made into a performance link to an "I"-function? It's not really me. Let's play a Spalding Gray drinking game. Raise a glass of water every time your mind ticks over into a rationale for repetition, the making the extraordinary seem ordinary.

There is a second obsessive-compulsive at the Passover table, who has been furtively watching me internally perform and now joins in the first person. It is Harvey Pekar, writer of the underground real-life comics series *American Splendor*, from which a movie by the same name will, in the future, have been made.[20] The film introduces "our hero" (as Harvey often calls himself in the comic) as a child being just who he is in contrast to a squad of kids dressed as Superman, Batman, and Green Lantern trick-or-treating in the neighborhood where he grew up. As he grows up, Harvey stands outside of a self whose inside is his ongoing subject/project and wonders why he is drawn in different ways by different illustrators of his angry, obsessive thoughts. He becomes a muse for underground comic artist Robert Crumb. Harvey's future wife Joyce hesitates to visit him for the first time because she can't tell what he really looks like from the various ways in which he is depicted. She doesn't know what (as in who) to expect. He tells her that if she comes to visit him he will try to be anyone she wants him to be. She says this is a dangerous offer, because she's "a notorious reformer"—another artist who wants to draw him differently. Joyce is a depressive hypochondriac and, like Harvey, a self-obsessed catastrophist. "My perspective, gloom and doom," Harvey says of himself. Joyce tells him that he is the

---

[20] *American Splendor* (dir. Shari Springer Berman and Robert Pulcini, 2003).

poster boy for obsessive-compulsive disorder (Finally, in Harvey Pekar, an obsessive-compulsive who, like me, doesn't/can't/won't clean), but then she believes that coming from a dysfunctional family qualifies her to analyze everyone. Is psychoanalysis just another form of other people drawing "you"? Or is it you drawing another version of yourself for someone else's "professional" edification? ("I" tell my therapist that I am just there to entertain her, to perform. "So, should I pay you?" she asks facetiously. "That would be great," "I" say.)

The real "Harvey Pekar" who appears on David Letterman's show on TV inside the film as "the real Harvey Pekar," is played by himself and not by the actor who is playing him in the film. And on air, Harvey hawks not just the book of his collected comics but the dolls his wife makes out of his own used clothing. Letterman says that Harvey looks "like every police artist sketch he has ever seen." Does this mean he resembles a type, as in a facsimile real? Isn't Harvey's entire person-as-persona a statement of not being like everybody else, of not being "like"? Harvey prides himself on being who he is and observing only what is, but then how and why does his bond with reality turn him into a comic book character? Harvey gets cancer, although he feels fine at the time of his diagnosis (as did I) and makes a comic book to get through it (with his wife), *Our Cancer Year* (1994). An OCD cancer patient who is not like everybody else and yet plays the part of someone who is. Cancer-minded Harvey wakes Joyce up to ask her the existential question, "Am I a guy who writes about himself in a comic book, or am I just a character in that book?" He asks her to tell him the truth. After all, how would *he* know? The truth may or may not be in the doing and whose doing is it in any case? Before they met, Joyce told Harvey how weird he looked as he was sometimes drawn with wavy lines coming off his body. Those, he told her, were "action lines," which I know is just a euphemism for anxiety. They are, as well, what Howard Jacobson calls the "Jewish terrors."[21] The Jewish terrors might be characterized as the four (Rhetorical) questions Jews (here slipping between the "we" and the "I") ask as part of a daily ritual of self-checking not reserved for religious holidays (e.g., Passover's regarding special food consumption): (1) Why must we always answer a question with a question? (Related: "Why must we always answer a negative with a negative?" Also: "Why must every argument have a counter-argument?") (2) Of what concretely

---

[21] Jacobson, *Shylock Is My Name*, 201.

are we afraid? (Where do "'I conjure up this dread from… this longing for this end of things,' this catastrophe, this chaos?" "Aren't all dreads half desires?") (3) Why must we understand everything? ("Where does it end, this *understanding*?") (4) Why must we make ourselves so neurotic? (Must we be "a hyperbolic people?") To this I would add a fifth question that like the others interrogates itself: "Why must it always be cancer?"[22]

When Harvey got his first phone and phone book in 1960, he found a second Harvey Pekar listed, a "purer" one not muddled by a middle initial. ("Lawrence" is our Harvey's middle name and, again, my father's first name.) In 1970, there was a third Harvey Pekar listed in the Cleveland phone directory—strange given that it is an unusual name and that there are three of them in the same city. "Then one day, a person I work with expressed her sympathy to me concerning what she thought was the death of my father." Lawrence? No, not *my* father "my father," *his* father Saul, but it was not his father either. The man whose obituary Harvey's co-worker read was for a man named "Harvey Pekar," one of whose sons was also named "Harvey." Six months later Harvey Jr. died. Our Harvey began wondering about who they were. "Two years later another Harvey Pekar appeared in the phone book. Who *are* these people? Where do they come from? What do they do? What's in a name? Who is 'Harvey Pekar'?"

Obsessive-compulsives depend upon routine and are uncomfortable with change. Cancer is change, and not small change either. It costs you everything. Cancer is a serial killer, a sociopath, a nemesis. Cancer invades the body because, like the scorpion on the frog's back crossing the river, it is its nature. It's ironic that Harvey's oncologist cousin Norman's cancer killed him, not because he was an oncologist but because Harvey was so obsessed with self-diagnosis and yet put off seeing a doctor about his growing lump for several years. Did Harvey fear the past (Norman's lymphoma) more than or even *as* the present (his own lymphoma)? Isn't this what we all do vis-à-vis our genealogy? Isn't this why we pay for genealogical testing—to see what we may already have or else may get? Was Harvey already halfway gone by the time of his own diagnosis, figuring that it takes a past as well as a present to make a future?

---

[22] See Mickey's (Woody Allen's) imagined scene in which his doctor tells him his hearing loss in one ear is the result of terminal cancer before we get the "real-life" corrective scene in which the doctor tells Mickey there is nothing wrong with him in *Hannah and Her Sisters* (dir. Woody Allen, 1986). Jacobson, *The Finkler Question*, 148, 155, 169, 215, 244, 245, 254, and 288.

Our cast of characters—Harvey's and mine and yours if you've had cancer—are the same: the surgery and the hallucination-causing drugs, the list of post-op meds and litany of chemotherapy-induced symptoms (fatigue, hair and weight loss, nausea, loss of interest and appetite—sweet things are sometimes good), cold sweats, insomnia, and depression (on top of what is already there), the prep for each round of treatment and the low white blood cell counts that interrupt treatment and call forth the $9000 Neulasta shots to counteract this (it's a twelve-week *protocol*, which is usually more than a twelve-week treatment—there is *waiting* involved), the wife or husband or life partner who bears the emotional burden of your physical suffering, the neighbor who says she's praying for you—even though you're not praying for yourself, only feeling sorry.

Multiples. I have had three friends in my life named "David." One taught me about adventure, taking me out of myself, another taught me loyalty since damaged by mystery, words unspoken in time, and the third thought like me and we wrote stories together, finishing each other's long-distance thoughts stretched out over years. I know him least well but most deeply through fictions. Each "David" can be located on a spectrum of brokenness—broken trust, broken commonality, and broken continuity. These are not flaws but functions of an extended self-imagining. There was no "David," there never was any "David." *I* was "David" *and* I was me too, lost to myself, giving up on myself, either letting myself or not letting myself off the hook. They often look like the same thing.

Unbreakable's Elijah Price is David's "David." Elijah is David Dunn's somatically broken self that David's unbreakable façade cannot allow. David dreams of saving others, but these are bad dreams, guilty secrets buried in the shallow grave of the subconscious. David nearly drowns in this waking dream (it's in the newspaper). He is pulled from the water with the help of a metal pole, a sort of walking stick absent the hand that gripped it. He is effectively saved by his alter-ego Elijah, underscoring the thought that a friendship forged between two miraculous survivors is in itself heroic. But heroic friendship on this mythic scale recasts friends as one another's nemesis, as Elijah points out to David when the latter discovers that his new "friend" engineered the train wreck that killed everyone other than himself so that he (Elijah) could attain proof positive that David was the heroic friend, the one whose very being overcame all (including Elijah's own) physical disability. Elijah had engineered other such accidents from which David did not emerge as the longed-for indestructible presence. Acceptable losses for the criminally insane Elijah, but not for David, who admittedly has been at a loss as to where he belonged, what he should be doing. He didn't think he needed a friend so much as a meaningful vocation. Had David and Elijah not played their discovery scene, they might wonder in future years why they had grown apart, not been in touch (as prescribed by haphephobia— Elijah at least does not allow himself to be touched). Each would feel like they had said or done something that made them so guilty that they dared not reach out to the friend they must obviously have betrayed. By revealing to David who he really was, Elijah believed that he was just being honest about their friendship that split the psycho/somatic right down the middle. But David knows as do I that darkening the character of your friend makes you somehow less responsible for keeping his friendship. And likewise, your friend's inflation of your merit was a charade your guilty heart could not abide, and so you cut him loose. When, in long-ago Flushing, Queens, my first best friend and I flew out of our apartments after watching TV's *The Adventures of Superman* (1952– 1958) wearing our pajamas and capes fashioned by our mothers from bath towels and safety pins, we were *both* playing the hero's role. There was as yet no nemesis.

In *Nemesis*, Philip Roth protagonist Eugene "Bucky" Cantor, a neighborhood superhero who protects his young playground charges from harm, becomes convinced that he is the source of the cancer epidemic that is killing them. When he abandons the playground to take a job at a summer camp where he can be with his fiancé, he first feels that he has betrayed the children he left behind in the stifling, carcinogenic New Jersey urban air, then becomes convinced that he has carried the cancer with him to bucolic Pennsylvania. When he abandons his playground job his boss refers to Bucky not as Cantor but as "Cancer." "You're an opportunist, Cancer," the boss says and truer words have never been spoken not about Cantor but about the illness whose namesake he is. In an elision worthy of a superhero/supervillain origin story, polio withers Cantor's own body and reinforces his belief that he is not just the instrument, the medium of the contagion but *the nemesis* itself. Having heard a woman shrieking in fear that her child would get polio, Bucky realizes that "he was the shriek."[23] Bucky, the pigeon-toed athlete an idealized extrapolation from someone else's fictional memory of "my best friend"

[23] Roth, *Nemesis*, 138 and 225.

elided with his older brother. Bucky, who nods when reuniting with a former charge who has beaten the mental limits imposed upon him by polio tells him, "What I wanted was the tritest thing in the world: to be like everyone else." Nodding as Ray Davies must have done when he gave his song "I'm Not Like Everybody Else" to his younger brother Dave to sing and then envied him for it as he did for everything else, for not being the one who was broken on the inside, who "never trusts his limits," whose complicated, guilty, obsessive mind is an arrow that is forever piercing the invincibility of the ordinary to which he thought in his prolonged dolorous youth he aspired.[24]

In *Hamletmachine*, Heiner Müller, paraphrasing Eliot's "Prufrock" voices the writer not being Hamlet by denying Hamlet's body, which is to say, his mortal self. In his reimagining Hamlet as a collective presence and his throwing off narrative history's equivalent second body, Müller is likewise paraphrasing Stein's *Everybody's Autobiography*, if everybody was a writer (as a special kind of public intellectual), that is filled with the guilt, anxiety, and the sense of personal responsibility that attend. The book you have been reading is, among other things, a mea culpa for not being more and better than I am and a personal and collective rationale for why that is. I am not Hamlet, nor am I Batman, but instead a counter-superhero from the "O-C" (Obsessive-Compulsive) Universe, whose cast of characters includes "Spalding-Man," "Roth-Man," "Union-Man," "Distracted-Man," "Broken-Man," "Dog-Man," and finally (what else), "Cancer-Man." These are only some of my multiples. "Embarrassed-Man" is, unsurprisingly, too reticent to wear a costume or even answer to his name. But he exists, as latency.

The thing about superhero franchises is that they keep reinventing themselves, with their origin stories beginning over and over again. They get second, third, and fourth chances to be reborn, making them im/perfect immigrant success stories. *The Amazing Spider-Man* (dir. Marc Webb, 2012), which followed an earlier Spider-Man trilogy, begins with Peter Parker playing hide-and-seek as a boy and finding, among other things, a pair of shoes sticking out from underneath curtains supporting a broomstick handle and wearing a hat. I was scared, but he wasn't of this reference to the Scarecrow, the Batman stories' purveyor of pure fear toxins. Jonathan Crane, a.k.a. Scarecrow, was raised by a scientist father who experimented on his son's fear to learn how it might be

[24] Ibid., 244, 267, 273, 275, and 280.

rooted out of other people or so the grown-up, fear-fixated child thinks, wanting to think "the best" of his father by giving him the best scientific intentions.[25] Both Peter "Spider-Man" Parker and his best friend Harry Osborn must unearth their own late fathers' intentions in order to become their own best men. In this particular version of the origin story, Parker gets bitten by a genetically mutated spider at Harry's father Norman's (a.k.a. Green Goblin's) Oscorp laboratory, where one-armed herpetologist Dr. Curt Connors (a.k.a. The Lizard) is trying to find a way to regenerate missing limbs. Connors is the author of a book whose last chapter is ominously entitled "The Final Solution." The man who killed Peter's gentle uncle and surrogate father Ben is tattooed with stars, the wrong stars, *not* Stars of David, but Peter has inwardly pledged allegiance to revenge and the motto "never forget." This is rendered problematic by Peter's masked identity as Spider-Man. Spiders are super-assimilationists. They "can change their color to blend into their environment. It's a defense mechanism." Peter learns this in an earlier version of his alter-ego's origin story.[26] So, aside from having to determine whether his best friend Harry is also his worst enemy (the New Green Goblin, fulfilling *his* father's legacy), whether his own father was conducting beneficial or malevolent genetic testing (a gloss on the mysteries of genealogy), on whether being not like everybody else is achievable only as a sort of antibody and whether this should ever be attempted even with the best intentions in mind, he must realize that he has only been made a teenager to test his desire to be assimilated versus his desire to master assimilation. According to his creator Stan Lee (New York City Jewish-born Stanley Martin Lieber), Spider-Man wears a mask so his enemies couldn't see his fear.[27] As a golem is he more Haganah or Irgun, defender or aggressor, and does he, like Scarecrow end by terrorizing himself? As young Parker's Aunt May tells him, "Secrets have cost. They're not free. Not now, not ever."

---

[25] "Jonathan Crane is the son of Dr. Gerald Crane, a biology teacher who, after being too afraid to save his wife from dying in a fire, began to murder people for their adrenaline glands in an effort to concoct a fear toxin he hoped would cure him of his fears. Testing an experimental version of the drug on his son Jonathan, the boy was rushed to the hospital after his father was shot dead by police, presumed by doctors to never be able to recover from his living nightmare." http://dc.wikia.com/wiki/Jonathan_Crane_(Gotham).

[26] *Spider-Man* (dir. Sam Raimi, 2002).

[27] *Spider-Man 2* (dir. Sam Raimi, 2004). http://www.imdb.com/title/tt0316654/trivia?ref_=tt_trv_trv.

In *Cast a Giant Shadow* (dir. Melville Shavelson, 1966), Colonel David "Mickey" Marcus is recruited by the Haganah to advise Israeli forces in their fight against the Arab nations (and, as in *Exodus*, in their internal fight with the Irgun). Marcus initially turns down the Haganah major who has been sent to recruit him, saying that he hadn't been in a temple since he made a speech at age thirteen and received hundreds of fountain pens. This is the M.O. of so many of us who later submit to our own personal law of return to the culture and collaterally the faith. This being still a pale shadow of the actual Law of Return that gives a Jew the right to emigrate to and become a citizen of Israel—i.e., to make a real life commitment.[28] I am the only member of my immediate family who has not been to Israel, let alone "returned" by law. I am the only one sitting at my sister's dinner table who struggles to recall the words to the Hebrew prayers I grew up reciting. At the rectangular table whose corners I have mentally rounded off to resemble an oval track, I feel like I have been lapped by those on whom as a bar mitzvah boy I had had an early head start. I am struck by the need to rebuild my Jewish identity. I have committed myself to Jewish rehab, where there are no locks on the doors and no curfews. I am allowed to bring in non-kosher food and even to continue seeing my non-Jewish psychiatrist. I find myself looking for landsmen and finding them everywhere, turning the whole world Jewish by shrinking it in size. I am as enthusiastic, even obsessed with returning to the fold as Nathan Englander's non-Jewish *gilgul* Charles Martin Luger was one evening in the back of a Manhattan cab when he discovered he had a Jewish soul.[29] Somehow this all figures in my overall theme of going back, more an obsession than an idea that I cannot explain away as merely a byproduct of advancing age. Marcus goes off to fight in Israel for reasons he cannot explain. It's not against someone but for something that is personal, that is sharper than the historical record. It is, in fact, something that is not on the record, that is, like my family's history, missing. Each of us carries within us a hall of records that contests "actual" memory, returning us not to a particular time and place but to a lifelong self-contested scene. This hall has within it unexpected doors and windows into rooms that do not logically configure in which relatives slip off the costumes in which I knew them, chant in languages

---

[28] Enacted by the Israeli Knesset (Parliament), July 5, 1950.

[29] *Gilgul* refers to reincarnation as described in Kabbalah or Jewish mysticism. Englander, "The Gilgul of Park Avenue," in *For the Relief of Unbearable Urges*, 109 and 110.

I don't understand, speak in broken sentences about things I did not know before and can only vaguely process now. I have tried to read the clues that I may have only constituted myself to give me something to read so as to occupy a mind preoccupied with disappearance and invisibility. I am like the actor who reclaims his heritage through a role he plays in a movie and when the project is completed moves on to the next part.

Stern's title character (who incarnates fear of domination and lack of self-mastery) is admitted to a medical clinic as an "intestinal" (an ulcer) rather than as a "mental" patient but the two share close quarters. There Stern observes, "beneath a great insect-covered bulb," a gray-haired old man who has lost his ability to walk and so drapes himself "over a wooden bannister like a blanket," clings "insect-like against poles," is "draped over rails, propped up against walls, but [is]never really standing." He "winks deeply" at Stern and "calls him forward" among these half-men, telling him "I had what you had, only now I'm here worrying about something else."[30] All of them spider-men, failed experiments in human regeneration, one-time thought by themselves to be supermen battling against the monstrosities of genetic re-engineering with which most if not all of Spider-Man's nemeses are involved. Well-meaning Nazis, they were, these mad scientists, and we of the extended Spider-Man Jewish family are the last defense against a final solution that sought the perfection of exclusion by annihilation.

"CLOSURE"

"Closure" it has been said, "is a concept foreign to Jewish tradition."[31] My grandfather, who I only recently learned had one earlobe shot off (how did I not notice *this*?), ended his living testimonial to fear, a scarecrow rooted in the corner of some dark memory, upon whose black cardigan sweater sleeve black crows roosted as if *they* had found a home, a dog at his slippered feet. He was buried in a plot bought for him as part of a group lot by some Jewish émigré society in a dark, skeletal pipe-cleaner cemetery on the side of a highway, in Queens, I think. It rained the day of his funeral and for a long time I thought that it rained at *all* funerals so that people would have to open black umbrellas. I remember

[30] Friedman, *Stern*, 117, 121, 124, and 125.
[31] Kushner and Mamet, *Five Cities of Refuge*, 5.

the sound of traffic competing with the Kaddish said over his grave. My grandmother died during the year I spent in Russia. She told me not to go, fearing that I would not come back. It just goes to show, you never know who's not returning. By the time my father's brother and two sisters died, we were dispersed. My maiden aunt Ruth had moved to live among the Russian Jewish community in Brighton Beach where she descended into full delirium. We were informed of my other aunt's funeral in Bayside only after she was buried for reasons that are known only to my cousin who was, I thought growing up, a great Jerry Lewis impersonator. While they lived, my father sought to avoid his sisters' phone calls, so I guess they didn't want to bother him with their deaths. My uncle, my father's brother died from a heart attack at age 65, although to me he just seemed to slip away. He had always been a quiet man who had apparently signed a non-compete clause with his spirited wife, a friend growing up in the Bronx of Anna Italiano before she became actress Anne Bancroft and became Jewish more by association than conversion through marriage to Mel Brooks. This uncle, who smoked a pipe and nearly died from carbon monoxide poisoning in his home garage years prior to his actual death, was lost somewhere between a nimbus and a penumbra. This was the sum of my father's family, all absent and accounted for. My father, of course, died of cancer, like his father before him. *Schindler's List* was the last film my father got to see. He notes Schindler's excellent memory for names. He looks for familiar names on his list, family names perhaps, or so I imagine. One name follows another. Generations of names on the other list, the wrong list. He sees a line of German Shepherds barking but muzzled, perhaps responding to the deafening, the deadening of his own life. They are trauma's echoic voice, identity's end, the insubstantiality of doors, walls, and windows, the rolling up of streets and paths, the hiding in that space to which his body will soon conform. No longer being followed, because no longer identifiable, not by *his* father or by the others who were following him. Everyone like everybody else. "You shouldn't get stuck on names," they tell him, tell Schindler. Names and dates no longer matter, nor place, nor story of origin. "There will be generations because of what you did." My father and my grandfather heard this, I know.

Don Celso Robles, the elderly protagonist of *Night Across the Street* (dir. Raúl Ruiz, 2012) is first seen sitting with his eyes closed behind a school desk along with the rest of the class of much younger pupils in what looks like a morose version of Woody Allen's satirical take on the ravages of time on the innocent in *Annie Hall* (1977). Rúiz's teacher, Professor Giono, rolls up his sleeves and is trying to elicit the response he has in mind from the class regarding the correct translation of "the setting sun" (quoted from Proust) in Spanish and in French. Likewise, "the canvas house of the exhibitor of things past." How does the translation determine not just meaning but relatability, mental concordance of the listener with the thought being expressed? "In Spanish one doesn't say 'exhibitor of shadows.' When someone says 'puppeteer of things past,' they are referring to the past, as though the past were a theater of shadows. If we say, 'The magician who makes us see the shadows of things past,' we're getting closer, aren't we?" With this, Don Celso's alarm rings and he frantically starts taking a succession of pills. With this, the school bell rings, and we are out of time, at least in terms of this particular lesson.

We next see Don Celso and the teacher walking slowly in each other's profile more *in* time than through it. Don Celso congratulates the disinterested teacher on the publication of his book, *The Horseman on the Roof,* an adventure novel published in 1951 in a good translation. The book's author, Jean Giono, shares his name but not his biography with the professor, as the latter suggests in his response to the old man congratulating him. "Why me?" "Because you are Jean Giono. The author of *The Horseman on the Roof.* Aren't you?" "Sometimes I get the impression that I am," says Giono. Professor Giono later says that he lives in this town of Antogasta alone, without his family, because *"Somebody has to write all those books that they attribute to me."* (This is complicated by the fact that the character is meant to be the real author Jean Giono who dreamed of living in Antogasta solely because of its name as he says in the film in which the surrogate Giono is granted the original's wish.[32]) For his part, Don Celso, who works in an office, is hearing voices that inflect his thoughts poetically, or as his colleague translates this, "incoherently." Celso, who says he has no ideas is cautioned by this colleague that this will cost the soon-to-be retiree his youth. Celso, whose image for ideas is seagulls, "recalls" as a boy meeting a man who called himself "Long John Silver" who points to his ship in the water which the boy can only see by closing his eyes and repeating the words "black spot" three times. He does and the ship appears *or rather a ship in a film the*

---

[32] "Lasting Elements on the Last Horizon," a visual essay by Kevin B. Lee, an extra on the Cinema Guild DVD of the film.

boy said he saw does. In the end, we die into our youth, something not regressed to but achieved.

Age extrapolates terminal images in their frames in the boarding house where the wind blows on the inside but not out on the street. We become haunted, like film itself. Like a human body that is wasting away, movies now show their theatrical bones: where people are standing relative to one another, how and where they are framed, who is illuminated and can be seen, who crosses in front of you or behind, where the furniture and the rugs are placed, and what the dialogue says about otherwise unseen natural elements inside these interior settings minus natural light with pumped in sound from "the outside." The image no longer moves faster than the tired eye can travel, because image is now transparently the mind's eye's product, all these lost images that have become unstuck in time. The dialogue speaks of emotions abstractly, at some distance from the character who is mentally composing it. The images speak a dialogue that seems random, as if images were themselves only ventriloquists of time deferred. The air has yellowed like the pages in an old library book which your allergies make it impossible to read. You hear the air around the thoughts being expressed. In your decrepitude, *the set shakes you.* Doors are no longer listened at but through because they are always open, more like gaps where the wall had been before things became more visible, less opaque. Synthesis of thought is matched by synchronicity of times and places. Space becomes poetic, time prosaic. You hear one not the other breathe. There are shadows in the room, but they are not cast by you. You have become a walking shadow. "Don Celso, do you walk?" "I do." "Every day?" "Every morning I come back to life and I walk." "How far?" "As far as a slingshot...As far as David's slingshot...When I go out to walk it's for a reason, a good one. I go out looking for words." But what word that has four letters, youth is anxious to know? Not "love," not "Adam," "damn," nor "wait." Dolorous youth presses the matter on the aged, impatient for the wor(l)d to be revealed. I am old enough now to know I am who "I" pretended to be.

DECOHERENCE (BOTH...AND)

"I don't want to sit next to the door to nowhere," I say inside the suddenly blacked-out room in James Ward Byrkit's *Coherence* (2013). (I have been meaning to get a door to nowhere but perhaps because there is no "where" to guide me, I have been unable to find one yet.)

The film deals with the unexpected appearance of metastatic selves released or else created by an event (the passing of a comet through the earth's atmosphere) that though theoretically predictable is also experientially unexpected. One (that is another) character in the house where we ("my friends" and "I") are gathered calls these selves "theoretical" since it is we and not they (we assume) who occupy the subject (viewing) position. (And yet someone is photographing us as subjects looking directly into the camera. Where *is* the camera?) Just as the back-up generator goes out in the house, causing the blackout and possibly before we ("my friends" and "I") discover that we are not necessarily the original subjects in this house's, in this room's narrative, I receive a CBS real-time Breaking News alert on the computer on which I am typing these words that says: "Chinese space authorities say Tiangong 1, the country's defunct and reportedly out-of-control space station, re-entered the Earth's atmosphere Sunday night, mostly burning up over the central South Pacific." But by this time, we have already lost all internet and cell phone service in the house, due to the intrusion of a foreign object into earth's atmosphere. A character named Hugh (a.k.a. "You" or "I" depending upon one's perspective) has likewise already cited Erwin Schrödinger's famous thought experiment in which, "A living cat is placed into a steel chamber along with a hammer, a vial of hydrocyanic acid and a very small amount of radioactive substance. If even a single atom of the radioactive substance decays during the test period, a relay mechanism will trip the hammer, which will in turn, break the vial of poisonous gas and cause the cat to die."[33] The thing is, though, that until you actually open the box, you don't know whether the cat is alive or dead; or alternatively, until the box is opened the cat is alive *and* dead. It is only once the box is opened and Hugh has brought a box into our house from a second house that turns out to be a duplicate of ours' (or ours' of theirs) that two separate but identical realities (the quantum physics principle of decoherence) collapse into a single event.[34]

---

[33] http://whatis.techtarget.com/definition/Schrodingers-cat.

[34] "Interference phenomena are a well-known and crucial aspect of quantum mechanics.... There are situations, however, in which interference effects are artificially or spontaneously suppressed. The *theory of decoherence* is precisely the study of (spontaneous) interactions between a system and its environment that lead to such suppression of interference." "The Role of Decoherence in Quantum Mechanics," *Stanford Encyclopedia of Philosophy*. https://plato.stanford.edu/entries/qm-decoherence/.

Hugh's referent for this is a book his unseen brother left for him called *Gravity: An Introduction to Current Research*. Hugh reasons that if he steals the same book from the subjects in the other house before they can read it, we (i.e., "I" and "my friends," including Hugh, played by an actor whose first name is really Hugo, "You go") can somehow dissolve their reality as being "us" or "we," or worst of all, "them." And then it suddenly dawns on me in the blackout that comes and goes like an edited life that the book to which they, to which we have been referring, have been reading, is this one—the book that you have just read. But which one of me has written it? I ask this question because "I" really want to know.

SYNCOPE

My uncle regains consciousness on the floor of his pharmacy down the block from my grandparents' apartment in the Bronx. He says that a tall, oddly angular-looking man in a long, dark leather coat hit him over the head with a glass cane. He says that moments before he had observed this man holding the tin acrobat to which I gravitated as a child whenever I would visit. The tinman spun around a tin pole, never falling but sometimes standing upside down atop the pole held up by the strength of his two hands, his body miraculously suspended in mid-air. My uncle called him, not the acrobat but the disabled figure, Anti-Gravity Man for want of a better name, not knowing the character's real name was "Glass," a Jewish-sounding surname which wasn't his real name either. It was "Elijah," like the prophet "Eliahu." Except that this man's name was "Elijah Price," like the profit, which, I suppose, determined who he was—a thief. But a thief of what? He opened the cash register, but he took nothing, instead leaving something, a note that read: "TELL ME WHEN SOMEONE COMES FOR IT." The note assumed my uncle knew what "it" was by making the tinman suspended vertically on the bar the last thing he saw before being rendered unconscious. The note is printed upside down, made clear because it is written on personal stationery with the letterhead standing on its head at the foot of the piece of paper, like the inverted tin acrobat on the bar. (Years later, I witnessed a human acrobat spin overhead on a bar connected only by his feet.) This note is left not to me but for an "I" created to replace the broken hinge that at some point must have joined the self and the world. It, and this is the real "it," is the "I" of the writer who left the door to the store that bore our revised family name ajar. At which point, it all went missing.

INDEX

CPI Antony Rowe
Eastbourne, UK
November 26, 2019